THE EXPERIENCE

A Devotional and Journal

Day-by-Day With God

Henry Blackaby & Richard Blackaby

BROADMAN
& HOLMAN
PUBLISHERS

Nashville, Tennessee

Ten-Digit ISBN: 0–8054–1846–6
Thirteen-Digit ISBN: 978–0–8054–1846–0

Published by Broadman & Holman Publishers, Nashville, Tennessee
Editorial Team: Leonard G. Goss, John Landers, Sandra Bryer
Page Design and Typesetting: TF Designs, Mt. Juliet, Tennessee

Dewey Decimal Classification: 242.64
Subject Heading: DEVOTIONAL EXERCISES

7 8 9 10 11 12 13 14 15 14 13 12 11 10 09 08 07 06 05

Contents

Preface

God blessed me with five wonderful children: Richard, Tom, Mel, Norman, and Carrie. At one point my four sons were all teenagers! I knew that all five children had great potential to make a difference in their world; God has gifted each of them in different ways. I also knew that the world would do everything it could to tempt them to accept less than God's best for their lives. I encouraged each child to love God and to follow him faithfully. My wife, Marilynn, and I did everything we could to model faithfulness for our children so they would know they could trust God with their lives. Ultimately, however, it was their choice. One by one, in different ways, each child chose to follow Jesus. They did it, not to please their parents, but because they had come to know and love Jesus for themselves. None of my children has had it easy. Each has faced unique hardships and challenges, but all five of them are faithfully serving their Lord in full-time ministry. I'm so grateful that the Lord is blessing them! My prayer is that this devotional book will encourage many young people to choose to follow Christ wherever he leads them as well.

Henry T. Blackaby

This book has been a special project for me because our family is just beginning those adventurous teen years! My son Mike is fourteen. He'll soon be in high school and entering an exciting new stage of his life. He's a great son. He loves God, and I'm extremely proud of him. God has incredible plans for his life, and I pray that God's Word will always be what guides his life choices. My son Daniel, twelve, and my daughter Carrie, eight, are terrific kids. Before long, they, too, will be reaching their teens. My prayer for them is a great future following God's will.

This book has also been special to me for another reason: I had the privilege of working on it with my wife, Lisa. She has the ability to condense my father's and my verbosity into one page per devotional thought. That's a gift, considering we're both preachers! You have her to thank that this book is light enough to carry. She's been immensely helpful to both Dad and me, and we owe her our deepest thanks.

The teen years are critical. I pray the words on these pages will be helpful to young people who earnestly desire to honor their Lord, Jesus Christ.

Richard Blackaby

Introduction

Could there be anything more exciting than to wake up each morning and know you are going to meet with God? How incredible to think that you can talk directly with the Creator of the universe, telling him your problems and listening to what he has to say about them! Yet that is exactly what you can do each day. God doesn't ask you to have a quiet time each day; he invites you to spend time with him! You are free to tell Almighty God whatever is on your heart. You can ask him any question. You can find comfort from any pain. God promises to respond to you with love. This makes meeting with God something you ought to look forward to each day with tremendous anticipation.

This devotional journal is meant to assist you as you meet daily with God. It assumes you already have a personal relationship with God. If you do not, you can begin a relationship with him by praying and asking God to forgive you of your sin. Then commit yourself to do whatever he tells you for the rest of your life.

This devotional book has Scripture verses that will introduce you to wonderful promises of God that can change your life. As you read the devotions, be sure to have your Bible with you so you can read the verses that come before and after the passage covered in that day's devotion. Have a pen with you as well so you can write your thoughts in the margins of your journal. When the Lord of the universe says something to you, it's important enough to write down! Later, you can look back over the things God has said to you during your times with him and see how he has been leading you, day by day. Your journal will become a source of comfort to you as you see how God has been guiding you and sharing his love with you.

Commit yourself to spend regular time with God each day. It will change your life!

Lessons from the Master Teacher

What words come to mind when you think about what God is like? *Awesome? Almighty? Omnipotent? Holy?* Did the word *Jesus* come to mind? When God the Father wanted to show us exactly what he was like, he sent his Son Jesus. When you have seen Jesus, you've seen what God is like. When you hear Jesus teach, you've heard the wisdom of God.

Have you ever had a favorite teacher? Was there someone under whom you studied who impacted your life in a significant way? Perhaps it was the example they set for you that challenged you to strive for excellence. Maybe you were encouraged by the care and attention they gave you. Maybe they inspired you by simply believing in you. A good teacher can touch your life in ways that will last forever. Jesus was not just a good teacher; he was God. When he spoke about holy living, he not only knew what he was talking about, but he was actually able to make his disciples holy. Every word Jesus spoke was backed by a life of total obedience to his Father. Every instruction he gave was given in unconditional love.

Even the best teachers can make mistakes. Not Jesus. When Jesus said something, you know it will always be true. As you read the following devotions, be aware that you are learning not just from a great teacher but from the holy Son of God. Jesus can teach you today just as effectively as he taught his disciples two thousand years ago. Be prepared to learn from the Master Teacher things that will forever change your life!

Lessons Teacher

January 1

Handling Your Blessings

From everyone who has been given much, much will be demanded; and from the one who has been entrusted with much, much more will be asked.

Luke 12:48b

It's not fair! From the time we're very young, most of us spend a lot of energy making sure things are fair. We watch our parents to make sure they don't give our siblings more than they give us. We watch our friends to make sure they don't have better toys, or nicer clothes, or more dates than we do. We do the same thing with God. We look at how he blesses someone else, and we can't resist the urge to compare it with what he's given us. We don't realize the audacity involved in accusing God of being unfair. The Bible leaves no question that God is completely just. Our problem is that we don't look at things the right way. Our problem is not that we have been given too little. Our problem is what we have done with what we've been given. Jesus made clear that we're responsible for what God gives us, not what he gives others. If any unfairness is involved, it's in the way we mishandle what God entrusts to us.

Take some time to consider how well you're handling your blessings. Remember, God holds you accountable for what he's given you, not what he's given your neighbor. If you've grown up in a Christian environment, with years of Bible study opportunities, God expects you to know his Word. He's not being unfair to expect obedience from you, because you clearly know what he wants you to do. The important thing in life is not who gets what but how well you manage what *you* get. As a Christian, you've received a lot, so be ready to give an account for what you've done with it.

But What About You?

"But what about you?" he asked. "Who do you say I am?" Peter answered, "The Christ of God."

Luke 9:20

Jesus had spent three years teaching his disciples. It was time to see if they'd learned what he wanted them to know. For three years they'd watched his life. They'd seen him face temptation without succumbing to sin. They'd seen him perform miracles, cast out demons, heal disease, and raise the dead. They'd marveled at his unparalleled wisdom as he taught the crowds. They'd seen him evade the cunning traps of the Pharisees. For three years, the disciples had observed Jesus live a pure, holy, and victorious life. Now Jesus wanted to know what conclusions they had drawn.

First, he asked a leading question: "Who do people say that I am?" The disciples had heard all sorts of theories from others on who Jesus was: possibly Elijah, possibly a prophet from long ago, or maybe John the Baptist raised from the dead. Perhaps they were trying to be polite by not mentioning the less flattering opinions: revolutionary, lunatic. It didn't matter. Jesus already knew the answer, just as he knew the answer to his second, more poignant, question: "But what about you? Who do you say that I am?"

Everyone has an opinion about Jesus. People say he was a great teacher, a moral man, a left-wing radical, or a fictional character who lived only in first-century literature. Who others think Jesus is, or was, is not the most important question. The most important question is, "Who do *you* say that he is?" When you meet Jesus face-to-face, he'll not ask, "Were your parents devout followers of mine?" or "Did you attend a dynamic, growing church where people loved me?" No. Jesus will look you in the eye and ask the same question he asked his disciples: "Who do you say that I am?" Are you ready with your answer? Will it be the same answer Peter gave: "You are the Christ"? If you've been hiding behind the opinions or the faith of others, it's time to step out and declare for yourself who Jesus is: the Christ, the Son of the living God.

January 3

What's That in Your Eye?

"How can you say to your brother, 'Brother, let me take the speck out of your eye,' when you yourself fail to see the plank in your own eye? You hypocrite, first take the plank out of your eye, and then you will see clearly to remove the speck from your brother's eye."

Luke 6:42

Most of us live by a double standard. We judge ourselves one way, but we use a different set of rules for others. When we sin, we're quick to explain the reasons behind our disobedience: "I was exhausted." "I didn't know what I was doing." "I was under a lot of stress." We feel that pointing to the cause of our sin will somehow make us an innocent victim rather than the guilty party. When it comes to other people, however, that's another case. Then we don our judge's robes and pronounce them guilty, regardless of the evidence: "He knew better." "This isn't the first time she's done this!" "There's no excuse for such behavior."

Jesus has no patience for such hypocrisy. He says it's as ridiculous as a person with a two-by-four in his eye who's trying to find a sliver in someone else's eye. Jesus doesn't deny that other people sin, but he directs us to take care of the two-by-four before we pick up the tweezers on our brother's behalf.

It's good to help your friends live the life God desires, but your priority should be to make sure *your* life pleases God. Be diligent to keep sin out of your life; then you'll be able to see others in the correct perspective. When you have sin in your life, it distorts everything you see. If your heart is pure, you won't condemn others for their sin, nor will you jump to conclusions without any evidence. You'll have the grace to help them without judging them.

Jesus' Secret to His Success

But Jesus often withdrew to lonely places and prayed.

Luke 5:16

People were always trying to figure out where Jesus' power came from. Some attributed it to the work of Satan. Others explained his miracles as simply illusions. Jesus made no secret about where his power came from. It came from his Father. That's why it was vital that Jesus spend lots of time in prayer, seeking his Father's will.

Many of us have difficulty establishing a daily habit of spending time with God. The problem is cramming one more thing into our already packed days. We lead busy lives, and there are a lot of demands on our time. It's not always easy finding a private place either, especially if we live with other people, or we have young children. And then there's the phone. . . .

Let's take a closer look at Jesus' life. It wasn't as though he had lots of extra time on his hands. Jesus was an extremely busy man! The more news spread that he could heal the sick and feed the hungry, the less privacy he had. Everywhere he went, there were crowds. People who were afraid to be seen with him would search him out late at night for private conferences. Jesus had to work hard just to be alone. In order to spend time with his Father, he had to get up unusually early and sneak away from the crowds to find a quiet place. If Jesus, the Son of God, needed time with his Father in order to live the victorious Christian life, why would we ever think we could do it alone?

January 5

Lord! Lord!

"Why do you call me, 'Lord, Lord,' and do not do what I say?"

Luke 6:46

In Jesus' day the term *Lord* was deeply meaningful. The Jewish people used the word to signify Almighty God. When the Roman Empire conquered Israel, they adopted the term, using the word *lord* to describe Caesar. Thus, Caesar was the lord of the Roman Empire. But to the Jewish people, there was only one Lord, and that was God. *Lord* was a term reserved for God alone. After Christ was raised from the dead, many Christians lost their lives because they refused to say, "Caesar is Lord."

Many would-be disciples followed Jesus while he walked throughout the countryside; they listened to him teach, but they never did as he said. Along with the true disciples, these pretenders would boldly call Jesus their Lord. Jesus confronted them for their hypocrisy; the word *Lord* easily rolled off their tongues, but their lives were unchanged. They were calling Jesus their Master, yet they refused to be his servants. They made no sacrifices; they continued to pursue their own goals; they carried on with the lifestyle that suited them. Once they met Jesus, they changed their vocabulary, but they didn't change their values. Jesus was not fooled by their show of loyalty. He likened them to a fool who builds a house on sand without taking the time to lay a solid foundation. At first, the house looks the same as the wise man's house, which has been carefully laid on a solid rock. But when the winds and the rains come, the fool's house collapses into a pile of rubble while the wise man's house stands firm.

Are you a wanna-be disciple? Do you say words you think Jesus wants to hear but refuse to do what he asks you to do? Perhaps you've been around genuine disciples enough that you've adopted their vocabulary without making Jesus your Lord. Jesus wants you to have much more than a new vocabulary. He wants you to have a new life.

Proven Right

"But wisdom is proved right by all her children."

Luke 7:35

At times, it seems like you just can't win. No matter what you do, someone will be quick to point out how wrong you are! This problem is nothing new; in fact, Jesus experienced the same dilemma. He compared his generation to children who get upset when they don't get their way, so they call out insults at those who won't dance to their music (Luke 7:32).

People criticized John the Baptist for being different. He didn't fit in: he dressed weird, and he ate bugs. His detractors concluded he must be demon possessed. Jesus, on the other hand, dressed and ate as others did. The same critics ridiculed Jesus for fitting in too well! They observed him spending time in the homes of those they considered riffraff, so they assumed he had to be a glutton and a drunkard! Jesus said there's no point in arguing with such absurd opinions. The best thing to do is exactly what God tells you to do, and let time vindicate your choices.

There are two lessons to be learned here. (1) Watch that you're not like the Pharisees; they condemned everyone who didn't live exactly as they did. Allow others to follow Christ's leading, and don't reject them because God's plan for them is not identical to his will for you. (2) When you know what God wants you to do, don't be distracted by the desire to please everyone who has an opinion. If you let others' criticism deter you from doing what is right, you're in a no-win situation. In trying to please one camp, you'll offend another. Instead, base your life on God's Word, and live with the confidence of God's approval. In time, the wisdom of your decisions will be evident.

January 7

Well Pleased

And a voice from heaven said, "This is my Son, whom I love; with him I am well pleased."

Matthew 3:17

Can you imagine what must have gone through John the Baptist's mind when Jesus asked to be baptized by him? The situation seemed backwards, so John tried to argue with Jesus: "But Jesus, it should be the other way around. You're the Master. I'm the servant. You should be baptizing me!" John knew his place. Perhaps he feared that by baptizing Jesus he would send the wrong message to those watching. It was important that the crowds see and understand that John was merely the messenger. Jesus was the Lord. This might confuse them. But Jesus had a Word from his Father that he should be baptized and that his cousin John should do it. So both men did as God said. The result? The people got the right message; they heard the audible voice of the Father, voicing his approval for his Son!

Sometimes God will ask you to do something that doesn't seem to make sense. You'll have a plan in your head that you think is more reasonable. It's far more important for you to obey God than it is to go with your reasoning. In your effort to follow your own best thinking, you can actually disobey God. This can happen in many ways. Perhaps God has called you to be a missionary, but you've always been a homebody; you don't think you're cut out for life in a foreign country. Maybe you have your career all laid out, but God tells you to go to seminary. Whatever it is that God tells you to do, don't try to convince him that he's got you pegged wrong. Just do it.

When you do what God asks, regardless of whether it makes sense to you, you'll experience his approval. No other achievement could ever match the joy of hearing your Father say he is pleased with you!

Hurry Home
January 8

"So he got up and went to his father. But while he was still a long way off, his father saw him and was filled with compassion for him; he ran to his son, threw his arms around him and kissed him."

Luke 15:20

We concoct many distorted images of God in our heads. We know God is love, yet we sometimes treat him as a stern, demanding judge. We're like Adam and Eve: the first thing we do when we realize we've sinned is to try to hide from God. Our shame causes us to run away from God when we should be running toward him. Jesus said that the Father is watching, all right; but he's watching for us to come home.

Jesus spoke of an arrogant young man who treated his father shamefully. This young man made a series of selfish choices that ultimately brought humiliation to his family and suffering to himself. When he came to his senses, he realized he could never undo the damage he'd done. He'd gone way too far. There was no hope in going back to the way things were before. He didn't even plan to try winning back his father's favor. The best he could hope for was a job with his father's business.

Do you ever feel that way? Do you ever wake up to realize that you've made a terrible mess? You've blown it so badly, you don't dare face God, let alone ask his forgiveness. So you decide to settle for life as a second-class Christian. You'll still go through the motions, but you'll never again enjoy the closeness with God that you once knew. After all, it's what you deserve, considering what you've done, isn't it? If that's your experience, read this entire parable (see Luke 15:11–37).

Even while the son was sinning his way to rock bottom, his father was watching for him, waiting to welcome him home. His father wasn't sitting at home planning how to punish that worthless boy—if he ever dared show up. The father was longing to see his son's face again. He was planning the party he'd throw in celebration if his son would just come home. When the day finally came and he recognized his son's silhouette on the horizon, the father took off at a run. He was filled with joy, not judgment!

Jesus was describing *your* Father. If you're a prodigal son, don't waste another day avoiding God. Just go home.

January 9

Thanksgiving

One of them, when he saw he was healed, came back, praising God in a loud voice. He threw himself at Jesus' feet and thanked him—and he was a Samaritan.

Luke 17:15-16

Don't you just love Luke's little postscript here—"and he was a Samaritan"? We know from Jesus' story of the good Samaritan that Jewish people despised the Samaritans. They were considered lowlife, the dregs of society. It's interesting that Jesus chose a Samaritan as the hero in his story, and now Luke gives this little by-the-way—"and he was a Samaritan." Here were ten men, all in the same boat. No matter who they'd been before, whether they'd been wealthy or poor, popular or outcasts, successes or failures, they all had one thing in common now. Their leprosy made them all outcasts. None of them had any hope of ever returning to his family or resuming normal life. Then they heard about Jesus, the miracle worker. In one loud, pitiful voice, they cried out for Jesus to notice them and to help them.

Jesus did notice, and he did help them. He sent them to show the priests their healed bodies. They were still lepers as they started off; their healing took place as they ran. As they realized what was happening, nine of them ran even faster toward their new lives. They couldn't wait to make up for lost time! But one man stopped. His first instinct was to run back to Jesus and thank him for this miracle of all miracles! It didn't matter that the one who'd healed him was from a rival ethnic group. The Samaritan shouted his praise and fell at Jesus' feet in a humble and moving gesture of thanksgiving. The significance of which man returned was not lost on Jesus. The others seemed to have a sense of entitlement, while this foreigner had a sense of gratefulness. Jesus praised him for his faith. At the end of the day, ten men had restored bodies, but only one had a restored soul.

Be sure you never assume a sense of entitlement with God. Think of all he has done for you—your family, your health, your talents, your friends, your church, your home. Think of the opportunities he's given you and the many times he's protected you from danger. Most of all, consider that he died on the cross to provide forgiveness for your sins and to give you a brand-new life. As you're rushing out to enjoy your blessings, don't forget to stop long enough to say thank you.

Weariness

"Come to me, all you who are weary and burdened, and I will give you rest. Take my yoke upon you and learn from me, for I am gentle and humble in heart, and you will find rest for your souls. For my yoke is easy and my burden is light."

Matthew 11:28-30

Even when you're young and strong, life can wear you down sometimes. Different things can cause you to get run down. Physical tiredness is probably the easiest form of weariness to remedy. Depending on how depleted you are, a hot tub, a good rest, or a vacation might build you back up. Emotional tiredness is a little harder to overcome, but it, too, can often be eased by taking time out to rejuvenate. Sometimes a counselor can help; in some cases just the passing of time brings emotional healing. There is one form of weariness, however, that no power nap, or bubble bath, or getaway can touch. That's spiritual exhaustion. Spiritual exhaustion happens gradually and imperceptibly. You might not even be aware that your spiritual strength is draining, but one day you realize that your soul feels heavy from all you have experienced.

How does it happen? When you stop spending time with God as you once did; when you allow unconfessed sin or unforgiveness to weigh you down; when you hold on to your anxieties, instead of giving them to God (1 Peter 5:7); when you wrestle with decisions that God has already made for you, these things can subtly eat away at your spiritual strength until you finally hit the wall. You'll know when you've hit the wall because you'll consider the Christian life a drain and a burden rather than a joy.

It doesn't have to be that way. Jesus offers you a perfect, peaceful rest such as no human therapy could ever give you. He can give you strength, not only to get back on your feet, but to soar like an eagle! (Isaiah 40:31). If you're spiritually exhausted, you're not walking with Christ as he wants you to. He loves you. He wants to carry your burdens. Go to him and find rest for your soul.

Chapter 2

Lessons from the Sermon on the Mount

Teaching. Preaching. Healing. Everywhere he went, Jesus explained the Scriptures, preached the good news, and made sick people well. Never had the people encountered a man like Jesus! Lots of rabbis taught in the synagogues but none with the authority that Jesus had (Matthew 7:29)! The other teachers droned on about keeping the Law, but Jesus taught about freedom and forgiveness. Other preachers had come and gone, but Jesus was in a class by himself. He seemed to understand the Scriptures as no one ever had before (Luke 2:47). Perhaps most amazing to the crowds was his healing power. With a mere touch, Jesus cured deafness, blindness, paralysis, epilepsy, and leprosy. He even cast out demons. No wonder the crowds followed him! They followed him partway up a mountain to hear what he had to say to his disciples. As they gathered, Jesus taught them with spellbinding insights into God's Word. Scholars have named his message the Sermon on the Mount. You can read it for yourself in Matthew's Gospel (chapters 5–7). For the next couple of days, we'll examine the profound wisdom of the greatest teacher in history—Jesus Christ.

Let Christ Teach You

Now when he saw the crowds, he went up on a mountainside and sat down. His disciples came to him, and he began to teach them.

Matthew 5:1-2

Everywhere Jesus went, masses of people followed. The sick would cry out loudly for healing. People would jostle one another to get a closer look at him. They'd press in on Jesus, trying to touch him and be healed. As news spread about this miracle worker, people from surrounding cities dropped what they were doing and rushed to Galilee to see for themselves. It never took them long to locate Jesus. The noise had grown to a deafening pitch. If Jesus was looking for a quiet spot to spend some time with his disciples, he didn't find it. Instead, he climbed partway up a mountain and sat down. His disciples gathered around him. The crowds closed in around the disciples. All became quiet. Then Jesus delivered a sermon that has seen no match in history: scholars have named it the Sermon on the Mount. You can read it for yourself in Matthew's Gospel (chapters 5–7). Jesus was actually teaching his twelve disciples, but the crowds were also treated that day to the most profound teaching in human history. Matthew records that Jesus' audience was amazed at his teaching.

This same Jesus is your Teacher. He has wisdom to share with you that will astound you too. What he has to teach you will change your life. You don't have to be sitting in a quiet sanctuary or a Sunday school class for him to teach you, though you can learn in both of those places. He can teach you something no matter where you are, even in a noisy crowd. Do you understand who your Teacher is? He is the Christ, the Lord of the universe! Pay close attention when he speaks so you don't miss a word he has for you!

January 12

The Poor in Spirit

"Blessed are the poor in spirit,
for theirs is the kingdom of heaven."

Matthew 5:3

Financial advisers will tell you one secret to monetary success: if you want to become rich, live like a pauper. Many billionaires are famous for their chintzy lifestyles; they live in modest homes and drive ordinary cars. They consistently live below their means, and the money they don't spend is invested to earn high returns. On the contrary, the bankruptcy files tell the sad story of many who lived as though they had much more money than they did. The rich didn't spend the money they had; the poor spent money they didn't have. The key to financial prosperity appears to be underestimating your worth!

The key to spiritual prosperity is much the same. Many people falsely assume their spiritual bank account is full simply because they're good people. They try not to hurt anyone. They don't break the law. They go to church every Sunday. They give to charity. But they are deceived. They're exaggerating their status in God's eyes. They conclude that God must be pleased with them because of their goodness. They need to understand that their good deeds won't cover their spiritual debt. Their spiritual debt is immense! It's overwhelming! In fact, they'll never be able to pay it off. You guessed it; they're spiritually bankrupt.

Jesus said we will inherit the kingdom of heaven only when we recognize our inability to pay our spiritual debt. When we admit our spiritual poverty and understand that without Christ we are spiritually destitute, we actually become wealthy. In fact, our riches will not be depleted in our lifetime or even in eternity. By assuming the attitude of a pauper, we'll build up a limitless bank account in heaven. This is what it means to be poor in spirit. Another word for it is *humility.*

Take Your Sin Seriously

*"Blessed are those who mourn,
for they will be comforted."*

Matthew 5:4

Jesus was preaching a sermon to his disciples. And what a sermon it is! He began by revealing the eight steps required to reach spiritual maturity. We know these eight steps as the Beatitudes of Christ. As scholars have pointed out, the brilliance of Christ's teaching is evident in the way he presented these eight progressive steps. There they are; Jesus and his disciples seated on the mountainside with multitudes of curious spectators all around them. Jesus used the visual imagery of their setting to describe the process each person must go through in order to reach spiritual maturity. It's like climbing a mountain; each step leads to the next as we continue to reach new heights in our spiritual development.

The first step is to recognize our own sinfulness. In the first beatitude, Jesus likened this step to being poor in spirit, or humble. Now Jesus said the second step is repentance—grieving over our sin. Today, we might use the term *remorse*. Jesus referred to it as mourning over our sin. Mourning is usually associated with death; when someone we love dies, we mourn the loss as a way of dealing with our emotional anguish. Grief counselors say that unless we mourn a loss, we'll never begin the healing process. Jesus said essentially the same thing concerning sin. When we face the gravity of our sin head-on and grieve over its devastating power, then we will find comfort and healing in Christ.

Some people want to skip the grief stage and go straight to rebirth. Sin is too depressing to deal with; they'd rather hurry along to the part about becoming a new creation. These people don't want to see their sin for what it is, so they try to gloss over it. "I never meant to hurt anyone. I haven't done anything really awful." Jesus said that in order to receive salvation, we must see our sin for what it is. We have to see sin the way God sees it—devastating and destructive. We have to understand that sin causes death. Only when we grieve over the depravity of our soul's sinful condition will we find comfort and renewal in Christ.

Step two isn't easy, but it's a necessary step in spiritual growth. If you've been taking your sin lightly or finding excuses for your sin, there's something you've not understood. Sin cost Jesus his life. Your sin. When you truly understand this truth, and it breaks your heart, you're ready for your next step up the mountain.

LESSONS the mount

January 14

Strength in Meekness

"Blessed are the meek,
for they will inherit the earth."

Matthew 5:5

Generations of comic strip fans knew the inside scoop on Superman, even though the citizens of Metropolis were unaware of it. The startling truth was this: meek and mild Clark Kent was really Superman in a very thin, but apparently convincing, disguise that consisted of a pair of eyeglasses. Clark Kent was meek, but he certainly wasn't weak. In fact, he went to great lengths to hide the superhuman power behind those spectacles. What did Jesus mean when he said the meek will inherit the earth? He meant those who surrender their lives to the control of the Holy Spirit will experience God's matchless power working in their lives.

This is beatitude number three in the eight steps toward spiritual maturity as outlined by Jesus in the Sermon on the Mount. This is the point in your spiritual climb when your life will start to look like Christ. Through the power of God's Holy Spirit, you'll have the ability to forgive others, which takes a much stronger character than getting revenge. You'll have the moral strength to overcome temptation. You'll have the self-control to resist your own sinful inclinations. Your life will be defined by strength, not insecurity. That's what Jesus meant by meekness. Jesus himself provided the ultimate demonstration of meekness. Though he was the Son of God, he willingly surrendered himself to his enemies in order to save the human race from its own destruction. The irony is heavy: his tormentors mocked him for lacking the power to come down from the cross (Mark 15:30), but Jesus showed infinitely more strength by remaining on the cross rather than crying out to his Father to rescue him from its horror. That's meekness.

People may try to convince you Christianity is fine for weaklings, but strong people don't need God. They have no idea what true strength is! Trusting in Jesus doesn't sap your strength; it empowers you in ways you'd never experience without Christ (Luke 9:1)! Don't be reluctant to let the Holy Spirit control your life. A Spirit-controlled life is evidence that you know Christ and that you're growing more and more like him.

Spiritual Hunger

*"Blessed are those who hunger and thirst for righteousness,
for they will be filled."*

Matthew 5:6

When we mention appetite, we're usually talking about food. Actually, the word *appetite* comes from the Latin word *petere*, meaning "to seek." An appetite is a strong desire that compels us to go after something. We can crave all sorts of things: food, love, attention, intimacy, power, money, and so on. Appetites can be good or bad, sometimes both. Hunger and thirst are necessary for survival, but when they're abused, they can lead to gluttony and disease. Love is essential to life, but when we go after the wrong kind of love, we're headed for disaster. God doesn't promise to satisfy every appetite we have, but he does promise that whoever seeks after him will find him (Matthew 7:7).

Have you grown discouraged because you've failed in some way to honor God? Are you disappointed with yourself for allowing peer pressure to coerce you into sinning? Maybe you've tried so many times, unsuccessfully, to overcome a sinful habit that you've resigned yourself to living with failure. Perhaps you've given in to a temptation so often you think you're powerless to overcome it. Jesus has a word for you: Don't give up! Don't let go of your desire to please God. If you truly desire a life that pleases God, keep seeking after it. You'll find it!

Righteousness means things are right with God and right with other people. When you became a Christian, God looked upon you as righteous because of the blood of Jesus. It wasn't your own righteousness that earned you eternal life; it was Christ's. From the moment you accepted Christ, God's plan has been for you to pursue righteousness yourself, to grow more and more like Christ. On your own, you could never live the way God desires, but the Holy Spirit will cause a deep craving for holiness within you. You'll experience conviction when you sin because the Spirit is guiding you toward righteousness. This appetite, which makes you long to please God, is a gift. It's a good thing! Don't get down in the dumps when you fail to measure up to God's desires. Take your failures to him, leave them there, and keep seeking righteousness. If you're genuinely longing for spiritual victory, Christ says you *will* be satisfied.

LESSONS the mount

January 16

Mercy

*"Blessed are the merciful,
  for they will be shown mercy."*

Matthew 5:7

At some point in our lives, we all need mercy. We all mess up. We all say foolish things that are better left unsaid. Every one of us has done something we wish we could go back and undo. When that happens, we know we deserve to pay the consequences for our thoughtlessness. That friend we let down shouldn't trust us again. The parent we disobeyed should punish us. The person we've offended should never forgive us.

Do you remember times like these, times when you braced yourself for the worst but you were met with loving forgiveness instead? Do you remember how thrilled you were to be given another chance? Do you remember the joy you experienced when you became a Christian and you realized your sins were forgiven. Every low-down, disgusting, nasty, despicable, mean, you-get-the-picture, thing you ever did was wiped from your record, and you received a brand-new start?

Jesus doesn't want you to ever forget what it's like to receive mercy when you deserve condemnation. When the shoe is on the other foot and you're on the receiving end of the hurtful words or the offensive behavior, stop and think about mercy. Sure, your friend said a nasty thing. Of course your sister did an irresponsible thing. If you don't feel like showing mercy for the sheer joy of doing so, remember this: Jesus warned that you'll be treated with the same measure of mercy that you give to others (Matthew 7:1–2). Are you a merciful person? That'll hold you in good stead when you need a dose of forgiveness yourself. What's more, when you're willing to extend mercy to others, no matter how badly they've treated you, you're another step farther up the mountain to maturity, and that's a step closer to being like Jesus.

Can You See Him?   January 17

*"Blessed are the pure in heart,
  for they will see God."*

Matthew 5:8

Sin causes many problems. It causes division between friends and between family members. It causes pain. It causes broken hearts. Did you know sin also causes blindness? Sin blinds us to the needs of others as well as to our own faults (Luke 6:42). Jesus said sin also obstructs our vision of God.

Many hard-hearted and bitter people have concluded with certainty that God doesn't exist. If he did, they claim, they would see evidence of his existence. They act on the assumption that God is obligated to make his presence known to them. The truth is, God is not obligated to reveal himself; he chooses to do so. Over and over, the Bible gives the assurance that those whose hearts are pure will see God, while those who close their hearts to him will not. When Jesus walked on earth, teaching the crowds and healing the sick, many were moved to discover the Messiah was in their midst. Others, who saw the same miracles and heard the same message, were equally convinced he was an impostor! It was the same Jesus; the difference was the way they saw him.

The question is not whether God makes his presence known but whether you're able to see him. If you've been blind to God's activity all around you, it's time to open your eyes! Have you been trying to hold on to your sin and then wondered why you can't see God? There is no mystery to finding God. From the beginning of time, he has made it clear that if we seek him first, above all else, we will see him as he really is (Jeremiah 29:13). Don't let sin obstruct your vision of God. Ask God to reveal every sinful thought or attitude within you so you can get rid of it. When your heart is pure and your motives are right, you will see God— and you'll never be the same again.

Making Peace

"Blessed are the peacemakers,
for they will be called sons of God."

Matthew 5:9

Have you ever noticed a strong family resemblance between a child and a parent, then you were surprised to discover the child was adopted? Even when families adopt cross-cultural-ly, family members can grow to resemble one another. That's because the similarity is not necessarily physical. It's behavioral. It's seen in the subtle things—gestures, expressions, pet phrases. Families spend so much time together that without realizing it they take on a certain collective identity.

God's family is no different. As believers spend time together, we develop our own family characteristics. First of all, we speak a common language based on our shared Bible knowledge. Unbelievers can guess, but they may not always understand what we mean by "good stewards," "prodigal sons," "broods of vipers," "the fall," and "the rapture." We also adopt common expressions, such as peppering our prayers with the word *just:* "Lord, we just ask that you just bless just those missionaries because they're just so . . . just . . . just mission minded!"

Certain behaviors should characterize every member of God's family. We should be kind, gentle, loving, forgiving, patient, and conspicuous for our self-control. We should also be known for our desire to bring peace. Jesus said every Christian should be known as a peacemaker. Despite all the foolish wars that have been waged in God's name, he is a God of peace. The entire gospel message is one of peace (Ephesians 2:14–16). Jesus has appointed every believer to a ministry of reconciliation (2 Corinthians 5:18). The world should know they can count on Christians to bring peace, not division. Being a peacemaker isn't always easy. We can be shot at from both sides, but our model is Jesus. He gave his life to give us peace with God.

Today's beatitude is the seventh of eight steps toward Christlikeness. According to Jesus' Sermon on the Mount, being a peacemaker is one of the Christian's highest callings. If you're growing in your faith, your life will have an influence on those around you. The environment you live in—your school, your workplace, your home—should be more peaceful because of your presence. If you're more prone to stir up dissension than to bring peace, you're not living up to your family name. Bring peace where there is division, and Jesus said it will be obvious whose child you are.

Blessed Are the Persecuted

"Blessed are those who are persecuted because of righteousness, for theirs is the kingdom of heaven."

Matthew 5:10

Imagine you were one of the disciples and you were listening to Jesus' Sermon on the Mount. Thus far, Jesus had served up some revolutionary thinking! Let's suppose, like all good students, you were taking notes. Maybe they'd read something like this:

Subject: Eight Steps toward Spiritual Maturity
Blessed Are the Following:

Qualifications	*Expectations*
1. Poor in spirit (humble)	kingdom of heaven
2. Mourners (remorseful for sin)	comfort
3. Meek (note to self: meek not equal with weak)	the earth
4. Those who crave righteousness	shall be filled
5. Merciful	mercy
6. Pure in heart	will see God
7. Peacemakers	known as children of God
8. Persecuted	?

Would you drop your quill at that point, or check your neighbor's notes to be sure you heard correctly? You'd seen persecution, and it didn't look like a blessing—people being whipped, beaten, and crucified for not toeing the party line. How, by anyone's imagination, could this be a blessing? But wait . . . Jesus said it again, "Blessed are those who are persecuted." He said that being persecuted because of him is cause to rejoice because the rewards for such suffering will be great in heaven.

When you're ridiculed and rejected for your faith, remember Jesus' words. Jesus listed persecution for his sake as the highest form of Christian maturity. Some find the climb too strenuous, the suffering too much to bear, and they turn back. But if you persevere to the top of the mountain, the flags you see will be those of the prophets—Moses, Joshua, Elijah; and your reward will be great, just as theirs is.

January 20

Salt

"You are the salt of the earth; but if the salt has become tasteless, how can it be made salty again? It is no longer good for anything, except to be thrown out and trampled under foot by men."

Matthew 5:13 (NASB)

Salt was a valuable commodity in Jesus' day. It was important for several reasons. First, it kept food from rotting. Meat, preserved with salt, would stay fresh much longer than without it. Second, as it is today, salt was used to bring out taste in food. A sprinkle of salt, and bland food had flavor. Finally, salt was used for healing. Applying salt to a wound would help it heal faster. Salt was considered so valuable in Jesus' day that it was used for money. That's where we get the phrase, "He's worth his salt."

Jesus often taught by using everyday stories and examples. In this case, he compared Christians to salt. Christians help to preserve people from sin and destruction. It may be that your friend is being tempted to sin but you urge him to resist. You are keeping him from the destructive effects of sin. Christians are also to add flavor to life by bringing joy to those around us. The world should be a better place because we are in it. Finally, we are God's instrument for bringing healing to people. When those who are hurting come to us, we are to share God's love with them. In doing so, we help to heal their wounded souls, and we bring them the life that is found in Christ.

Just as salt was highly valued in Jesus' time, we make a valuable difference in the lives of those around us. Jesus cautions us not to lose our saltiness lest we lose our good influence for God's kingdom. It's crucial that we act as God intended and enrich the lives of others.

Lighting Things Up

"You are the light of the world. A city set on a hill cannot be hidden; nor does anyone light a lamp and put it under a basket, but on the lampstand, and it gives light to all who are in the house. Let your light shine before men in such a way that they may see your good works, and glorify your Father who is in heaven."

Matthew 5:14-16 (NASB)

Few things are as important to people as light. When people want to be secure from crime, they turn on lights. When people can't see things clearly, they turn on a light. People who are deprived of light can become depressed and even suicidal. Without enough light, people get sick. Light is something we take for granted—until it is no longer there.

Jesus described Christians as light. There are things that cover people's lives with darkness—things such as sickness, loss, guilt, and failure. When people are living in darkness, they need hope. Christians can be the light for them. We can offer them Christ's hope. We can bring light to those who don't know Jesus—those who are living in spiritual darkness—by letting Christ shine through us.

No problem is so dark that God cannot bring victory, no sin so evil that God cannot forgive it and make the sinner clean. As a Christian, you have the opportunity to be light in a darkened world. Everywhere you go you ought to be enlightening people about God. Will you be that light today?

Whom Do You Believe?

"You have heard that it was said to the people long ago, 'Do not murder, and anyone who murders will be subject to judgment.' But I tell you that anyone who is angry with his brother will be subject to judgment."

Matthew 5:21-22

Everyone has an opinion about what's right and wrong. People can hold inflexible views about what's acceptable in society and what's not. They can get highly charged emotionally while arguing their point. Listen to a call-in program on any number of subjects, and you'll hear the whole gamut of opinions. One caller will be adamantly in favor of something; the next will be vigorously opposed to the same thing. Both are convinced they know the truth.

You'll encounter people with all sorts of value systems. Because you're a Christian, many people will appoint themselves as your liberators and try to free you from your old-fashioned mind-set. Many university professors pride themselves on challenging the Christians in their classes. The world will offer you all kinds of proof for its way of thinking. What should you do? Don't be afraid of people's opinions, but always remember this: until you've heard from Christ, you've not heard the truth (John 14:6).

In Jesus' day the Law was very important. The Ten Commandments, as handed down to Moses, and ancient Scriptures provided the definitive word on what was right and what was wrong. Some people made a career out of explaining the Old Testament Law to the common people. As far as the Jewish people were concerned, the Mosaic Law was God's final word on any subject. Then, along came Jesus. He took the Scriptures to a completely new dimension. He didn't dispute what the Law-teachers taught; he expanded it. He presented God's Word, not only what it said about outward practice but also what it said about the heart. The Law said don't murder; Jesus said don't even hold hatred in your heart. The Law said don't commit adultery; Jesus said don't even lust in your heart. The law said keep your oaths; Jesus said don't even make them. The Law said love your neighbor but go ahead and get revenge on your enemies; Jesus said love both your friends and your enemies (Matthew 5:43–47).

Over and over, Jesus took popular opinion and added, "But I say to you. . . ." If someone is trying to convince you of something, don't agree until you've heard from the Truth. If God's Word differs from what you're hearing, you know whom to believe.

Lessons ⌐⌐⌐ ⌐ ⌐⌐⌐⌐⌐⌐ e mount

Making Things Right

"Therefore, if you are offering your gift at the altar and there remember that your brother has something against you, leave your gift there in front of the altar. First go and be reconciled to your brother; then come and offer your gift."

Matthew 5:23-24

To a Jew nothing was more important than worshiping God. Since Old Testament times, the nation of Israel had offered sacrifices as a way to show reverence for God. There was no better place to be than kneeling at the altar with an offering for God. How Jesus' words must have shocked them!

Jesus said if you're in the midst of worship and you realize that someone is offended at you, stop worshiping and go mend the relationship. After you've made things right in the relationship, *then* God is interested in your gift.

To us this might not seem so radical, but to Jesus' audience this was scandalous! Nevertheless, we can be just as guilty of trying to satisfy God with our good deeds—going to church, attending a Bible study, living a moral life—while refusing to be reconciled with someone who is angry with us. Jesus' message is clearly directed at us too. He's not asking for nominal attempts at reconciliation, where we offer a feeble or partial apology: "I'll admit I was wrong if you will" or "I tried to reconcile with her but she was still angry." He's calling for us to restore the relationship completely, no matter who was right and who was wrong, no matter how long it takes. Then we can return gladly to worship, with hearts free from guilt or bitterness. Then our offering means something. Before you attend another worship service, is there someone with whom you need to be reconciled?

LESSONS the mount

January 24

Be Perfect!

"Be perfect, therefore, as your heavenly Father is perfect."

Matthew 5:48

"Christians aren't perfect, just forgiven." So says the bumper sticker, and it may be an accurate description for you at this point. But that's not an excuse to settle for just being forgiven. God wants you to strive for perfection. Jesus said so himself, and Matthew recorded it. When you read this, you might think something was lost in the translation: *I'll never be perfect. Perhaps Jesus said to be as close to perfect as you can be or to be a perfectionist.* No, Jesus said it *is* possible to be perfect. Saying otherwise is saying God is unable to make you like his Son. That's a statement about God as much as it is about you.

Biblically speaking, to be perfect means to be complete, lacking in nothing. To be perfect means to reach spiritual maturity. It doesn't mean you never make mistakes. It means the fruit of the Spirit will be evident in your life (Galatians 5:22), so your life will be characterized by the same things that characterized Jesus' life: love, joy, peace, patience, kindness, goodness, faithfulness, gentleness, and self-control. In other words, to be perfect means to be like Christ. A tall order? You bet. But God wants to fill it. His Word says so (Galatians 2:20).

Throughout history, the human race has accepted a lower standard for ourselves than God's standard for us. Our sin has caused us to fall short of becoming the people God meant for us to be. The Bible is filled with accounts of those who chose to disobey God instead of cooperating with him, and it always led to their destruction. We still do it. We still don't trust that God can make us complete, so we choose our own way. We do what we think is best, and we get what we bargained for—our own best wisdom. Jesus said it doesn't have to be that way. God has a plan to make us spiritually mature. We just have to trust him and follow it. If we will allow him, he will rid us of every selfish and sinful attitude in our hearts. Then he'll remake us into the image of his Son.

Where Is Your Heart?   January 25

"Do not store up for yourselves treasures on earth, where moth and rust destroy, and where thieves break in and steal.

But store up for yourselves treasures in heaven, where neither moth nor rust destroys, and where thieves do not break in or steal;

for where your treasure is, there your heart will be also."

Matthew 6:19-21 (NASB)

Your heart can be a battleground! Many people want to control it. Whoever or whatever owns your heart will determine what you do with your life. One of the great temptations for your heart will be in the area of money and possessions. The world will bombard you with advertisements of wonderful things you could buy if only you had enough money. Slick advertisements will promise that your life would be perfect if only you had a particular product. Society will affirm that whoever has the most money will be the happiest and most powerful. The world can make the pursuit of money and possessions tempting!

Jesus has a warning for you if you are preoccupied with gaining wealth: Wealth doesn't last. Money doesn't satisfy. It is only temporary. Possessions can be stolen. Money can be lost or wasted. Even if you do obtain wealth, you will find that it disappoints because it cannot truly satisfy you.

Jesus taught that true happiness comes not from collecting possessions but from investing our lives in things that are eternal. Spiritual things last forever; no one can take them away. They don't depreciate over time. Investing in God's kingdom is the smartest investment anyone could make.

Where have you been investing your time and effort? What is it you really care about? Have you set your heart to care about things that will last forever?

January 26

Don't Judge

"Do not judge so that you will not be judged.

For in the way you judge, you will be judged; and by your standard of measure, it will be measured to you."

Matthew 7:1-2 (NASB)

Jesus warned us not to judge one another. He said we should be careful because the standard we use to judge others will be the same standard used to judge us. This doesn't mean we can never say anything when someone else is sinning. If a friend is sinning, we don't have to agree with his activities because we know we're not supposed to judge anyone. That isn't what Jesus meant. Some people like to quote this verse as an excuse to do whatever they want without being corrected.

Jesus was talking about the attitude of immediately condemning someone without hearing all the evidence. It's an attitude that shows no mercy to someone who has done wrong. It's an attitude that takes delight in condemning those who do not live the way you think they should.

Remember, God is perfectly fair. It's his job to judge people's actions and the motives behind them, not ours. We've been duly warned. If we act as judge over others, we'll be measured by the same harsh standards that we use to condemn others. Be as generous as you can with your attitude toward others, and God will respond with grace toward you.

Are You Listening?

"Therefore everyone who hears these words of mine and puts them into practice is like a wise man who built his house on the rock."

Matthew 7:24

Hearing and listening are two completely different things. Hearing is a physical process in which sound waves go into your ears, vibrate for a while, then head for your brain. Listening is a mental process; listening is what your brain does with the message it gets. Igor Stravinsky, a Russian music composer, said it this way: "To listen is an effort, and just to hear is no merit. A duck hears also." A deaf person may not hear, but she can be an excellent listener. On the contrary, a hearing person may have sound waves entering his head, but that doesn't make him a good listener.

In his Sermon on the Mount, Jesus explained the huge difference between hearing his words and listening to them. He compared the wisdom of those who act on his words to the foolishness of those who hear what he says but follow their own plans. Jesus used the analogy of two men who were both building houses. The first man understood that a house built on a solid foundation could withstand the storms when they came. Sure enough, the rain fell, and the winds blew, but the wise man's house, built on a rock, was unshaken. The second man was too foolish to plan ahead. Without considering the possibility of storms, he built his house on sand. The same rain fell on his house, and the same winds blew against it. The foolish man's house fell with a mighty crash because there was nothing under it to hold it up.

Don't be like the foolish builder. Don't think your job is done once you've heard what Jesus has to say. When you hear a great message or when you read a profound truth in your Bible, these are nothing more than sound waves tickling your eardrums unless you apply what you hear. The evidence that you've listened is a changed life. God's Word has more than enough wisdom to see you through life's storms. Jesus has so much to tell you! Are you listening?

Chapter 3
Great Moments of Decision

Your life will be the sum of all the decisions you make. The studies you pursue and how far you extend your education will determine the direction your career takes. The person you choose to marry will obviously affect your future considerably. Financial choices—how much to spend and how much to save—will establish your standard of living. Your decision to forgive someone or to hold a grudge, to give in to temptation or to resist it, to work hard or hardly work, to take the high road or to blame someone else—all of these choices will have an impact on your life.

Life calls for scores of decisions every day. Most are rather minor, such as what to wear or what to eat (though these are major issues for some people!). Other decisions are much weightier, such as whether to drive recklessly or whether to steal from your employer. In these weighty situations, your choices will change your life forever. The Bible tells about people who faced such monumental decisions. Consider what you can learn from their experiences as you face similar choices.

Rich Young Ruler

So when Jesus heard these things, He said to him, "You still lack one thing. Sell all that you have and distribute to the poor, and you will have treasure in heaven; and come, follow Me."

But when he heard this, he became very sorrowful, for he was very rich.

Luke 18:22-23 (NKJV)

God knows what is most important to us. We may say that our relationship with him takes precedence over everything else, but is it true? God knows. A wealthy young man approached Jesus with the claim that loving God and keeping his commandments were his top priorities. Jesus knew immediately this was not true. He instructed the young man to get rid of everything he owned so he would be free to join Jesus and his disciples. Jesus zeroed in on what mattered most to the young man. This fellow loved God, but he loved the security that his riches brought him even more. Jesus was forcing him to decide what would have first place in his heart, his devotion to God or his love for money. Sadly, the young man chose his wealth. This momentous decision changed his life forever. He must have felt a deep sense of loss, knowing he was missing out on an incredible opportunity. Luke tells us that the young man went away sad. Perhaps he understood that he was trading in eternity with God for temporary earthly comfort.

Jesus knows your heart as well. He knows if your friends matter more to you than God does. He knows if sports, good grades, or parties are more important than your relationship with him. He will give you the same option that he gave the proud young man two thousand years ago. Would you be willing to give up the most important thing in your life if it were keeping you from loving God as you should?

Cain

So the LORD said to Cain, "Why are you angry? And why has your countenance fallen? If you do well, will you not be accepted? And if you do not do well, sin lies at the door. And its desire is for you, but you should rule over it."

Now Cain talked with Abel his brother, and it came to pass, when they were in the field, that Cain rose up against Abel his brother and killed him.

Genesis 4:6-8 (NKJV)

The most dangerous decisions are made in the heat of anger. Anger makes us reckless and causes us to foolishly disregard the possible results of our actions. Only after we have cooled down do we recognize the damage we have done.

Cain was furious! His kid brother, Abel, could apparently do no wrong. Their parents always seemed pleased with Abel and disappointed in Cain. Even God appeared to favor Abel over his older brother. Finally, Cain's jealousy boiled over into rage, and he lost perspective. That's when he made an irrational decision: if he couldn't match up to his brother, he'd get rid of him! Of course Cain should have realized that he couldn't hide a murder from God. However, anger blinded him to the point that even when God warned him of the outcome of his diabolical plan he took no notice! At that moment he didn't care what the consequences would be.

When you allow yourself to become angry and lose your self-control, you are in great danger. No one can make you angry. It is a choice you make. Anger is never your only option: you can choose to forgive; you can decide to change your attitude; you can even pray for the one who has provoked you. Do you sometimes find that being angry at someone else is easier than making changes in your own life?

When you find your heart is filled with rage, go immediately to God. Ask him to remove the anger from your heart and to replace it with patience, forgiveness, and love. Through his Holy Spirit, God will warn you, as he did Cain, of the danger in acting out your anger. Be wiser than Cain was, and you won't have to live with regret.

Josiah

Josiah was eight years old when he became king, and he reigned thirty-one years in Jerusalem. His mother's name was Jedidah the daughter of Adaiah of Bozkath. And he did what was right in the sight of the LORD, and walked in all the ways of his father David; he did not turn aside to the right hand or to the left.

2 Kings 22:1-2 (NKJV)

Josiah had every excuse to live an evil life. His grandfather, Manasseh, was arguably the most wicked king ever to rule Judah. The Bible says he "shed so much innocent blood that he filled Jerusalem from end to end—besides the sin that he had caused Judah to commit, so that they did evil in the eyes of the LORD" (2 Kings 21:16). Josiah's father, Amon, was as wicked as Manasseh had been (2 Kings 21:20). What a terrible heritage to have as a child. Josiah was only eight years old when he became king. Could you blame him if he had chosen a reign of wickedness as his father and his grandfather had before him? He was surrounded by a family who mocked God and laughed at those who tried to live a godly life.

Amazingly, the Bible says that Josiah chose to reject the hedonistic ways of his heritage in order to do "what was right in the eyes of the Lord." It must have been intimidating to go against the practices that his family had begun. By the time Josiah inherited the throne, the nation of Judah had rejected God and adopted the idol worship of his father and grandfather. Josiah had to oppose his family, his royal court, and the very nation he governed in order to follow the true God. He was surrounded by distractions, yet the Bible says he persevered in his faith.

Can you identify in some way with Josiah? You may not have been raised in a Christian family; perhaps your parents oppose your choice to follow Christ. If you are the only Christian in your family, your desire to live the Christian life may be misunderstood, even ridiculed. Don't let the resistance of others keep you from following your Lord. Your relationship with God is a choice you make, not one that your parents or your friends make for you. No matter how the people around you choose to live, you still have a choice regarding your own life. Choose to begin a family heritage of faith in God.

David

And the Philistine said to David, "Come to me, and I will give your flesh to the birds of the air and the beasts of the field!"

Then David said to the Philistine, "You come to me with a sword, with a spear, and with a javelin. But I come to you in the name of the LORD of hosts, the God of the armies of Israel, whom you have defied."

1 Samuel 17:44-45

Sooner or later we all have to choose whether to believe what the giant tells us. Can you picture the scene? Across the field looms a growling, menacing hulk of a man. He's nine feet tall and dressed in magnificent bronze armor. He wields a huge sword and a deadly spear. His massive shield appears impenetrable. His name is Goliath, and he wants to eat you for breakfast. "Your corpse will make a nice meal for the birds and wild animals tonight!" he sneers.

You, on the other hand, are a skinny teenager, dressed only in sheepskin. Your arsenal is a slingshot and a few small stones. You have to decide whether you believe the giant's taunts. Probably everyone watching believes him! What do you do? David chose to believe that God would give him the victory despite the lopsided odds. He was right.

Sometimes your problems look like giants, and giants come in many forms. One of your giants could be a broken relationship that seems impossible to mend. Perhaps you must take a stand for your faith in the face of strong opposition. Maybe you have an enemy who seems to have all the weapons. Whatever your situation is, things don't look good, but you know in your heart what God wants you to do. The decision you make next reveals what you really believe about God. Don't believe what the giant tells you! Believe God instead, and he will give you victory. It's significant that God did not help David by making Goliath smaller; he gave David victory over all nine feet of him! That's the kind of God you serve!

John

When He had gone a little farther from there, He saw James the son of Zebedee, and John his brother, who also were in the boat mending their nets. And immediately He called them, and they left their father Zebedee in the boat with the hired servants, and went after Him.

Mark 1:19-20 (NKJV)

Sometimes you must make decisions quickly. You can't take several days to respond to an invitation from God. When John was a teenager, he worked with his older brother James and their father, Zebedee, in the fishing industry. Their business was successful; they had servants and business partners to help them. John had everything in place for a great future. One day he and James would inherit their father's possessions, and John could live out his days in peace and comfort.

Then Jesus came along with an invitation: "Follow me." John had been watching Jesus. He probably had some idea what following him would involve. A dozen questions must have flashed through John's mind: *Where would they sleep? What would they eat? What would happen to the family business? What would his father think?* The problem was that Jesus wanted an answer now. There was no time to weigh the options. The Bible tells us that John did not hesitate but got up and followed Jesus immediately. It was the single most important decision John would ever make, and he had to make it instantly.

Are you ready for the invitations Jesus has for you? Some opportunities don't offer a long time for deliberation. Do you know Jesus well enough that when he invites you to join him, you're ready to say yes right away? John could later testify that if he'd stayed in the boat he would have regretted it forever. Don't get left in the boat when Jesus invites you to join him. If the invitation comes from Jesus, you have all the information you need to make your choice.

Peter

Then after about an hour had passed, another confidently affirmed, saying, "Surely this fellow also was with Him, for he is a Galilean."

But Peter said, "Man, I do not know what you are saying!"

Immediately, while he was still speaking, the rooster crowed. And the Lord turned and looked at Peter. Then Peter remembered the word of the Lord, how He had said to him, "Before the rooster crows, you will deny Me three times."

Luke 22:59-61 (NKJV)

You can't help but like Peter. He was impulsive, outspoken, and passionate. He was never at a loss for words, always ready to speak his mind. He had his problems, but a lack of confidence wasn't one of them. And he really loved Jesus! No wonder he was shocked when Jesus predicted that Peter would not stand up for him in his hour of need! Surely not he! He had enough courage to take a swipe at the thug who came to take Jesus away. Instinctively, when he perceived Jesus was in danger, he pulled out a sword and cut off the man's ear! (John 18:10). Certainly that proved he had the courage to take a stand for Jesus.

How then could this burly, opinionated fisherman be reduced to trembling by the questioning of a servant girl? When he was with Jesus and the other disciples, he could not imagine ever denying Jesus. Yet, when he was all alone and Jesus was imprisoned, he lost his bravado. Peter tried to pretend he didn't even know Jesus!

Isn't it the same way for us? When we're surrounded by other believers, it's easy to claim Jesus as our Lord. It's not quite as easy at school or at work, though, when we're the only Christian there. Others might laugh at us or ask tough questions to try to trip us up. We don't want to be rejected, so sometimes it's easier to pretend we're not Christians.

When Peter realized what he had done by denying Jesus, even as Jesus was being tortured for his sake, it broke Peter's big, tender heart. He vowed it would never happen again, and it never did. Standing up for Christ can be one of the hardest things you do. That's why you need to decide in advance that you will stand up for Christ, no matter what the cost.

Judas

Then Satan entered Judas, surnamed Iscariot, who was numbered among the twelve. So he went his way and conferred with the chief priests and captains, how he might betray Him to them. And they were glad, and agreed to give him money. So he promised and sought opportunity to betray Him to them in the absence of the multitude.

Luke 22:3-6 (NKJV)

Judas will go down in infamy as the most treacherous friend in history. He had the unbelievable privilege of spending three and a half years as a friend and confidante of the Savior. He knew Jesus better than almost anyone. Yet he readily betrayed him for the price of a slave. How could Judas do such a horrible thing? How could he betray the Son of God for a few pieces of silver? We cannot know for certain what motivated him. Perhaps it was jealousy. Perhaps he thought that turning Jesus in would bring him a measure of respect, even fame, among the Jewish leaders. Perhaps greed had provoked him. One thing is certain; Judas let selfishness block out his loyalty to the one who had been his friend for years. When Judas sold out the one who had loved him and trusted him, it was not Jesus' welfare he had in mind; it was his own.

Selfishness is immensely destructive. It can blind you to the truth that you are hurting those who love you. Could self-centeredness lead you to betray a friend the way it did Judas? Certainly. Perhaps it already has. Could it cause you to ignore those who need your help? Of course. Are there people you have let down? Did you hurt them because you were thinking only of yourself? Was there something you wanted badly enough to betray a friend to get it? Were you so preoccupied with your own desires that you were oblivious to the needs of your friends and family?

Be careful that you never justify selfish actions. When Judas finally realized what he had done, he was devastated. Selfishness, left unchecked, will devastate you too. Keep watch over your heart so that greed and selfishness do not control your actions and hurt those around you. If you put the needs of others first, you will be free of the guilt and regret that destroyed Judas.

Paul

Then Jews from Antioch and Iconium came there; and having persuaded the multitudes, they stoned Paul and dragged him out of the city, supposing him to be dead. However, when the disciples gathered around him, he rose up and went into the city. And the next day he departed with Barnabas to Derbe.

Acts 14:19-20 (NKJV)

Paul winced in anguish as rocks flew at him, one after another from every direction, lacerating his flesh until it was raw, covering his entire body with oozing wounds. His moans of agony were lost amid the din of the angry, shouting mob that surrounded him, taunting him as they hurled the deadliest stones they could find. There was no way to escape the pain, no hiding from the humiliation. Finally, Paul could stand no longer, and he crumpled to the ground. The angry mob, satisfied that they had killed the blasphemer, dropped their rocks and dragged Paul's broken body out of the city.

Then the other disciples gathered around him, including his friend Barnabas, with whom he had been traveling. A few questions might have crossed Paul's mind at that moment: *Where were you guys when I was being tortured all alone? Why did the Jews pick me and not Barnabas as the brunt of their anger?* The situation was enough to tempt even the most devout Christian to get a little bitter. Perhaps even to call it quits.

So what did Paul do next? He got up, wiped away the blood, and headed back into the city. Without even taking a sick day, he carried on with his missionary journey the very next day. The Bible tells us that when Paul and Barnabas reached Derbe they preached there and "won a large number of disciples." Later verses reveal that "God did extraordinary miracles through Paul" (Acts 19:11). How fortunate for those new Christians—and for the thousands who would follow—that Paul was no quitter!

Paul had a choice in the way he would respond to pain and suffering. He had obeyed God, but look where it had gotten him! Still, he chose to trust God in the midst of hardship, and God blessed him for it. How do you respond when others hurt you? What is your attitude when your Christianity brings jokes and ridicule? Do you get angry at God? Do you run and hide? Do you quit? God has not promised that if you obey him no one will ever hurt you. He does promise never to abandon you. He kept his promise to Paul, and he will keep it to you as well.

Paul and Silas

And when they had laid many stripes on them, they threw them into prison, commanding the jailer to keep them securely. Having received such a charge, he put them into the inner prison and fastened their feet in the stocks.

But at midnight Paul and Silas were praying and singing hymns to God, and the prisoners were listening to them. Suddenly there was a great earthquake, so that the foundations of the prison were shaken; and immediately all the doors were opened and everyone's chains were loosed.

Acts 16:23-26 (NKJV)

Some people love to focus on their misery. They find immense pleasure in recounting, in full detail, every ache and pain, every discomfort, to anyone who'll listen. Do you know anyone like that? Do you know someone who takes pride in finding the negative in every situation? Such people are at a loss for conversation topics if something isn't going wrong in their life. Fortunately for them, there is usually something to gripe about!

Paul and Silas didn't have to look far if they wanted a reason to grumble. Their situation was a complainer's dream! They'd been wrongly accused and beaten with rods until their bodies throbbed with pain. They were shackled in the darkest, gloomiest section of the prison, under the constant surveillance of a hardened jailer. They had everything they needed for a great pity party!

They chose to praise God instead—not just silently or in whispers to one another but loudly so that everyone could hear them! They sang hymns; they prayed. Their environment made no difference; they loved God, and they wanted everyone to know it, including the scowling jailer. Paul and Silas understood an important life lesson that we would all be better off understanding: You can't always choose your circumstances, but you *can* always choose your attitude about those circumstances. A positive attitude is ours for the choosing.

Rehoboam

Then the king answered the people roughly, and rejected the advice which the elders had given him; and he spoke to them according to the advice of the young men, saying, "My father made your yoke heavy, but I will add to your yoke; my father chastised you with whips, but I will chastise you with scourges!"

1 Kings 12:13–14 (NKJV)

Rehoboam was getting advice from both sides. On the one hand were the elders, those who'd been counselors to his father, Solomon, the wisest man in Israel's history. On the other hand were the young men he'd grown up with and whom he wanted to please. The older set was advising him to treat his subjects kindly and to ask less of them. His friends urged him to push the people even harder than his father before him had done. More than likely, Rehoboam knew which advice was the wisest.

He chose to please his friends anyway. He did what they urged, and his nation was split in two. Israel would be torn apart for hundreds of years and left too weak to defend itself from its powerful enemies. All this happened because Rehoboam chose to appease his friends rather than follow the wise advice he received.

Good advice doesn't always come from your favorite source. As hard as it may be to admit, your parents, your teacher, or your pastor may be giving you far wiser counsel than your friends. They might not be telling you what you want to hear, but the best counsel is not always the most appealing. Don't just seek advice from those who will tell you what you want to hear. Be receptive to those who tell you what you need to hear. Make wise choices about where you seek guidance. Your future, as well as the future of others, could be at stake.

Chapter 4
Great Friendships

What can you tell about people by the friends they choose? Quite a bit.

Jesus chose his friends carefully. That didn't make him a snob; he cared deeply about each person he met. However, he was closer to some people than to others. Lazarus and his sisters, Mary and Martha, were privileged to be close friends of Jesus, as were Peter, James, and John. These friendships brought Jesus joy and encouragement. Not one of his friends was perfect, but Jesus loved each of them dearly enough to forgive their imperfections and to help them become better people. That's what friendship is all about.

Some people have trouble making friends. Others have trouble keeping them! The best way to have friends is knowing how to be one. The Bible has a lot to say about friendship. Proverbs urges people to be careful in the friendships they form. The Bible gives several examples of friendship, some healthy and some not so healthy. As you study these friendships in the Bible, examine your own relationships to see if they measure up to God's standards.

Jonathan and David

Now it came about when he had finished speaking to Saul, that the soul of Jonathan was knit to the soul of David, and Jonathan loved him as himself. . . . Then Jonathan made a covenant with David because he loved him as himself. Jonathan stripped himself of the robe that was on him and gave it to David, with his armor, including his sword and his bow and his belt.

1 Samuel 18:1, 3-4 (NASB)

Jonathan and David came from two different worlds. Jonathan was a prince, raised in affluence, wanting for nothing. David was accustomed to sleeping under the stars as he watched over his father's flock of sheep. Other things might have kept them from being friends. Jonathan, as King Saul's son, might naturally have expected to follow his father on the throne. Yet David was chosen to receive that honor. Both David and Jonathan were valiant warriors, yet David received the nation's praise for his heroic battles, not Jonathan.

It's remarkable that Jonathan could rise above these circumstances and not only accept David but actually make a vow to protect his life. In forging a friendship with David, Jonathan revealed a great deal about his own character. He proved that he was kind, generous, above petty jealousy, and genuinely unselfish. He also showed wisdom beyond his years by helping David become the next king of Israel. Jonathan understood and accepted that God had chosen David, not him, and anointed David as Israel's future king. He never worried that David's success might take away from his own. He went beyond merely accepting David as God's chosen king; he even donated his own sword. In doing so, Jonathan gave up his own security, asking nothing from David in return.

There is much to learn about friendship from Jonathan's example! A true friend seeks to give, rather than to take. In true friendship there is no keeping score. A real friend cares as much for his friend's well-being as for his own life. A friend finds joy in the success of her friends, even if their accomplishments outshine her own. Are you examining your friendships? How do you measure up so far?

David's Mighty Men

David had a craving and said, "Oh that someone would give me water to drink from the well of Bethlehem, which is by the gate!"

So the three broke through the camp of the Philistines and drew water from the well of Bethlehem which was by the gate, and took it and brought it to David; nevertheless David would not drink it, but poured it out to the LORD; and he said, "Be it far from me before my God that I should do this. Shall I drink the blood of these men who went at the risk of their lives? For at the risk of their lives they brought it." Therefore he would not drink it. These things the three mighty men did.

1 Chronicles 11:17-19 (NASB)

First of all, there's the obvious question: After these guys risked their necks to get David that water, why didn't he at least drink it instead of wasting it? It seems that David was so humbled by the sacrificial gift of his loyal friends that he could not accept it for himself but instead he offered it to God. These three men thought so highly of David that they endangered their own lives to meet his needs. What kind of person would inspire such loyalty? These were the elite of the army. They were superior soldiers in their own right. They spent much of their time helping David flee from wicked King Saul. They didn't have to do that. They could have joined Saul's army. The pay certainly would have been better, and they could say they worked for a king, not a fugitive.

What was it about David that moved his friends to sacrifice their very lives for him? We may agree that it would be nice to have the kind of friends David had, but what kind of persons would we have to be in order to evoke such loyalty? David proved by his reaction to their venture that he certainly did not take their loyalty lightly. He could not even bring himself to drink the water they had retrieved under such dangerous circumstances. He probably made a mental note not to voice his longings quite so readily in the future once he realized just how loyal his comrades were.

Think about your own friendships. Are your friends willing to take risks for you? If so, do they know that you'll appreciate their efforts? Do they have the assurance that you'd do the same for them?

Four Friends

And many were gathered together, so that there was no longer room, not even near the door; and He was speaking the word to them. And they came, bringing to Him a paralytic, carried by four men. Being unable to get to Him because of the crowd, they removed the roof above Him; and when they had dug an opening, they let down the pallet on which the paralytic was lying. And Jesus seeing their faith said to the paralytic, "Son, your sins are forgiven."

Mark 2:2-5 (NASB)

What would you do to bring a friend to Jesus? This paralyzed man was fortunate to have the friends he did. These guys would stop at nothing to get him to the one who could help him. Even when it looked impossible to get close to Jesus through the thick crowd, they didn't give up. They found a way because they were certain that Jesus would take pity on their crippled friend and heal him.

Jesus admired their faith. He didn't just heal the man's paralysis as they hoped; he did something much better: he forgave the man's sins. It's notable that Jesus forgave the man, not when he saw his faith, but when he saw his friends' faith. This man had his friends to thank for the new life he found in Jesus. The four friends believed so fervently in Jesus' ability to heal that their friend had come to believe as well and had been healed.

You probably have friends who need to know Jesus. It might seem impossible to you. Perhaps they are hostile to Christianity. Maybe they are filled with doubts about whether God can help them. You might feel inadequate to answer their questions. When your friends are hurting and you know that Jesus is the only one who can bring healing and forgiveness to them, what will you do to bring them to him? Have you allowed obstacles to discourage you from bringing a friend to Jesus? Ask God to show you what you need to do so your friends encounter Christ in the same life-changing way that the paralytic did.

Jeremiah and Baruch   February 10

Then Jeremiah took another scroll and gave it to Baruch the son of Neraiah, the scribe, and he wrote on it at the dictation of Jeremiah all the words of the book which Jehoiakim king of Judah had burned in the fire; and many similar words were added to them.

Jeremiah 36:32 (NASB)

Do you have a friend you can always count on to support you as you seek to obey God? When you are tempted to give up on your faith, is there someone who will encourage you to stay faithful? Some friends don't like to get too serious about following Christ. If the cost gets too high, their advice is to give up. Perhaps they worry that you'll be hurt or disappointed. But there is a kind of friend who will back you up every time you try to do what is right.

Jeremiah had only a few friends. He was a prophet whom God appointed to tell people things they didn't want to hear. When you have to tell the king he will be soundly defeated and his family will be killed, there aren't many people who want to go along to deliver the message! Jeremiah did have one friend who was willing to stand with him. His name was Baruch. Baruch wrote down God's message to the people of Judah as Jeremiah dictated it. When the king had Baruch's painstaking work destroyed, a lesser friend would have concluded he'd done enough. Not Baruch. Jeremiah dictated his letter all over again, and Baruch carefully wrote down everything a second time. Baruch knew he was risking his own safety by helping Jeremiah, but he did it anyway. It's not easy finding a friend like Baruch!

Jeremiah didn't have a lot of friends, but he had a genuine friend. Do you have a friend like Baruch? Do you appreciate the friend who consistently encourages you to do the right thing? Are you the kind of friend who helps others when they try to do what honors God? A true friend is a gift from God. If you have a faithful Christian friend, be thankful. Remember, it's not the number of friends you have that matters; it's the kind of friend you have that really counts.

Philip and Nathanael

Philip found Nathanael and said to him, "We have found Him of whom Moses in the Law and also the prophets wrote—Jesus of Nazareth, the son of Joseph." And Nathanael said to him, "Can any good thing come out of Nazareth?" Philip said to him, "Come and see."

John 1:45-46 (NASB)

What's the first thing you do when Jesus teaches you something? Philip told his friend. As soon as Philip met Jesus, he was so excited he immediately rushed out to find his friend Nathanael. When Nathanael heard what Philip had to say, however, he was skeptical. "Can anything good come from such an insignificant town as Nazareth?" he scoffed. Philip could have been insulted by his friend's less-than-enthusiastic response. He could have argued with Nathanael; after all, Philip knew the truth. Instead, he simply gave Nathanael an invitation to come and see for himself.

There will be times when you, like Philip, will encounter Jesus in a life-changing way. This may happen in a worship service, at home as you read your Bible, or as you pray. However God speaks to you, it is natural to want to share your excitement with your friends. Don't be discouraged or insulted if they are skeptical or indifferent to what you tell them. Don't try to argue with them about the truth of what God has told you. You alone can never convince someone of the truth; you can only bear witness to the truth. Be faithful to share with your friends what God has taught you, and be obedient to what he asks you to do. Trust that he will work through your obedience to teach others the truth he has taught you. It's up to God to prove that what he says is true. Your job is to obey what God tells you.

Paul and Mark

Now Paul and his companions put out to sea from Paphos and came to Perga in Pamphylia; but John left them and returned to Jerusalem.

Acts 13:13 (NASB)

Have you ever blown it as a friend? Have you ever assured a friend he could count on you, only to let him down? Mark had that painful experience. He had been thrilled when Paul, the zealous missionary, and his own highly respected uncle, Barnabas, had invited him to join them on their next exciting missionary journey. It had begun with such promise! Then everything fell apart.

Mark grew homesick and feared the dangers they might encounter, so he abandoned his friends and fled home. When Paul suffered greatly for his missionary efforts, Mark was not there to help. As Paul prepared for his next journey, Mark offered to go again, promising to do better this time. To his dismay, Paul refused (Acts 15:36–41). What was Mark to do? How do you prove to someone you won't let him down again? All Mark knew to do was to prove himself faithful in every opportunity he had. The Bible doesn't say how, but at some point Mark had an opportunity to befriend Paul again. This time he proved to be trustworthy. By the end of Paul's life, when he needed a friend, he sent for Mark (2 Timothy 4:11).

Have you disappointed a friend? You can't change the past, no matter how painful, but you can choose, like Mark, to strive from now on to be the best friend you can be. Your words may never convince someone whom you have hurt that you have changed, but your actions will, in time. Be ready for the opportunities God will bring you to prove that you are a trustworthy friend.

February 13

Peter and His Friends

So Peter was kept in the prison, but prayer for him was being made fervently by the church to God.

Acts 12:5 (NASB)

Peter faced the most dangerous moment in his life. He had been thrown into prison by King Herod, the same king who ordered the beheading of the disciple James. Now it was Peter's turn. There seemed to be no escape and no hope. Back at his church, Peter's friends began to pray. They gathered in the home of John Mark's mother and prayed fervently for Peter's safety.

God heard the prayers of Peter's friends and sent an angel to release him. It was a miracle! So miraculous was Peter's escape that, when he arrived at their prayer meeting, his friends did not believe it was him! What can match the thrill of seeing God do a miracle in a friend's life? There is nothing more exciting than seeing God miraculously answer the prayers we lift up for a friend. We receive the blessing along with our friend.

What do you think God wants to do in your friend's life? Does God need to rescue her from something? Does God want to strengthen your friend for a difficult task? Does God want to open your friend's eyes so she sees what things are really like? Does God want to convict your friend of his sin? Are you willing to pray until it happens? One of the greatest acts of friendship is to pray for God's will to be done in your friend's life.

Chapter 5
Love: The Greatest Force on Earth

Power is intoxicating. Many of us may not realize it, but we all want power to a certain extent. Why? Power is control. Power puts us in the driver's seat. It helps us get what we want. We go after power in different ways. Some of us try to exert influence on others by using our strength to bully them. Some of us are master manipulators; we use subtle emotional maneuvers on people to get what we want from them. We may enlist the help of our money or our friends or our status to assist us, but our goal is to dominate others. However we go about getting the upper hand, we do it because we think there is strength in power.

People sometimes mistakenly equate love with weakness. We think doing the loving thing, such as forgiving another person, or putting others first, is a sign of giving in—of surrendering control. We're afraid really to love others because it makes us vulnerable. We assume we can be loving, or we can be in control, but we can't be both.

Can love and power coexist? Most certainly! God is the most powerful One in the universe. He is also the most loving. In fact, God is more than loving: he is love (1 John 4:8). God said there is strength in his love that is superior to anything else (Romans 8:38–39). Over the next few days, let's see what God has to say about the power of love. It could be life changing!

God's Love

Who shall separate us from the love of Christ? Shall trouble or hardship or persecution or famine or nakedness or danger or sword? . . .

No, in all these things we are more than conquerors through him who loved us. For I am convinced that neither death nor life, neither angels nor demons, neither the present nor the future, nor any powers, neither height nor depth, nor anything else in all creation, will be able to separate us from the love of God that is in Christ Jesus our Lord.

Romans 8:35, 37-39

Just about everything in this life is subject to change without notice. Your friend can become your enemy. Your family can be removed from you. Your health can go. You can lose your job. Nothing is guaranteed to remain the same, except one thing. There is one constant, one thing you can count on, now and forever, and that is the unfailing love of God.

There is nothing you can do and no place you can go where God's love for you is not there. The apostle Paul tried to imagine a way that God's love would not be available or sufficient. He couldn't think of one. No matter what your situation is right now, whether you are healthy or suffering from disease, employed or unemployed, on top of the world or feeling like a failure, living the Christian life victoriously or suffering the consequences of sin, *no matter what*, God loves you.

God's love isn't altered by your circumstances. It doesn't depend on your environment. It is steady and unchanging. Even demons cannot stop God from loving you. God is not intimidated by your problems or your faults. If there is anything the Bible makes crystal clear, it is that God loves his children. That's why the psalmist could proclaim with confidence, "Give thanks to the LORD, for he is good; / his love endures forever" (Psalm 106:1).

You may feel at times that even God couldn't possibly love you. You may look at your circumstances and wonder why a loving God would allow you to go through such difficult times. Always remember that your state of mind is not what determines God's love. Nor is his love decided by your situation. God's love is the one thing in life you can safely count on. Base your security on this one unchanging truth: nothing can separate you from God's love. That's a promise.

Love

Love is patient, love is kind. It does not envy, it does not boast, it is not proud. It is not rude, it is not self-seeking, it is not easily angered, it keeps no record of wrongs. Love does not delight in evil but rejoices with the truth. It always protects, always trusts, always hopes, always perseveres.

Love never fails. But where there are prophecies, they will cease; where there are tongues, they will be stilled; where there is knowledge, it will pass away.

1 Corinthians 13:4-8

The problem with love is that so many people don't have a clue what it is. Love is not a feeling; it's an attitude. Basing love on emotions, as the world does, has caused immeasurable pain to countless numbers of people. It's like building a sand castle on the beach. It might look solid, but when the high tide rolls in, the sand castle isn't strong enough to hold up, and it washes away.

Feelings come and go. We all experience a wide array of emotions on any given day. Obviously, basing any human relationship strictly on feelings is asking for trouble. Parents who love their children only when the mood hits them are poor parents. A friend who remains loyal only until a better offer comes along is not much of a friend. A husband who deserts his wife and children because he finds another woman more attractive has missed the point of marriage. The world gives love a staggering amount of attention. Movies, songs, and books about love generate billions of dollars in revenue. The problem is, love is presented as something to be "fallen into" and "fallen out of." There is no solution given for what to do when the emotion fails you and the warm fuzzies are gone— other than bailing out and starting over with someone else. You can recognize worldly love by how unpredictable it is.

The Bible offers a different kind of love. This love says I am committed to act lovingly toward this person regardless of how I feel. You'll be able to recognize biblical love: It is patient, unselfish, and loyal. It doesn't keep score; it assumes the best motives. It gives without seeking in return; it always seeks to honor God, and it endures through thick, thin, and in-between. Feelings change. Feelings don't last, but biblical love is eternal. Ask God to take you beyond the world's way of loving so you can love others in a totally new dimension, as God does.

February 16

Everything in Love

Do everything in love.

1 Corinthians 16:14

Christians play by a different set of rules than the world does. The world says it's good to be honest, moral, and loving, but there are certain times when it's OK to make an exception. When you are threatened or mistreated, the world gives permission to respond in anger. The world accepts revenge when someone hurts you first. It tolerates immorality as long as you don't hurt anyone else. In the world there are lots of gray areas that are left up to the individual's discretion. The standard for Christians, however, is straightforward. Do everything in love. No qualifiers. No exceptions.

"How is that possible?" you ask. "After all, aren't there times when people hurt you and take advantage of you? Don't you have to look out for yourself? Why does it matter as long as no one gets hurt?" The Bible doesn't give a single example where acting with love is inappropriate. If anyone ever had an excuse to make an exception, it was Jesus. People hated him so much they tortured him and killed him. Jesus loved them and forgave them. People ridiculed him and betrayed him. In return, he loved them. No one else in human history was as powerful as Jesus, yet not once did he take advantage of another person. Jesus never based his actions on what others did to him or around him. He lived by one truth: love.

As Christ's followers, we too must base our lives on Jesus' standard. A Christian should never be known as an angry or selfish person. The one thing that should characterize each one of us is that we love (John 13:35).

True Love

And this is my prayer: that your love may abound more and more in knowledge and depth of insight, so that you may be able to discern what is best and may be pure and blameless until the day of Christ.

Philippians 1:9-10

Love without discernment is not really love; it actually causes more harm than good. Parents who show love to their children by overindulging them and refusing to discipline them are really hurting them in the long run. The guy who asks his girlfriend to prove her love by having sex is not loving her; he's using her. A person who lies in order to keep a friendship is not acting as a true friend.

What a tragedy to hurt those you love simply because you lack the wisdom to treat them as you should. Love has to be discerning, for love always seeks the best for others. If you ask him, God will help you know how to love others. He will tell you when to be gentle with someone and when to be firm. The Holy Spirit will help you know when to get involved in someone's problems and when to leave them to God. He will show you how to give without asking for something in return.

For your part, you should seek to be blameless in all your relationships. This means you will guard your thoughts, your words, and your actions to make sure you have the other person's best interests at heart. When you love others this way, you will be loving as Christ loves. Examine your present relationships. Have you been treating people with the kind of love that comes from God? Ask God to teach you how to love people with discernment.

LOVE: the earth

Distracted

As Jesus and his disciples were on their way, he came to a village where a woman named Martha opened her home to him. She had a sister called Mary, who sat at the Lord's feet listening to what he said. But Martha was distracted by all the preparations that had to be made. She came to him and asked, "Lord, don't you care that my sister has left me to do the work by myself? Tell her to help me!"

"Martha, Martha," the Lord answered, "you are worried and upset about many things, but only one thing is needed. Mary has chosen what is better, and it will not be taken away from her."

Luke 10:38-42

Christians love to take this story about Mary and Martha and play armchair psychologists. We cluck our tongues at Martha's preoccupation for getting the job done, and we nod in approval at Mary for sitting at Jesus' feet and listening to him. We conclude there are two types of people in the world: those who love to learn (Mary) and those who love to labor (Martha).

We're a little too quick to hang up our shingle, and we're being too hard on Martha. In fact, both sisters loved Jesus dearly. Martha, most likely the mistress of the house, was doing what was expected of her. She was showing her love for Jesus by being a good hostess to him and his disciples. No doubt, she wanted to spend time with her Lord as much as Mary did, but someone had to do the work. Perhaps she thought if her sister would help out, they'd both have time to sit at Jesus' feet. Perhaps she could hear the muffled sounds of Jesus' voice in the other room. She longed to hear what he was saying, but she was stuck in the kitchen. So the more she worked, the more agitated she grew. Finally, she couldn't stand it, and she took her frustrations to Jesus. She did the right thing. And Jesus helped her, but not in the way she expected. With his gentle words of correction, Jesus took away her burden. He gave her the freedom to take off her apron and join Mary at his feet. Jesus' concern was not food, but people. He knew Martha loved him; she didn't have to prove it by constantly working. Jesus wanted her to forget the feast and simply spend time with him.

Jesus offers you the same freedom he gave Martha. If your efforts to show Jesus how much you love him are keeping you from spending time with him, hang up your dish towel. Mary probably didn't stay out of the kitchen for the rest of her life, and Martha probably didn't stay in it. Both sisters learned a lesson in priorities that day.

Loving the Same Way

My command is this: Love each other as I have loved you.

John 15:12

Most of us like to think of ourselves as loving people. We probably assume we are lovable. The world considers love to be a good thing. People spend a lot of time and energy pursuing love. There is a difference, however, between God's love and the love that the world knows. If we are not careful, Christians can begin to adopt the world's way of loving instead of God's. The world says love is a feeling. When you stop feeling love for someone, it means you no longer love them. The world doesn't understand how this happens and doesn't offer a good solution for getting love back. The world encourages you to love the lovable but gives you permission to hate your enemies. Jesus said loving those who love you is no great feat; it's loving your enemies that proves you are a loving person (Matthew 5:46).

Jesus commanded those who wanted to be his disciples to follow his standard for loving people rather than the world's standard. Jesus directs us to love others in exactly the same way he loves us. When Jesus saw us hopelessly enslaved to sin, he didn't say, "I don't feel like dying on a cross for them. I think I'll wait until the feeling comes." He didn't say, "I have tried and tried to love them, but they always reject me. I give up!" Jesus saw that without him we would perish, and he acted lovingly toward us despite our rejecting him. His love did not depend on what we did to deserve it, or even on whether we accepted it. Jesus freely and unconditionally gave us his love.

This is how God wants us to love others. Not with strings attached, as the world loves. Not just love as long as they are lovable. Not just love as long as they appreciate it. God wants us to give our love freely and unconditionally. Only God can help us to love people in this way. Think of someone who doesn't deserve your love, someone who is unlikely to repay your love. Today, ask Christ to love that person through you.

Chapter 6

Lessons from the Life of Joseph

Joseph is seventeen when the Bible first introduces him to us. He was Jacob's eleventh son but the first child of his mother Rachel. Rachel was Jacob's favorite wife, and Joseph became the apple of his father's eye. The situation was ripe for spoiling, which is exactly what happened. As Jacob showed favoritism toward Joseph, his other sons naturally became jealous. Joseph made matters worse by bragging about his dreams that predicted his brothers would one day serve him. Finally, the animosity between Joseph and his siblings grew to a crisis point. When Joseph was sent to the field to check on his brothers, they saw their chance to get rid of their spoiled little brother. Originally they intended to kill him, but they ultimately settled on a kinder plan; they would sell him to foreigners as a slave!

Egypt was full of slaves in those days, but most did not know God. Joseph distinguished himself as someone who knew and heard from God. He was falsely accused of a crime and thrown into prison, but God did not forget him. God helped Joseph find favor with the pharaoh by interpreting his dream when no one else in the nation could. Ultimately Joseph became a respected world leader and the most powerful person in Egypt, next to the pharaoh.

Life was not always kind to Joseph. He was betrayed by his family, misrepresented by his boss's wife, misjudged by his boss, and forgotten by his friends. Nevertheless, God used Joseph to make a difference in his world. Even through the toughest times, Joseph never gave up hope in God. Eventually his trust was rewarded. Joseph attained power and status, but—more importantly—he learned forgiveness and received God's blessing.

Unexpected Heroes   February 20

This is the history of Jacob.

Joseph, being seventeen years old, was feeding the flock with his brothers. And the lad was with the sons of Bilhah and the sons of Zilpah, his father's wives; and Joseph brought a bad report of them to his father.

Genesis 37:2 (NKJV)

"Joseph is a spoiled brat who'll never amount to anything." If you had asked one of Joseph's brothers about the youngest child in their large family, this would probably have been their response. Everyone knew that the oldest child, not the youngest, would someday inherit the family wealth and become the leader of the family. Besides, Joseph was a troublemaker. A tattletale. He seemed to think God had something special in store for him that was different from God's plan for the rest of the family.

Life was pretty lonely for Joseph. His mother had died. His stepmother disliked him. He was, after all, Jacob's favorite son and a living reminder that Jacob had loved Rachel the most. His jealous half brothers despised him. Joseph alienated his family even further by bragging about all the incredible dreams of his glorious future.

On the outside, Joseph didn't look much like a candidate for a world leader. But God doesn't look at the outside; he looks much deeper. In Joseph, God saw potential for greatness. God had big plans for Joseph, so he set to work developing Joseph's character to match the assignment that awaited him.

What do others see when they look at you? Lots of problems? Immaturity? What do you see when you look at yourself? All the imperfections? Don't be discouraged! You may think others are much smarter, wealthier, or more attractive than you are. Others may readily agree with you, but those things don't matter nearly as much as God's opinion of you. Trust him, as Joseph did, to honor you. He wants to do things with your life that will amaze you!

February 21

Dreams

Now when they saw him afar off, even before he came near them, they conspired against him to kill him. Then they said to one another, "Look, this dreamer is coming!"

Genesis 37:18-19 (NKJV)

It can be frustrating when people misunderstand you. It hurts when they question your motives and criticize you. It really stings when the opposition comes from your own family! Joseph knew the feeling.

God told Joseph in a dream that he would one day hold a position of such great power and influence that even his older brothers would show him respect. Joseph naively rushed to tell his older brothers of God's message. They were not impressed. They ridiculed him and sarcastically labeled him a dreamer. When they looked at their kid brother, God's apparent plans for him seemed not only ridiculous, but impossible.

Of course we know that God's revelation to Joseph happened exactly as he said it would. Unlike Joseph's brothers, God knew the future. When he spoke about his plans, they were as good as done.

Have you received a message from God? Has he called you to full-time Christian ministry, perhaps as a missionary or a pastor? Has he told you to be baptized? If you have received a word from God, don't let the opposition of others deter you, even if it comes from your family. Take your cue from Joseph. Don't give up doing what God has asked you to do. If you're patient, God will make everything he promised you come to pass exactly as he said it would. One day your critics will have to admit that they underestimated what God could do through your life!

God Is with You

The LORD was with Joseph, and he was a successful man; and he was in the house of his master the Egyptian.

Genesis 39:2 (NKJV)

"Lord, be with the missionaries in Africa. Lord, be with the pastor as he preaches today. Heavenly Father, be with me during my exam today." We pray for God to be with us and others, but what do we mean? God is everywhere, is he not? How could he not be with us?

The Bible says God was with Joseph. This is especially significant, considering Joseph's situation. His father assumed he was dead. His brothers had no idea where he was. His mother was dead. He had no friends. He was in prison on a false charge. Joseph must have felt awfully alone. Where could he turn? Joseph discovered that even when everyone else abandoned him, God remained. God made his presence with Joseph obvious through what he did in Joseph's life. He didn't give Joseph an easy life, but he blessed him nonetheless. When Joseph was a slave, God made him chief slave. When Joseph was a prisoner, he became assistant to the jailer. When there seemed little reason to have confidence, God gave Joseph courage.

God's presence doesn't mean you won't experience hard times. It does mean that no matter what you are going through, you will know that he is with you, just as Joseph knew he wasn't alone. God's presence will give you security when everything is going wrong. His love will be obvious to you even when it seems no one else cares. God's wisdom will guide you to make the right choices in the confusion of life.

The Bible says Joseph prospered because God was with him. In other words, God's presence made a visible difference in Joseph's life. God's presence will make an obvious difference in your life as well. No matter how tough your circumstances, you can have confidence because you're not alone.

February 23

Temptation

And it came to pass after these things that his master's wife cast longing eyes on Joseph, and she said, "Lie with me."

But he refused and said to his master's wife, "Look, my master does not know what is with me in the house, and he has committed all that he has to my hand. There is no one greater in this house than I, nor has he kept back anything from me but you, because you are his wife. How then can I do this great wickedness, and sin against God?" . . .

But it happened about this time, when Joseph went into the house to do his work, and none of the men of the house was inside, that she caught him by his garment, saying, "Lie with me." But he left his garment in her hand, and fled and ran outside.

Genesis 39:7-9, 11-12 (NKJV)

Joseph had recovered from the terrible thing his brothers had done to him. After they sold him into slavery, a kind master bought him and quickly promoted him. Joseph was thriving in his new environment when, suddenly, he found himself in a dangerous and awkward situation. His master's wife took notice of him and invited him to her bed. She had the power to make Joseph's life unbearable if he refused her, but if he gave in, he'd be deceiving his master and dishonoring God. It was a no-win situation.

Temptation comes in many forms, sometimes from completely unexpected sources. There will be times when you, like Joseph, will be innocently going about your business only to be caught off guard by an invitation to do something that goes against God's standards. It may be a friend who entices you, and you're reluctant to risk the friendship by standing firm. Perhaps the temptation will come from a boss whom you want to please in order to keep your job. As a Christian, you should always base your choices on God's desires. Be careful that you don't let others set the agenda for your life. Don't live your life based on someone else's values. Rather, when you are confronted with an invitation to sin, respond as Joseph did. He was in a tough spot, but he never entertained the option of agreeing to sin. For Joseph, the issue was not whether he'd get caught or whether it would be a smart career move. He knew what God wanted him to do, and he wouldn't let anyone change his mind. He was not deceived into giving in, just to keep the peace. Instead, he did the smartest thing he could do; he ran as fast as he could in the opposite direction. It cost him his cloak, but it saved him from sinning.

It's Not Fair!

So it was, when his master heard the words which his wife spoke to him, saying, "Your servant did to me after this manner," that his anger was aroused. Then Joseph's master took him and put him into the prison, a place where the king's prisoners were confined. And he was there in the prison.

Genesis 39:19-20 (NKJV)

Joseph should have won a promotion, or at least his master's admiration, for what he'd done. He'd worked hard. He'd remained loyal, both to God and to his master, while at the same time keeping Potiphar's wife out of a sinful liaison. Imagine the sense of betrayal he must have felt when Potiphar chose to believe his crafty wife, though he surely knew Joseph's character by that time. Instead of praise, Joseph's reward for his loyalty was a prison cell on death row!

It would have been easy for Joseph to become bitter and to blame God for not protecting him. Yet Joseph was wise enough to look beyond the circumstances of the moment. His spirit undefeated, he continued to trust in God's character. As he waited for God to bring justice, he worked hard, even in jail. The result? God "showed him kindness and granted him favor in the eyes of the prison warden" (Genesis 39:21). His jailer admired his work ethic and promoted him; he put Joseph in charge of the prison, responsible for the well-being of the other prisoners. Once again, Joseph's faithfulness had earned him God's blessing.

Sometimes you will suffer even though you've done the right thing. When you are teased, criticized, even ridiculed for refusing to compromise your faith, remember Joseph. His faith in God remained solid, no matter how things appeared, and God rewarded his allegiance. Have you been mistreated though you've done nothing wrong? Hold on tightly to your faith! God is completely just; he will take care of you just as he took care of Joseph.

Giving Glory to God

And Pharaoh said to Joseph, "I have had a dream, and there is no one who can interpret it. But I have heard it said of you that you can understand a dream, to interpret it."

So Joseph answered Pharaoh, saying, "It is not in me; God will give Pharaoh an answer of peace."

Genesis 41:15-16 (NKJV)

It was the opportunity of a lifetime! "I've heard a lot about you," observed Pharaoh. "I understand you are very talented." Here was Joseph's ticket out of jail—his big break! It would be easy to take credit for figuring out Pharaoh's troublesome dreams. Without actually lying, Joseph could become famous for his wisdom! And it wouldn't hurt to have the pharaoh in his debt either. It would most certainly shorten his jail sentence and maybe earn him national fame.

As tempting as it may have been, Joseph chose to give credit where credit was due. He used the opportunity to tell the pharaoh about God's wisdom rather than to blow his own horn. In the presence of the most powerful men in the country, Joseph explained that he held no supernatural powers himself but that his wisdom came directly from God. Joseph knew better than to take the credit for something God had done! Joseph wasn't about to abuse this incredible opportunity by focusing on himself instead of on God.

How has God blessed you? Are you a musician? A good athlete? Are you gifted academically? Resist the temptation to use your talents selfishly. Instead, seek to honor the Lord with your gifts. The abilities God has given you are not for you alone. He has given them to you so that you can use them to bring glory to God. God promises that if you honor him, he will honor you (1 Samuel 2:30).

Perseverance

Joseph was thirty years old when he stood before Pharaoh king of Egypt. And Joseph went out from the presence of Pharaoh, and went throughout all the land of Egypt.

Genesis 41:46 (NKJV)

How long are you willing to wait until you receive what God has promised? Is it worth the wait? Joseph spent thirteen years in slavery and in prison waiting for God to deliver him. That's a long wait; but by the time he was thirty, he had reached the highest position possible in Egypt. He was able to use his influence to save the lives of his family as well as thousands of other lives. Would Joseph say it was worth the wait? Undoubtedly!

God did an amazing work in Joseph's life during those thirteen years in Egypt. He developed Joseph's character to a point where he could be entrusted with the fate of his country and the surrounding nations as well.

The years you spend as a teenager and as a young adult are crucial. The decisions you make now will determine your future as well as the future of others. Why not submit your life to God to be used in an extraordinary way? Allow him to prepare you and teach you so you'll have an impact on society and so you'll make a difference in his kingdom. This may involve some challenges, as it did for Joseph. It may mean resisting shortcuts and spending some time in the trenches, but the result will be a walk with God that will sustain you through the toughest circumstances. Don't be satisfied with a mediocre life lived in a mediocre way with mediocre results. Do you want God to use you in a powerful way, as he did Joseph? Be patient and allow him to develop your character. When things don't go the way you think they should, don't assume God has abandoned you. Trust him as Joseph did. Your perseverance will pay off.

Lesson Joseph

February 27

Perspective

But as for you, you meant evil against me; but God meant it for good, in order to bring it about as it is this day, to save many people alive.

Genesis 50:20 (NKJV)

Perspective: It makes all the difference. We may look at our problems and wonder how anything good could possibly come out of them. Joseph might have wondered the same thing. His life was turned upside down again and again as he bounced from beloved son to slave, from favored employee to prisoner. For thirteen years his life seemed to be at the mercy of other people's whims. As he sat awaiting execution on death row, he certainly might have questioned what God was doing. Later, when Joseph became the second most powerful man in Egypt, answering only to the pharaoh, it all made sense.

After their father Jacob died, Joseph's brothers were terrified that he might seek revenge for the heartless way they had treated him. But now Joseph could see things from God's perspective. Had it not been for his brothers' cruelty, Joseph would not have gone to Egypt. As it was, God used Joseph to save the lives of thousands of Egyptians. Joseph's willingness to listen to God and to act with integrity saved his country from imminent ruin and saved his own relatives from starvation at the same time.

Are you in the middle of confusing circumstances? Does it seem as though God is not in control? Pray that God will help you to see things as he sees them. Trust him to lead you, for he sees the whole picture. In time you will look back and realize that God was in control all the time, guiding you into his perfect will.

Jesus' Words to His Disciples

Jesus was saddened when he looked at the needy crowds who followed him. *Like sheep without a shepherd,* he observed. It was time to send out some help. Only God knows what Jesus thought when he looked at the twelve who were to be his answer to the seeking multitudes. *A tax collector, a few fishermen, a member of a radical political movement . . . not a preacher among them!* It was time for a serious talk.

Jesus called his men together and gave it to them straight. First, the good news: they would have power to heal the sick, to drive out demons, even to raise the dead! Then the other news: "I am sending you out like sheep among wolves" (Matthew 10:16). He talked of floggings, arrests, and persecution. Jesus laid it all out for them—the good, the bad, and the scary. He told them exactly what to expect and how to respond. There would be lots of incredible experiences, but no surprises.

It's all there, in Matthew, for us too. Jesus' words are relevant to us because we, too, are his messengers to a hurting world. Let's give Matthew a closer look and see what we can learn about what it means to be a follower of Jesus.

February 28

Free Gifts

"Heal the sick, raise the dead, cleanse those who have leprosy, drive out demons. Freely you have received, freely give."

Matthew 10:8

You're probably familiar with the term *oxymoron:* "sweet sorrow," "uniquely uniform," "cute in an ugly sort of way"; some words don't go together. The term *selfish Christian* is an oxymoron, or at least it should be, because there ought to be no such thing. But why should Christians be unselfish? Because we're filthy rich? Not likely. Because we have more time than everyone else? Very unlikely! Maybe it's because we've received more; therefore, we have more to give than anyone else.

We Christians are experts at receiving. We've soaked in God's love, forgiveness, and healing. We've eagerly accepted eternal life. We've been adopted into God's family, and we gladly claim the myriad of promises the Bible says are just for us. We don't pretend to have earned any of these things; they're all free gifts from God, and we know it. Nor are we dense enough to suppose we could ever repay God. In fact, God doesn't ask us to pay him back. He does ask one thing, however. He wants us to become experts at giving as well as receiving.

Selfishness is a sign that we've forgotten who we are. If we give only to people we consider worthy of our gift, we've missed the whole point. Whether the person in need deserves our help is irrelevant. The evidence of genuine Christianity is the willingness to give whatever it takes to whoever needs it.

Be on the lookout today for a way to share with someone else something God has given you.

Sheep Among Wolves

"I am sending you out like sheep among wolves. Therefore be as shrewd as snakes and as innocent as doves. Be on your guard against men; they will hand you over to the local councils and flog you in their synagogues."

Matthew 10:16-17

Do you ever feel like the world is out to get you? It is. Some people think Christians are naïve because we're supposed to be meek, mild, and submissive. We're like sheep, right? And who ever heard of a killer sheep? So people try to take advantage of us, assuming our only option is to turn the other cheek. Or they try to manipulate us into sinning to prove we're no different than they are. Jesus has two words of advice: Wise up! Yes, we are to be kind and loving, but we are not to be foolish. In the same breath, Jesus tells us to be like sheep, like snakes, and like doves.

The sheep part we know all about. We've read all the biblical analogies that say we're the sheep and Jesus is the Good Shepherd. But maybe that's so familiar we don't really get it: as sheep we must understand that there are wolves in the bushes and that they're not looking out for our best interests. That's why Jesus warns us to be as shrewd as snakes. Biblically speaking, snakes don't have a great track record; they're usually the bad guys. They're also very clever. Jesus alerts us so we don't fall blindly into the traps of cunning, evil people. We're unlikely to be flogged in a synagogue anytime soon, but people will take advantage of us if we let them.

If you're beginning to feel paranoid, don't panic. The key is to remain innocent as a dove. In other words, guard your heart. Don't go looking for evil, or worse, get into evil yourself. Stay close to Jesus and don't let anyone, even your friends, manipulate you into sinning. Be kind, be loving, but be smart!

March 1

What Will You Say?

"On my account you will be brought before governors and kings as witnesses to them and to the Gentiles. But when they arrest you, do not worry about what to say or how to say it. At that time you will be given what to say, for it will not be you speaking, but the Spirit of your Father speaking through you."

Matthew 10:18-20

Some things just seem too good to be true. Christians love to grab onto this verse from Matthew, assuming that anytime we're at a loss for words, God will intervene. What a deal! No more studying, no more preparing for presentations, no more planning ahead. The words will come automatically, courtesy of God. This eliminates the need for Bible study because God will zap the appropriate verse into our minds at the right time. Don't we all sometimes expect God to cover for our own laziness?

The truth is, Jesus was addressing a specific situation here; this is not a blanket promise. He was talking to friends who would soon be hauled before kings and governors. They would be beaten, interrogated, and expected to explain their faith under threat of death. They were all new Christians; none of them had known Jesus for more than a few years. Unlike Paul, who was well schooled in the Scriptures, these men were blue-collar workers. They had no tracts or pocket New Testaments to pull out when they were in a bind. Most significantly, they would be in danger because of witnessing for Christ, not because of their own shortcomings. As long as they were obeying God, Jesus assured them that God would intervene. This promise was not just for the disciples; it was also for the sake of their listeners who would need a word from God.

What does this mean for us? Obviously there is no open-ended guarantee that God will always bail us out when we have not prepared ourselves. However, if we are living as God wants us to live and our faith is challenged, God will not only give us the words we need; he'll also give us the courage to say them.

Not for the Fainthearted

"Brother will betray brother to death, and a father his child; children will rebel against their parents and have them put to death. All men will hate you because of me, but he who stands firm to the end will be saved. . . .

"A student is not above his teacher, nor a servant above his master. It is enough for the student to be like his teacher, and the servant like his master. If the head of the house has been called Beelzebub, how much more the members of his household!"

Matthew 10:21-22, 24-25

Following Christ is not for the faint-hearted! Some may tell you that becoming a Christian guarantees a problem-free existence, but Jesus shatters that illusion. In fact, he presents Christianity as not only difficult but downright dangerous!

In Bible times, following Christ was perilous. Constant persecution separated serious disciples from would-be Christians. The threat of arrest, torture, and even death didn't make Christianity all that inviting. People took their commitment to Christ very seriously because their lives and the lives of their family members were on the line. Yet thousands and thousands of people considered it worth the hazards to know God personally. Christ himself was hated and persecuted, so his disciples didn't expect that they would avoid persecution themselves.

Times have changed, but persecution still separates the true disciples from the wanna-bes. In some parts of the world, being a Christian is still a life-threatening venture, but for most of us it's not as dangerous. Still, there is a cost involved in following Christ, and each of us has to decide if knowing Christ is worth the price.

Is your faith costing you anything? Are you willing to stand up for Christ, even when it's an unpopular thing to do? Will you remain faithful to Jesus, even if it causes you to lose friends? If you are truly Christ's disciple, you will pay a price. But stand firm; the reward is worth the cost.

March 3

The Hairs of Your Head

"Are not two sparrows sold for a penny? Yet not one of them will fall to the ground apart from the will of your Father. And even the very hairs of your head are all numbered. So don't be afraid; you are worth more than many sparrows."

Matthew 10:29-31

Have you ever been in a stadium surrounded by thousands of screaming fans? Did you wonder how God could possibly know every person there? It is pretty mind-boggling; there are billions of people in the world, and the Bible says that God knows everything there is to know about every one of us!

We might consider our lives insignificant in the global scheme of things, but Jesus would disagree. In fact, he made a point of showing the disciples just how intimately the Father knew them. Tiny and weak, sparrows are among the least important creatures on earth. Their life span is so short, who even notices when it's over? God does. If that is true, God is more than capable of loving each and every person he has created.

In case his friends still didn't get it, Jesus went on: God even knows the number of hairs on our heads. The truth is, God knows us better than we know ourselves. God doesn't see us as a massive crowd; he sees and loves each of us individually. The disciples were going out to a hostile world. They would deal with dangerous, evil people. They would be mocked and threatened; they would even be face-to-face with demons. Jesus wanted to assure them that their heavenly Father was in control, that he loved each one of them, and that he was watching over them. This promise is for you too. Don't ever assume you are just one of the crowd or that God isn't intimately acquainted with your life. You are precious to God. He knows everything about you. He loves you more than you know. You can trust him with your life.

Enemies at Home

*"Do not suppose that I have come to bring peace to the earth. I did
not come to bring peace, but a sword. For I have come to turn*

> *" 'a man against his father,*
> *a daughter against her mother,*
> *a daughter-in-law against her mother-in-law—*
> *a man's enemies will be the members of his
> own household.'*

*Anyone who loves his father or mother more than me is not worthy
of me; anyone who loves his son or daughter more than me is not
worthy of me."*

Matthew 10:34-37

It's one thing when strangers, or even friends, challenge our
faith. But when our own family opposes us, that cuts deep.
Would Jesus really ask us to oppose our parents' wishes
when we've been commanded to honor our father and our
mother? Aren't we to be peacemakers? Sometimes the
biggest obstacle between us and obedience is not the
demons out there; it's the resistance we face in our own
homes. That's an obstacle that some of us aren't willing to
face. It's not worth it to us because it's too painful. Jesus
doesn't ask us to stop loving our families or to treat them
with disrespect. He does insist that our first loyalty be to
God.

Non-Christian family members won't understand your
choice to follow Christ. They may consider you a fanatic or,
at best, tolerate your decision because they think you're just
going through a phase. They may even see your loyalty to
Christ as a rejection of them. It's critical to continue loving
your family, but Jesus said that if you are to be worthy of him
you must make the hard choice: God first, family second.
When your family asks you to put them before God, they
are, in a sense, your enemy. Even Christian family members
can come between you and God. For example, if you're
called to missions, your family may dissuade you because
they want you nearby or because they fear what you will
face "over there." If your family is asking you to disobey
God, ask God for the strength you need to put him first.

March 5

The Cross

"And anyone who does not take his cross and follow me is not worthy of me. Whoever finds his life will lose it, and whoever loses his life for my sake will find it."

Matthew 10:38

When you see a cross, what image does it bring to mind? Christians often wear crosses as jewelry or on the bumper of their car as a sign of loyalty to Christ. For you it's probably a welcome sight because it stands for your resurrected Lord. It's a victory symbol.

When Jesus referred to a cross, his disciples likely had a different mental picture. No one had to tell them what a cross meant; they'd seen plenty of crosses. In their day, the cross was a torture device. Condemned criminals had to carry their own crosses to their place of execution. It was a grim sight. To the condemned person, the cross was the ultimate humiliation. It meant his life was no longer his own. Any future plans were now irrelevant because the cross he carried would soon end his life.

Today the cross is both a victory symbol and a sign of what Christ requires of us. When he says to take up our cross, he means we are to turn our lives completely over to him. Our own plans are no longer important; it's what Jesus has planned for us that matters. If we are unwilling to go where he wants us to go and to do what he asks us to do, Jesus says we're not worthy to be his followers.

If you have your future all figured out, you need to check with Jesus. Ask him what his plans are, and begin following him today. Trust that his way is the best way.

Receiving Jesus

"He who receives you receives me, and he who receives me receives the one who sent me."

Matthew 10:40

Why does it matter how Christians behave? Aren't we being phony when we try to act perfect all the time? Aren't we trying to fool others into thinking Christians are perfect? There is a good reason for Christians to act with integrity. It's because of who we represent.

There are people who will never know what Christ is like unless they see Christ in you. If you are a Christian, you take Christ with you everywhere you go. When you are at school or at work, Christ is with you. Whether you are out with your friends or speaking to a stranger, Christ is with you. Whenever people meet you, they also meet Christ. How tragic for a non-Christian to see Christ in you and be unimpressed! If you don't represent Christ to others in a way that honors his name, some people might never know what he is really like.

That's why it's so important that you always represent Christ as he is. Others will be attracted to Christ when your life shows that he is loving, forgiving, patient, and kind. The only way some people will ever believe God is forgiving is when they experience Christ's love as you forgive them. There are many people around you who need to receive Jesus, and you're the one who can introduce them to him. Have people been impressed with the Christ they have seen in you?

March 7

For or Against?

"He who is not with me is against me, and he who does not gather with me scatters."

Matthew 12:30

According to the world, there are three ways to believe about God. You are either a *believer*, an *atheist* (unbeliever), or an *agnostic* (undecided one way or the other). You'll find the term *agnostic* in the dictionary, but you won't find it in the Bible. Jesus says there are two options, not three. He has drawn a clear line in the sand, and we choose one side or the other. According to Jesus, whoever does not stand with him is automatically against him. There is no middle ground.

Some people prefer to remain neutral when it comes to Christ. They don't want to come right out and reject Jesus, but they're not quite willing to accept him either. They pick and choose what they will believe about God and what they will obey from his Word. They choose to live a good life, at least by worldly standards, but they don't want to get "bogged down" by Christianity. Such people are deceived. Jesus said that in not choosing, they have made their choice.

If you are not for Christ, you are against him. If you've considered yourself in the neutral zone when it comes to trusting God, understand that you've actually been Christ's enemy. God has given you all the information you need to make your choice for him. Choose now—before it's too late—to live for Christ.

The Overflow of Your Heart

"You brood of vipers, how can you who are evil say anything good? For out of the overflow of the heart the mouth speaks. The good man brings good things out of the good stored up in him, and the evil man brings evil things out of the evil stored up in him."

Matthew 12:34-35

Why was Jesus so critical of the Pharisees? They tried to live by God's law. They weren't thieves or murderers. They were respected members of society. Yet Jesus had more patience for outright criminals than he had for the Pharisees. He treated tax collectors and prostitutes kindly, but he called the Pharisees a bunch of venomous snakes!

The Pharisees loved to impress people with their lengthy public prayers and their religious practices, but Jesus knew their hearts. They were preoccupied with how pious they appeared on the outside, while on the inside they were critical, judgmental, and proud. They were religious teachers, but their goal was not to lead others closer to God. It was to show everyone how spiritual they were. They pitied everyone else for being wretched sinners, but they were blind to their own sin. They had no clue how they looked in God's eyes.

Self-deception is a crafty enemy. We may think we're fooling everyone around us with the spiritual act we put on, but we are usually the only ones deceived. It's hard to keep what's in our hearts from coming out through our words. If we're filled with jealousy, we can't help cutting down others. If we're judgmental, we criticize others more often than we realize. In unguarded moments, our anger slips out in bitter, hurtful words. There's no sense wasting our energy trying to say all the right things if our hearts are not right with Jesus. We need to get our hearts right before God, and good things will follow naturally.

By Your Words

"But I tell you that men will have to give account on the day of judgment for every careless word they have spoken. For by your words you will be acquitted, and by your words you will be condemned."

Matthew 12:36-37

Speaking without thinking is like playing with a loaded gun. Careless words are the bullets. When the gun goes off and injures someone, the damage is done. You can retrieve the bullet, but you can't undo the harm it caused. Have you ever hurt someone's feelings with careless words, then shrugged it off as their problem because they're too sensitive? Have you ever spread gossip about someone, embellishing just a little to spice up the story? Have you cut down a friend's self-confidence with your repeated, "all in fun" jabs? Have you dishonored God by speaking his name disrespectfully even though you knew better?

Most of us will admit that we don't always choose our words wisely. If we really understood the power of our words, we would never shoot them off as carelessly as we do. God knows how damaging careless words can be, and he takes them far more seriously than we do. Jesus cautions us that one day we will be required to account for every word we've spoken. Imagine standing before holy God in heaven and having every careless and hurtful word we ever spoke revealed before the hosts of heaven! If we're wise, we'll get in the habit now of thinking before we speak.

If you tend to shoot off your mouth without thinking, ask God today to help you gain control over your tongue. Begin choosing your words wisely, and there will be no need for regrets.

Good Soil

A farmer went out to sow his seed. As he was scattering the seed, some fell along the path, and the birds came and ate it up. Some fell on rocky places, where it did not have much soil. It sprang up quickly, because the soil was shallow. But when the sun came up, the plants were scorched, and they withered because they had no root. Other seed fell among thorns, which grew up and choked the plants. Still other seed fell on good soil, where it produced a crop—a hundred, sixty or thirty times what was sown. He who has ears, let him hear.

Matthew 13:3-9

Good teachers don't just deliver lectures; they help their students picture the material, and they speak in terms their listeners will understand. When Jesus had an important lesson for his disciples or for the crowds who gathered around him, he showed them what he wanted them to know by painting word pictures (parables) for them. He talked about things that were part of their experience, such as farming, fishing, food, and nature.

The crowds following Jesus were the first generation to hear the gospel, and many of them were confused about how to respond. Jesus used a parable to teach them about genuine faith. He talked about four types of soil: all four received the same seed, but only one produced a crop. He compared this to the four ways people respond to the same gospel. First are those who don't accept Christ because Satan prevents them from understanding the gospel when they hear it (see v. 19). Second are people who hear the gospel and respond immediately, but for whatever reason they don't grow in their faith. God's Word enters their minds but not their hearts. These people start out with enthusiasm, but they lack the depth to persevere in their faith, so they fall away. Third are those who accept Christ but fall victim to worldly thinking. They choose to rely on their own resources rather than on God, so their lives are no different from nonbelievers.

The first three types of soil produce no crop, but Jesus explained what happens when the seed falls on good soil. Those who hear the gospel, accept it, and grow in their faith are the people who make a difference in God's kingdom. You can read Jesus' explanation of his parable for yourself in Matthew 13:18–23. Consider each of the four soil types. Think about your own response to the gospel. Has God's Word produced everything that it could in your life?

jesus' ...ciples

March 11

Genuine Faith

"I tell you the truth, if you have faith as small as a mustard seed, you can say to this mountain, 'Move from here to there' and it will move. Nothing will be impossible for you."

Matthew 17:20

Faith is measured by quality, not quantity. It's not how much faith we have that counts, but where we put our faith. Sometimes we put our faith in faith, instead of in God. We think if we just believe hard enough we'll get whatever we want. That's trusting in ourselves rather than in God. Faith by itself is as worthless as a solar-powered flashlight or an inflatable dartboard. The power to move mountains is in God, not in our faith.

When the disciples asked why they'd been unable to cast a demon out of a boy, Jesus pointed to their faith. The disciples had false confidence in their own faith. Jesus explained that they had grown to believe in themselves and their ability to do things for God, instead of believing in God's ability to work through them. They were treating their faith like a magic wand that they pulled out whenever they needed another miracle. They had placed their faith in faith rather than in God.

Be careful you don't fall under that same misconception. Don't even try to work up enough faith, thinking that at some point God will say, "You've reached the minimum faith requirement; now you can move a mountain." Instead, put your faith where it belongs: not in yourself, but in God. Then stand aside and watch *him* move the mountain!

The True Meaning of Greatness

"Instead, whoever wants to become great among you must be your servant, and whoever wants to be first must be your slave—just as the Son of Man did not come to be served, but to serve, and to give his life as a ransom for many."

Matthew 20:26-28

Wanted: Male or female to be model of success for the world. Qualifications: Must be attractive, charming, bright, and physically fit. Only the wealthy need apply; money can be either earned or inherited but not stolen. May be required to show evidence of greatness, such as how many persons are serving you. Good dose of luck helpful but not essential. Fame definitely an asset. Send resume, full-length picture, medical records, and list of important friends.

Wanted: Male or female to be model of success for Christians. Qualifications: Must be kind, patient, and generous. Good dose of humility essential. Selfish applicants need not apply. May be required to show evidence of greatness, such as how many persons you are serving and how you have been persecuted for your Christian lifestyle. Only servants will be considered. Send resume; no picture or medical records or list of influential friends necessary. It doesn't matter what you look like or how healthy you are or who you know.

If anyone had a right to be served, it was Jesus. Yet he didn't come to be served. He came to serve. If you're looking for a genuine model of success, you'll find it in Jesus. If you want to have the success Jesus had, you will have to live like he did, as a servant. Who are you serving right now?

The Greatest Commandment

Hearing that Jesus had silenced the Sadducees, the Pharisees got together. One of them, an expert in the law, tested him with this question: "Teacher, which is the greatest commandment in the Law?"

Jesus replied: "'Love the Lord your God with all your heart and with all your soul and with all your mind.' This is the first and greatest commandment."

Matthew 22:34-39

The Pharisee had a question for Jesus: "Which is the greatest commandment in the Law?" It was a loaded question, designed to trap Jesus and discredit him. No doubt the Pharisee expected Jesus would have to choose one of the Ten Commandments over the other nine, opening the door for debate. Then he'd have this unschooled carpenter's son right where he wanted him. The Pharisee was an expert in the Law; he had scrutinized the Scriptures for years and had memorized many passages. The Law was his life. This uneducated carpenter would be no match for his expertise. It was going to be an easy victory.

Jesus showed who the expert really was. He condensed all ten commandments into one statement that targeted the Pharisees' most vulnerable spot. The Pharisees were adept at keeping the letter of the law but fell pitifully short in following the spirit of the law, which was love. The Pharisees were doing the right thing for the wrong reasons. In God's eyes, this was still sin. God expected them to obey his commands because they loved him, not because they were trying to be perfect. God was more concerned with their hearts than with their actions.

Sometimes we're like the Pharisees. We make Christianity too complicated. Although God has the right to demand anything he wants, he asks one thing of us: love. If we devote our hearts, minds, and souls to God, we will fulfill the law as it was meant to be followed, and everything else will fall into place.

Love Those Neighbors

"And the second is like it: 'Love your neighbor as yourself.' All the Law and the Prophets hang on these two commandments."

Matthew 22:39-40

When you consider Jesus' audience, his message was revolutionary! The Old Testament Law was everything to the Pharisees; they devoted their entire lives to following the Law to the letter. Now Jesus was telling them that all their efforts were futile unless they loved their neighbors. The Pharisees weren't in the habit of loving their neighbors; they were actually in the habit of criticizing them, judging them, even pitying them. After all, their neighborhood included some pretty unsavory characters. How could they love prostitutes, beggars, or tax collectors—those traitorous Jews who'd sold out to the Roman government? These were nasty, sinful people. The Pharisees had their standards.

God has standards too—high standards. He expects us to treat others exactly as we want to be treated. It's tempting to avoid those we find hard to love and to stick with people who are more like us. That way we can still be loving, but it doesn't really put us out. That's not what Jesus was talking about; he said anyone can do that. God expects us to show love to our neighbors, no matter who they are.

Do you find some people impossible to love? Jesus used the word *love* as a verb—an action word. We like to think of it as a noun—something we have (or don't have), not something we do. Don't waste your time considering whether someone is worthy of your love; that's not your concern. Instead, ask God to help you act lovingly today toward everyone you encounter, even when it's difficult.

March 15

Exalting or Humbling?

"The greatest among you will be your servant. For whoever exalts himself will be humbled, and whoever humbles himself will be exalted."

Matthew 23:11-12

We can always count on the Bible to turn human reasoning inside out. The Scriptures are full of paradoxes; over and over we read phrases that seem to contradict themselves: "The first shall be last," "The greatest will be the servant," "The one who holds onto his life will lose it." To the world, such thinking is nonsense, but it is crucial for Christians to understand these truths if we are to live as Christ desires.

Today, let's tackle the concept of humility as Jesus sees it. Nobody is born humble; humility is a trait that we have to learn. Instinctively, we want to present the best possible picture to the world, so we go to great lengths to hide our weaknesses and highlight our strengths. Sometimes we go even further by trying to make a good impression at someone else's expense. We're threatened when others receive praise, so we set out to prove that we, not they, deserve the attention. It's the way we've always done things because life has taught us that if we don't promote ourselves no one else will. God says the opposite is true: If we act proud and build ourselves up, we'll be brought down. It's inevitable. But if we stop worrying about impressing everyone and, instead, seek to be genuinely humble, others will end up thinking highly of us.

If you've been preoccupied with your image, trying to impress those around you, you've been duped by the world's thinking. From now on, seek to humble yourself and to put others first. That's God's way, and when you think about it, it really does make more sense than the way the world does things.

Lessons from the Apostle Paul

Some people have lived diverse lives, filled with such rich experiences that you would love to talk with them all day long. When you spend time with people who are truly wise—people who walk closely with God—you find yourself motivated to live your life more fully as well. God's power is so evident in some people that you find yourself drawn to them. You learn from them, and you're a better person because you know them.

Paul was such a person. He'd seen it all. He'd been everywhere. He'd witnessed miracles and experienced miracles himself. He spoke God's word with authority and boldness. As you spend the next several days with Paul, understand that you're learning from a well-traveled, experienced, wise man. He has a lot of good advice for you. Enjoy your time with Paul. You won't easily forget what he has to say!

Abba, Father

For you did not receive a spirit that makes you a slave again to fear, but you received the Spirit of sonship. And by him we cry, "Abba, Father." The Spirit himself testifies with our spirit that we are God's children.

Romans 8:15-16

Your personality is partly the result of the way you were parented. Of course other factors are involved, but parents have a bigger influence on their children than some would like to admit. Children from abusive homes usually suffer from severe insecurity. They may struggle with anger just like their parents and repeat the cycle when they have children. On the other hand, parents who are kind and loving tend to pass on these traits to their children.

When you become a Christian, you are adopted by a perfect Parent. Your heavenly Father loves you perfectly. He has no regrets for what he says to you; he never wishes he could have done more for you. You have nothing to fear because he watches over you, and he is more powerful than any problem you will ever face. You will not live in want because your Father's resources are unlimited.

As God's child, your life ought to reflect God's character. The more time you spend with your Father, the more your life will reflect your new heritage. As God's child you should become more and more like him: loving, patient, giving, and fair. As you grow in your faith, your heavenly Father's influence should have increasingly more impact on how you live than your earthly parents' model does.

Don't use imperfect parents as an excuse for not living up to God's standards. You do have a perfect parent who will teach you how to be loving, forgiving, and patient, just like him—your Father.

The Glory to Come

I consider that our present sufferings are not worth comparing with the glory that will be revealed in us.

Romans 8:18

Many of Paul's friends suffered because they were Christians. Some lost their jobs; others were beaten; many were killed. In light of the dangers involved, some were questioning whether Christianity was worth it. At least it would be easier to be silent Christians, outwardly following the crowd to avoid persecution. Paul assured them everything they were going through was worth it, as they would see when they were with Christ in heaven. He promised that their present suffering would be more than compensated by the rewards that awaited them in heaven.

In light of an eternity in heaven, this life is only a blip on the screen. If only we could fully understand how magnificent heaven will be! No tears. No pain. No suffering. When we reach our eternal home, we will realize that everything the Bible said was true. Everything God promised will be ours. Then we will know that living the Christian life was well worth the effort.

If you are going through a difficult time right now, keep in mind that this life is only temporary. Nothing you might be suffering now can compare to the reward you will receive for having patiently endured. One day, you will enjoy eternity with God, and eternity will be more wonderful than anything you could imagine. Don't become disheartened by the problems you face right now. God has things for you to learn and to do for him. Remain faithful to him today, and your reward in heaven will be beyond comparison!

March 18

All Things

And we know that in all things God works for the good of those who love him, who have been called according to his purpose.

Romans 8:28

People often misunderstand Romans 8:28. Some assume this promise means God will turn every bad situation into a good situation. The Bible doesn't say that. It says that God can use any situation, even the worst experience, to produce good results in a Christian's life. This verse is not about freedom from difficulties; it's about the kind of person who emerges from life's pressures. Some misunderstand this verse by assuming it applies to everyone. It doesn't. It is only for those "who love him, who have been called." If you are angry at God or do not love him, God does not promise to work all your experiences out for good.

Paul knew what he was talking about. He had endured some horrid experiences: insults, threats, beatings, arrests, stonings, shipwrecks. Yet in every bad situation, God brought about something good. For example, as a result of Paul's imprisonment, a jailer found new life in Christ. Paul's own character grew stronger, and his relationship with God grew deeper because of the way God worked through trials (Acts 16:22–40). Through Paul's hardships, he discovered something: God could take the worst experiences and use them to build his kingdom and to teach Paul something new about God.

If you're seeking to do what God has called you to do, this promise is for you. Whatever experiences you go through, whether good or bad, you can have confidence that God will bring something good out of them. Don't expect God to remove every difficult situation; watch instead to see how he uses the tough times to bring about good in your life.

Back Talk

But who are you, O man, to talk back to God? "Shall what is formed say to him who formed it, 'Why did you make me like this?' " Does not the potter have the right to make out of the same lump of clay some pottery for noble purposes and some for common use?

Romans 9:20-21

Asking questions is a natural part of growing up. When you were younger, you probably accepted things more readily than you do now. But as you grow toward independence, you begin to think more for yourself. You no longer want others to make your decisions for you. This is a normal step as you advance toward maturity. Paul warns, however, that there is one line you should never cross: you should never challenge God's wisdom. Paul is adamant that no one has the right to talk back to the Lord of the universe.

God is in control of all that exists, including you. He has had a plan for your life since before you were born. This plan is as unique as you are, and it involves the very best that God has to give you. Don't get caught up in comparing your place in God's plan to the place he has for others. That will make you either proud or envious. You'll lose sight of the truth that God loves you just as he loves your friends.

You may feel that your friends are more gifted than you are. Some may be called to serve God in glamorous ways, while God's plan for you seems more commonplace. Don't ever doubt that God knows what he's doing. Just as the potter has total mastery over the clay in his hands, God has the absolute right to your life. He wants to mold you and stretch you to suit his plan for you. That is his right as your Creator. Trust him; he knows what he's doing. Choose to serve the Lord cheerfully in everything you do, no matter how mundane, and you will discover the secret to a joyful, meaningful life.

March 20

Jesus Is Lord

That if you confess with your mouth, "Jesus is Lord," and believe in your heart that God raised him from the dead, you will be saved. For it is with your heart that you believe and are justified, and it is with your mouth that you confess and are saved.

Romans 10:9-10

Many people are confused about what it takes to become a Christian. They think accepting Christ is a complicated process, but salvation requires only two things: belief and confession. With his usual directness, Paul sums it up this way: believe in your heart that Jesus is who he said he was, and willingly share this truth with others. Then you will know you are a Christian.

Millions of people through the centuries have proclaimed Jesus as Lord without following him personally. They have declared Christ to be God without ever believing he could make a difference in their lives. Their words were empty because they were not backed up by personal faith. Sadly, words without faith are not enough.

Likewise, the Bible doesn't recognize secret Christians. Believing that Jesus is alive and risen from the dead is only part of the equation. According to Paul, true followers of Jesus will confess him before others. Jesus said that in heaven he will confess his relationship with those who confessed him on earth (Matthew 10:32–33). Confessing Christ doesn't require eloquent speeches or theological training. It simply requires acknowledging before others that we know Jesus, not only as Lord of the world but also as Lord and master over us personally. Baptism is one way of showing publicly that we belong to Christ. In Paul's day, confessing Christ was dangerous business. We are free to declare our allegiance to Jesus in ways that Paul could never have imagined.

If you or your friends have been unclear about what is involved in becoming a Christian, Paul teaches that it is a combination of two things: believing and confessing. Take a few moments to examine your heart. Do you believe with all your heart that Jesus is alive, that he loves you, and that he is guiding you today? Are there ways you need to make your faith public?

Everyone Who Calls

For, "Everyone who calls on the name of the Lord will be saved." How, then, can they call on the one they have not believed in? And how can they believe in the one of whom they have not heard? And how can they hear without someone preaching to them? And how can they preach unless they are sent? As it is written, "How beautiful are the feet of those who bring good news!"

Romans 10:13-15

Everywhere Paul went, people accepted Christ and new churches were started. Why? Because Paul never assumed his job was done. He did not rest as long as there was someone, somewhere, who had not heard the good news of Christ.

We tend to make two mistakes that limit our effectiveness in telling people about Christ. Mistake number one is this: we assume that everyone has heard the gospel. After all, Christianity is everywhere; how could they not have heard? If we actually understood how many people around us have no idea who Jesus really is, it would astound us. Christianity was brand new in Paul's day, so he saw everyone as someone who needed to hear about Christ for the first time. Our generation too often assumes that because we have heard the gospel, others have heard it too. This error in our thinking causes us to miss many opportunities to share our faith. Mistake number two is this: we assume that some people are so hard we can't imagine them ever accepting Christ's love. Paul knew better. Paul had topped the list of least-likely candidates for salvation, yet Christ had softened Paul's heart and completely turned his life around. The Bible says that salvation is available to everyone, no matter how young or old or how deeply caught in sin.

It's critical that we understand, as Paul did, that others are depending on us to tell them the good news. The only thing that prevents some people from knowing Christ's love is our unwillingness to share it. Look around you today: is there someone who needs to hear the good news of Christ?

Lessons from the Apostle Paul

March 22

Don't Be Conformed

Therefore, I urge you, brothers, in view of God's mercy, to offer your bodies as living sacrifices, holy and pleasing to God—which is your spiritual worship. Do not conform any longer to the pattern of this world, but be transformed by the renewing of your mind. Then you will be able to test and approve what God's will is—his good, pleasing and perfect will.

Romans 12:1-2

Don't let the world give you your values. If you let that happen, non-Christians will determine how you think, how you spend your money, and how you spend your time. The world will tell you what is important in life and what your priorities should be. Don't think so? Turn on your TV. Flip through a magazine. Read the newspaper. The media isn't the only way the world wants to squeeze you into its mold. Spend some time with non-Christians and consider what they value. Think about your own values. Do they reflect God's priorities, or do they look more like the world's values? Is there any difference in the way you live and the way an unbeliever lives?

Paul says there is a way to prevent the world's thinking patterns from taking over your own: offer yourself every day to God. Just as Old Testament believers gave animals on the altar as gifts to God, make your life a living sacrifice every day. As you get up each morning, say to God, "Here is my body, my mind, my heart, my time and my money. Everything belongs to you." As you turn your life over to God, the Holy Spirit will clean out the garbage in your mind and replace it with God's Word. The Bible promises that God will transform you by renewing your mind. The world will no longer determine the way you live. Instead, your life will be an act of worship that brings glory to God.

Hate Evil, Love Good

Love must be sincere. Hate what is evil; cling to what is good.

Romans 12:9

The Christian life is not nearly so complicated as we sometimes make it out to be. It really comes down to two things:
hate what is evil, and love what is good. You know the difference between good and evil. The Bible pictures evil as
being darkness and righteousness as being light. Even the
world separates good from evil. The hero in the western
movies wears the white hat; the bad guy gets the black one.
The hero in science fiction refuses to cross over to the dark
side.

What makes something evil? It brings pain. It's destructive.
God hates evil. From Adam and Eve, down through the
centuries, evil has systematically destroyed people. Evil has
caused people to lie, cheat, steal, abuse, and even kill one
another. We know God is love, but we need to understand
that because he loves us God hates the evil in our lives.
Only God knows the great suffering that evil has inflicted
on people throughout history.

The more you become like Christ, the more you should see
evil for what it is. You should not simply avoid evil; you
should despise it, as Christ does. You should hate sin for
what it does to you and to others. You should have no tolerance for evil in your own life. Rather, as Paul says, you
should cling to what is good. Have you become comfortable
around evil? Are you tolerating sin in your life? Ask God to
give you a holy aversion to sin.

March 24

Pay Your Debts

Give everyone what you owe him: If you owe taxes, pay taxes; if revenue, then revenue; if respect, then respect; if honor, then honor.

Let no debt remain outstanding, except the continuing debt to love one another, for he who loves his fellow man has fulfilled the law.

Romans 13:7-8

There are all kinds of people in the world. Some are easygoing—definitely not the worrying type. They have a casual attitude about everything. They don't concern themselves with what they have coming or with what they should do for others. Their live-and-let-live attitude saves them from anxiety, but it can also make them irresponsible. They don't always consider the way they treat others. They're late for appointments. They break their promises and borrow things without returning them.

Then there are others who lean toward the opposite extreme. These are ultraresponsible people who keep a mental account of everything they do for others. They watch carefully to see that they always get what's coming to them. They put heavy demands on themselves. They can also be petty and demanding of others as they're always keeping score. People with this type of personality remind you continually of all that they do for you. And they always know whose turn it is.

The Bible says that Christians should not fall into either category. We should be careful how we treat others. We should respect their time and their possessions. We should be true to our word and honest in our business dealings. This means we won't cheat. It means we repay what we borrow and we give to others whatever God asks us to give them. It means we pull our weight rather than being a burden to others. According to Paul, it is our obligation as Christians to love one another. That's a debt we owe our fellowman; it's not something we give in hope of repayment. The bottom line is this: we are called to be considerate of others. Maybe you lean toward one of the above extremes. Do you tend to be undependable? Or are you a demanding scorekeeper? If you lean either way, pray that God will help you to show proper respect to those around you. In doing so, you are showing respect to God.

Every Effort for Peace

Let us therefore make every effort to do what leads to peace and to mutual edification.

Romans 14:19

Which is more important to you—to win an argument or to win a friend? Do you know someone who always has to be right, no matter how trivial the debate? How do you feel when you're with someone who is always pointing out your faults?

Some people seem to cause disruption wherever they go. They look at life as a contest, and they're always sizing up the competition. Everyone becomes their rival. The only way to win the contest is to disqualify everyone else. Disruptive people love to argue because it gives them a chance to show that they are the smartest. They love to criticize because it makes them look better by comparison. They were the bullies on the playground in school. Sadly, the people we're talking about are often adults, who should know better.

Even Christians sometimes act this way. In fact, sin causes all of us to be contentious at times. Christians are to bring peace wherever we go. Dissension does not come from God; it is rooted in our own insecurity. God calls us to look for ways to build up other people, but we will never do so as long as we're always trying to prove how good or how right we are. Satan wants us to believe we're worthless, or at least not worth as much as everyone around us. That's a lie, and we must not believe it. Instead, we must understand who we really are as children of God. We are deeply loved; we are God's priceless treasure. Because we have no cause for insecurity, we have no reason to tear down others.

Do you struggle with a critical or argumentative spirit? If so, give it over to God. Ask God to help you see others as he sees them. Ask him to make you a peacemaker, one who looks for ways to build up others. God will open your eyes to see that if you build up others everyone wins. They will be stronger, and you'll feel better about yourself as well.

Lesson from the Apostle Paul

The Failing of the Weak

We who are strong ought to bear with the failings of the weak and not to please ourselves.

Romans 15:1

The world loves to divide people into two camps: rich against poor, smart against dumb, attractive against ugly, strong against weak. Usually, only one of the two categories is considered desirable. For example, the strong rule the weak. As it often does, the Bible turns worldly thinking completely around. The Bible tells Christians that the strong are not to dominate the weak but to serve them!

You may be a strong Christian. Perhaps you were raised in a Christian family, and you have extensive Bible knowledge. Maybe some in your church family took extra time to teach you God's ways. You may grow frustrated with weaker Christians who constantly seem to struggle with issues you dealt with long ago. They may be tempted by things that have no power over you. You may sometimes grow impatient and be inclined to leave them behind as you move forward in your Christian life. Paul said that's not the way Christians operate.

The Bible recognizes that some people are stronger than others. Some Christians are stronger because they've been Christians longer or because they've had good role models. Perhaps they've simply put in more effort. In any case, God expects them to help weaker Christians. Christians show true strength when they help carry their brothers and sisters, not when they forge on ahead, oblivious to the needs of those who are struggling.

Think about it. Does someone need the strength and encouragement that you have to offer?

Famous Obedience

Everyone has heard about your obedience, so I am full of joy over you; but I want you to be wise about what is good, and innocent about what is evil.

Romans 16:19

Is there anyone, anywhere, who has it all together? Some people think they do. Paul has some good advice for people like that. No matter how strong they are, there is always a weak spot somewhere. The church in Rome was earning a reputation as a sturdy, obedient bunch of believers. But Paul saw potential danger around the corner. He warned the Romans about those who would come and try to deceive them to disobey God. Paul must have had some concerns about the church's gullibility, for he cautioned them about smooth-talkers who could "deceive the minds of naive people" (v. 18). That doesn't sound very flattering!

Paul's advice to the Romans is well taken by us also. No matter how far we've come, we're never all the way there. There is always something to learn. It's crucial that Christians never stop growing in wisdom. Just as there were in Paul's day, there are deceivers today who will try to cause division between us and our fellow believers. There are silver-tongued preachers whose message sounds great but is contrary to God's Word. We are to hear them out and try to find the good in what they are saying, right? Wrong! Paul warned his friends in Rome to learn all about what is good and to stay away from anything evil.

Many Christians spend far too much time becoming experts in evil. They seek to learn everything they can about Satan in order to avoid his snares. They end up thinking, reading, and talking more about evil than about God. They are deceived. God does not ask for blind obedience from us, but he does want us to be completely innocent of evil. Our efforts should be spent getting to know him through his Word. We should test everything we hear against God's Word, and we should avoid anything that has the appearance of evil.

Lessons from the Life of Joshua

Joshua spent his teenage years as a slave in Egypt. His parents had been slaves as had his grandparents and great-grandparents. His family had always worked hard and lived in poverty, with no hope of seeing life get any easier. Then along came Moses, who was perhaps the greatest hero of the Old Testament. Moses enlisted young Joshua as his assistant. He took Joshua with him wherever he went and taught him how to walk with God. When Moses was preparing to die, he made Joshua responsible for leading the Israelites into the Promised Land. What an incredible honor! Even the revered Moses had been denied this privilege. Joshua did as he was instructed, and led the Israelites into Canaan. They conquered mighty cities, such as Jericho, and defeated formidable armies. Throughout Joshua's outstanding life, he trusted and obeyed God.

Joshua's story can be a model for you in many ways. His is a tale of overcoming great odds. It's an example of what can happen when a mature Christian mentors a younger one. As you learn more about Joshua, watch to see how his trust in God helped him overcome the many obstacles he faced.

As I Was with Moses

"No man will be able to stand before you all the days of your life. Just as I have been with Moses, I will be with you; I will not fail you or forsake you."

Joshua 1:5 (NASB)

Moses was a tough act to follow. He had performed spectacular miracles, called down plagues, and brought the powerful pharaoh to his knees. He had even been in God's glorious presence. Never had the people of Israel had such a leader! When they needed guidance, Moses asked God, and God sent clouds and pillars of fire to lead them. When they were hungry, Moses went to God, and God produced manna and quail. When the people were thirsty, their leader secured water for them—from a rock! Who could have watched Moses raise his staff to part the Red Sea and doubted his leadership abilities? God trusted Moses enough to be the one to deliver his law, which would guide God's people for centuries to come. Never had there been such a man as Moses!

Now Moses was dead, and the people looked to Joshua as their next leader. Can you imagine how Joshua felt? *Who, me? I'm no spiritual giant like Moses. Moses was a prince! I was a slave! I'm no hero!* Joshua had plenty of reasons to feel inadequate, but God thought otherwise.

God reminded Joshua that every mighty and spectacular thing Moses had done was due to God's presence. God promised to make the same power available to Joshua. As you read about heroes such as Moses and Joshua, do you understand that their God is your God? God did not lose his power somewhere between the Old Testament and the present. The God who parted the Red Sea for Moses now lives within you. His promise is available to you as well: "I will never leave you nor forsake you."

Be Strong and Courageous

"Only be strong and very courageous; be careful to do according to all the law which Moses My servant commanded you; do not turn from it to the right or to the left, so that you may have success wherever you go.

"This book of the law shall not depart from your mouth, but you shall meditate on it day and night, so that you may be careful to do according to all that is written in it; for then you will make your way prosperous, and then you will have success.

"Have I not commanded you? Be strong and courageous! Do not tremble or be dismayed, for the LORD your God is with you wherever you go."

Joshua 1:7-9 (NASB)

Joshua had good cause for fear. The Hebrew nation was not an easy lot to lead. The Israelites had proven unfaithful and rebellious. The enemy had chariots and skilled horsemen. Their cities were fortified with formidable walls. Forty years earlier, the Israelites had attempted to enter the Promised Land under Moses' leadership. That effort had ended in weeping, fear, and failure. Now, after four decades of wandering the desert, would they be ready to take on a war against experienced enemy armies? If Moses had been unsuccessful, why should Joshua expect to do any better?

Then God spoke to Joshua. If he wanted victory, Joshua had to do two things. The first was to be brave. This was not an option; it was a command. God knew Joshua would face situations that could scare him to death, but he had nothing to fear because God would be with him. It was a matter of faith. God was telling Joshua to trust him completely. Fear would be a sign that Joshua doubted God, and there was no need for doubt. Second, God cautioned Joshua to stay absolutely faithful to the Scriptures. This would require knowing God's Word and meditating on it day and night. In this way, Joshua would not be swayed by man's thinking but would instead remain in the center of God's will. In other words, God was asking for Joshua's unfaltering obedience.

Faith. Obedience. These were the two things God required of Joshua. In return, God promised him victory and prosperity. If you are facing an overwhelming problem, trust God and do what his Word tells you. You will experience God's presence, and he will give you victory.

Reminders

Now when all the nation had finished crossing the Jordan, the LORD spoke to Joshua, saying, "Take for yourselves twelve men from the people, one man from each tribe, and command them, saying, 'Take up for yourselves twelve stones from here out of the middle of the Jordan, from the place where the priests' feet are standing firm, and carry them over with you and lay them down in the lodging place where you will lodge tonight.'"

Joshua 4:1-3 (NASB)

Have you ever flipped through the family photo album and thought, *Oh yeah! I'd forgotten all about that trip!?* Or, *Dad, were you really that skinny?* Have you ever been disappointed at a special event because you didn't have your camera? You take pictures to preserve good memories, not only for yourself, but also to share with others. A spiritual journal functions as the photo album of your walk with God. If you've never kept a spiritual journal, now is a great time to begin the habit. It doesn't have to be elaborate, with a dozen subdivisions, an index, and cross references; a simple notebook will do.

No matter how good your memory is, it will be impossible to remember all that you'll experience as God leads you through the years. Keeping a journal will help you in several ways. It will provide a record of answered prayers. When you experience doubts or when you are discouraged, read back through your journal and see that God has never failed you yet. Each day, as you spend time with God, jot down your prayer requests. As God answers them, go back and write in his answer. Your journal will also reveal a pattern in the way God is leading you that you might otherwise miss. As you look back at how God has guided you in important decisions, you will see that each new encounter with God builds upon the last. Making big decisions will be easier when you understand how God has been leading you. Finally, your spiritual journal can be a source of encouragement to others. When your friends—or later, your children—are struggling, you'll have a record of how God helped you through a similar situation. You'll be able to share what you learned that may help them.

God had Joshua build a stone altar as a reminder that God had done a great miracle at that spot. The pile of twelve stones served as a spiritual marker; it represented one step in a miraculous journey as God led his people to freedom. There would be more markers to come, all attesting to God's love and guidance of his people. Today is the perfect day to begin recording your own miraculous journey.

Closed Doors

Now Jericho was tightly shut because of the sons of Israel; no one went out and no one came in. The LORD said to Joshua, "See, I have given Jericho into your hand, with its king and the valiant warriors. You shall march around the city, all the men of war circling the city once. You shall do so for six days. Also seven priests shall carry seven trumpets of rams' horns before the ark; then on the seventh day you shall march around the city seven times, and the priests shall blow the trumpets. It shall be that when they make a long blast with the ram's horn, and when you hear the sound of the trumpet, all the people shall shout with a great shout; and the wall of the city will fall down flat, and the people will go up every man straight ahead."

Joshua 6:1-5 (NASB)

There it was—the impenetrable city of Jericho. The gates were closed tight. The guards were in place. The walls seemed invincible. There Joshua was, with no army to speak of and zero siege equipment. As Joshua was pondering his ridiculous situation, he heard a voice:

God: "See, I have delivered Jericho into your hands."

Joshua: "Excuse me????"

God: "Here is your battle plan. All you need are loud trumpets and comfortable walking shoes . . ."

If Joshua had come up with this plan on his own, he'd have been laughed out of camp! It sounded preposterous! Yet it was God's plan, so the Israelites did as they were told, and the rest is history: they won.

When God tells you to do something that doesn't appear to make sense, do it anyway, even if it seems impossible. All you need to know is that God said it.

The Sin of One   April 1

So about three thousand men from the people went up there, but they fled from the men of Ai. The men of Ai struck down about thirty-six of their men, and pursued them from the gate as far as Shebarim and struck them down on the descent, so the hearts of the people melted and became as water. Then Joshua tore his clothes and fell to the earth on his face before the ark of the LORD until the evening, both he and the elders of Israel; and they put dust on their heads.

Joshua 7:4-6 (NASB)

True or false: When you disobey God, it's a private matter between you and God. It doesn't affect anyone else. This is one of Satan's biggest whoppers; don't believe it! Your sin can, and does, affect those around you, probably more than you realize. The same goes for your obedience; when you do as God says, others are blessed in ways you might not know. The Christian life is not an individual pursuit; it's a group project.

Joshua learned this lesson when he attempted to capture the village of Ai. After taking on Jericho, Ai was going to be a cakewalk! Joshua didn't even send his entire army to this insignificant little dot on the map. But to Joshua's horror, Ai soundly defeated the Israelites. Joshua was astounded! Where did I go wrong, God? Then he learned the whole story. It hadn't been Joshua's fault. One of his men, Achan, had disobeyed God's orders not to keep any plunder when they conquered Jericho. Achan's greed got the better of him, and he hid a bit of treasure in his tent. It wasn't much, and Achan figured as long as no one knew, nothing would happen. God knew, and Achan's sin caused an entire army to march confidently into battle without God's hand of protection.

Whether we like it or not, we Christians are interconnected. What one Christian does will affect those around us. Our friends, our family, and our church need us to be walking closely with God. Let's not let them down.

Building Altars

Then Joshua built an altar to the LORD, the God of Israel, in Mount Ebal.

Joshua 8:30 (NASB)

Do you find it inconvenient sometimes to worship God? It can mean you have to get up early on your one day off to sleep in. It can mean traveling across the city or missing the first half of the football game. It can cut into your studying time or make you miss certain activities. Does it have to involve so much effort? Can't you worship God by taking a walk and enjoying nature? What about spending time at home instead, reading your Bible and praising God? Or tuning in to a service on television? Aren't these all forms of worship?

In Joshua's day, worshiping God involved a lot of work. There were no church buildings, no Christian radio stations, no traveling evangelists. Worship services in those days were of the do-it-yourself variety. Each time God gave Joshua a great victory or guided him to make a wise decision, Joshua would go to great lengths to build an altar and show his thanks. He would painstakingly gather large stones and build them into a mound. Then he would gather branches and sticks and offer a burnt sacrifice to God.

Everything is relative, isn't it? Surely we love God as much as Joshua did, yet we sometimes find attending worship too strenuous. In stark contrast, Joshua would have marveled at us for not wanting to attend our beautiful church building to worship God. The bottom line is that God is worthy of our very best. Next Sunday, when your alarm goes off and you're tempted to snuggle down deeper under the covers, think about Joshua.

Outnumbered

So the five kings of the Amorites, the king of Jerusalem, the king of Hebron, the king of Jarmuth, the king of Lachish, and the king of Eglon, gathered together and went up, they with all their armies, and camped by Gibeon and fought against it.

Then the men of Gibeon sent word to Joshua to the camp at Gilgal, saying, "Do not abandon your servants; come up to us quickly and save us and help us, for all the kings of the Amorites that live in the hill country have assembled against us." So Joshua went up from Gilgal, he and all the people of war with him and all the valiant warriors. The LORD said to Joshua, "Do not fear them, for I have given them into your hands; not one of them shall stand before you."

Joshua 10:5-8 (NASB)

Most problems aren't too bad if they come one at a time; it's when they seem to be coming from all sides that things get overwhelming. It happens that way sometimes. Life is moving along quite nicely, then something goes wrong. Then something else goes wrong. Before you've sorted out the first two problems, along comes a third, and a fourth, and so on. You feel as if everyone is conspiring against you: your friends, your family, your teachers, your boss. You may be overwhelmed by the pressure, but God is not.

Joshua and his army had successfully defeated their enemies when they had faced them one at a time. But now there were five Amorite kings with their armies. Joshua's enemies could attack him from five different directions. Yet God was just as faithful to give Joshua victory over five enemies as he was to give him victory over a single enemy. Numbers don't intimidate God. The more enemies, the greater opportunity for God to demonstrate his power.

Don't focus on how many challenges you face. Focus on God instead. Don't allow the various challenges that are coming against you one after another to discourage you. God is watching over your life, and he is more than able to handle your problems, whether they come one at a time or in bunches.

Hill Country

"I am still as strong today as I was in the day Moses sent me; as my strength was then, so my strength is now, for war and for going out and coming in. Now then, give me this hill country about which the LORD spoke on that day, for you heard on that day that Anakim were there, with great fortified cities; perhaps the LORD will be with me, and I will drive them out as the LORD has spoken."

Joshua 14:11-12 (NASB)

Can't you just picture Caleb? His skin brown and wrinkled from forty years in the desert, his hair gray and thinning, his eyesight not quite as good as it used to be. He and Joshua were the only two adults still alive from their generation. Everyone else was much younger. Joshua and Caleb had waited and longed for this day—to do something they'd been ready and willing to do forty years earlier. They were much older than when Moses had sent them to stake out the Promised Land. Back then they had returned with their report, full of excitement, eager to take on the enemy. But the other ten spies had held them back, weeping in fear. Thanks to their timid colleagues, these two brave and faithful men had just spent forty years at camp, waiting for an entire unfaithful generation to die off. Now, at last, they were in the land they had waited four decades to occupy.

You'd think Caleb would ask for a peaceful valley, where farming was easy and enemies were few, leaving the more dangerous areas to his younger comrades. But Caleb hadn't changed much. He looked to the hill country. He saw fortified cities occupied by fierce Anakites. He'd been ready to take them on long ago, and he was still ready!

Some people never know the thrill of conquering the hilltops because they prefer to live comfortably in the valleys. Some people never see God's power demonstrated in their lives because they never attempt anything that requires God's strength. If you want to see God move in power, bypass the valley and look to the hilltops.

Not One of God's Promises

Not one of the good promises which the LORD had made to the house of Israel failed; all came to pass. . . .

"Now behold, today I am going the way of all the earth, and you know in all your hearts and in all your souls that not one word of all the good words which the LORD your God spoke concerning you has failed; all have been fulfilled for you, not one of them has failed. It shall come about that just as all the good words which the LORD your God spoke to you have come upon you, so the LORD will bring upon you all the threats, until He has destroyed you from off this good land which the LORD your God has given you."

Joshua 21:45; 23:14-15 (NASB)

God keeps his promises. That sounds like a warm and fuzzy thought, but let's examine what Joshua had to say about it. Joshua had walked with God his entire life—from the time he was a child slave in Egypt through his days as a Hebrew spy, through his forty-year stint in the desert, and as he led his army to victory all across the Promised Land. Joshua had seen it all. He saw how many times the Hebrews pleased God and how many times they failed him. He saw their faith and their disbelief, their obedience and their disobedience. He was there for the good days and the bad days. Joshua also observed God's ways over his long lifetime. He saw that God kept, to the letter, every single promise he made. He concluded that God had been faithful, without exception, to his people.

Joshua also saw that God would indeed judge his people for their sin, just as he said he would. Half of Joshua's life had been spent in the back country leading a nation that was paying the penalty for its disbelief. As he looked back over his life, Joshua could say with confidence that God was completely trustworthy to do as he said he would. According to Joshua, this could be troubling or it could be comforting. It all depends on whether you've been faithful.

Are you aware of how many promises God has made to you? It's important that you never take his faithfulness to you for granted. It's equally important that you don't take your faithfulness to him for granted. Strive to be faithful to God, and you will enjoy fully God's incredible faithfulness to you.

April 6

Choose for Yourselves

"If it is disagreeable in your sight to serve the LORD, choose for yourselves today whom you will serve: whether the gods which your fathers served which were beyond the River, or the gods of the Amorites in whose land you are living; but as for me and my house, we will serve the LORD."

Joshua 24:15 (NASB)

Joshua would have made an excellent jury member because he had the confidence to make his own decisions. He could think for himself, and he was not afraid to defend his beliefs. When Moses sent a dozen spies into Canaan, ten came back with their verdict: "Forget it!" Joshua was in the minority, yet he had the courage to stand by his belief in God's ability to give them victory.

No matter who he was up against, Joshua resolved to stand boldly for the truth. When Israel's respected leaders were ready to give up and head back to slavery in Egypt, Joshua knew this wasn't what God wanted, so he challenged them to persevere. When those around him were falling into the Amorite religion, Joshua remained faithful to the true God. Joshua was never one who looked around to see what others were doing before making up his own mind. It made no difference to him if he stood alone; he was determined to do what was right.

From time to time you will find yourself in Joshua's position. Everyone around you will be rejecting God's way. Some of your friends may choose acceptance by the majority over taking a stand for God. They may go against their better judgment and follow the crowd. Think for yourself; don't be swayed by the foolishness of others. Even if you are the only one, don't be afraid to choose God's way. It's far better to be in the minority that pleases God than in the majority that dishonors him.

Chapter 10
Paul's Advice

Timothy was a young man from the city of Lystra, a province in Galatia. His father was Greek and probably not a Christian. Timothy's grandmother, Lois, and his mother, Eunice, were devout Christians. They had taught Timothy much about Christ. The apostle Paul had traveled through Lystra on his first two missionary journeys, helping to start a church there.

Paul saw lots of promise in young Timothy, and he spiritually adopted him as a son. This must have brought great comfort to Eunice and Lois. Since Timothy's father was not a believer, Timothy needed a good role model of how the Christian life should be lived. Paul took Timothy along on his journeys and wrote at least two letters to him that we find in the Bible.

Timothy faced many challenges to his ministry. He was eager to serve God and was gifted to do so, but some people felt he was too young to be a pastor (1 Timothy 4:12). His health was weak (1 Timothy 5:23), and he was shy (2 Timothy 1:7). Nevertheless, Timothy followed Paul's advice and became one of the great saints of the Bible. As you read Paul's wise counsel to this young man, let the apostle Paul advise you as well. You might be surprised to find advice that speaks directly to the problems you face as a young person.

April 7

The Strength You Need

I thank Christ Jesus our Lord, who has given me strength, that he considered me faithful, appointing me to his service.

1 Timothy 1:12

What does God look for in his servants? Cleverness? Ability? Strength? Talent? Above all, he looks for faithfulness. If you are willing to obey him in whatever he asks of you, he will see to it that you have all the ability and strength you need to succeed in what he asks.

Serving God is a privilege, not a burden. If God gives you an assignment, count yourself blessed that he considers you faithful enough to trust you with it! Don't concern yourself about whether you have the ability needed to get the job done. That's in God's hands. He has more than enough strength to carry out his plans. What's important is that he chooses to include you in his activity.

If you have failed to do what God has asked you to do, don't be surprised if he doesn't give you a new assignment. If he led you to serve in some capacity in your church and you refused because you felt inadequate, you were really saying God is unable to carry out his plans. Do you wonder why no new word is coming from God for your life? If you will go back and do the last thing he told you, trusting him to give you the strength, you will then be ready for what he has in store for you next. You will know that God considers you faithful when he trusts you with a new opportunity to serve him.

Old Wives' Tales   April 8

Have nothing to do with godless myths and old wives' tales; rather, train yourself to be godly.

1 Timothy 4:7

In first-century society, people, especially the Greeks, loved to spend hours debating different topics. They would discuss bizarre theories and philosophies. They would fritter away hours talking about ideas that had no relevance to their daily lives. They thought these discussions broadened their minds and proved how intelligent they were. The problem, according to Paul, was that they were wasting valuable time that could be spent pursuing godliness. Paul was a very practical person. Even though he was a brilliant theologian and could have debated with the best minds of his day, he refused to waste his time. Instead, he urged Timothy to invest his efforts where they could do the most good, in learning to be like Christ.

Modern Christians can fall into this first-century trap. Christian fads and theories can distract us from what is really important. For example, some Christians devote more time theorizing and speculating about Christ's return than preparing themselves for it! Others argue vehemently over a single point of theology though their lives dishonor Christ. Sometimes we can spend so much time talking about godliness that we have little time left to become like Jesus.

We would all do well to follow Paul's advice and focus our mental energy on the things that are really important. Let's not become so bogged down with frivolous speculations and theories that we neglect the very clear instructions in the Bible. It's usually not what we don't know that causes us problems. For many Christians it is what we do know God wants us to do that troubles us! Let's stop speculating and begin doing what we already know God wants us to do.

Paul's Advice

April 9

Godliness

For physical training is of some value, but godliness has value for all things, holding promise for both the present life and the life to come.

1 Timothy 4:8

What is it about athletes that draws our admiration? Is it the glory of their victory? Is it the substantial salaries their accomplishments often generate? For most of us, it's their determination. We respect them for their willingness to train so rigorously and to push their bodies to the point of excellence. We envy the discipline involved in training and practicing long after the faint-hearted have gone home.

The Olympic Games were famous in Paul's part of the world. Young people would push themselves to the limits of their physical endurance in order to be ready to compete in various sporting events. Each athlete knew that a half-hearted effort would never be sufficient. In order to win a prize, he would have to strive harder than all other competitors. While others were snug in their beds, the conscientious athlete would be up and training. Even when the athlete was exhausted and feeling tremendous pain, he would continue to push himself until he could go no further.

Paul asks you an important question: If athletes are willing to discipline themselves to such great lengths in order to win a temporary prize, shouldn't you be willing to do at least as much in order to become godly? How much do you want to become like Christ? Are you willing to get up earlier in order to spend time with him? Are you willing to make time for Bible study? Will you be teachable and open to learn from those more mature than you? Will you extend the effort to change unhealthy habits? Like physical excellence, godliness comes at a price. You cannot simply decide to be like Christ, announce it to your church, then sit back and wait for it to happen. It is an excellent pursuit, with a prize reserved for those who are disciplined enough to attain it.

The Problem with Youth

Don't let anyone look down on you because you are young, but set an example for the believers in speech, in life, in love, in faith and in purity.

1 Timothy 4:12

In our day youth is admired. People spend enormous amounts of time and money trying to stay young. No one wants to grow old, so we put our energy into fighting the aging process. Timothy's problem was exactly the opposite. He was a young man in an old man's world. The elders were most respected in his society. They were the ones with wisdom and experience, and they held the power and influence to control the community.

As young Timothy set out to follow God's will, he came up against opposition because of his age. His critics claimed that God wouldn't use him until he had put in his years. Do you ever find yourself in the same position? Are there things you know God wants you to do but others discourage you because you're too young? Do you ever feel that you don't have the experience or respect from others to do what God is asking? If so, Paul has some advice for you.

First of all, don't bother arguing with your detractors. Paul says the best way to handle them is to prove them wrong! Strive even harder to be faithful to God. Become a model for others of what a Christian life ought to be like. In your speech, be careful that everything you say is godly and that your words give grace to those who hear them. In your lifestyle, seek to honor God in all that you do. By your love make it obvious that you know the Lord. Persevere in your faith, striving to encourage others to trust God as you do. Live a life of purity, so upright that even your harshest critic can find no fault in you. If you will concentrate on these things, God will use your life in significant ways, regardless of what anyone else thinks.

Watch Yourself!

Watch your life and doctrine closely. Persevere in them, because if you do, you will save both yourself and your hearers.

1 Timothy 4:16

We all know we're supposed to be careful about how we live, but did you know it is equally important to be careful about what you believe? Paul was very intentional about how he lived. He kept watch for sin that might creep into his life. He diligently obeyed everything God told him to do. Paul was aware that one day he would have to give an account for his life, so he was cautious about everything he did (2 Corinthians 5:10). Paul was also careful about what he believed.

What you believe about God is your *doctrine*. Paul knew from experience how easy it was to get false ideas about God. In fact, he had been so disoriented to God at one point in his life that he was actually killing and imprisoning Christians. What's worse, he thought that doing so would please God! This explains why Paul urged young Timothy to be careful about the views he had about God. What Timothy believed about God would affect not only his own life but also the lives of those he was teaching—for better or worse.

There are many false doctrines today. There is the false teaching that because God loves you he will not punish you for your sin. Another falsehood is that God does not have a specific purpose for your life. Lots of theories sound good but are actually unbiblical. Be careful to examine each teaching based on the Bible. Don't accept a belief just because someone claims it is true and quotes some Scripture verses to prove it. If you're not careful, you will accept falsehood as truth, and your faith will be weakened. Take ownership of your faith in God; it is far too important to allow anyone else to work out for you.

Respect Your Elders

*Do not rebuke an older man harshly, but exhort him as if he were
your father. Treat younger men as brothers.*

1 Timothy 5:1 (NASB)

You've heard the saying "Respect your elders." Sometimes
that's easier said than done, would you agree? As a young
man, Paul was extremely ambitious, eager to make his mark
on the world. He saw the way many older men and women
were living, and he was not impressed. He set out to show
them what a man of vision and energy could do! Maybe
they were content to sit around, but he would make things
happen! And Paul did! He had saintly Stephen stoned to
death. He threw Christians into jail, devastating their families. In his youthful exuberance, he became one of the
church's greatest enemies!

Maybe it was his past that made Paul so sensitive to the
need for respecting the older generation. Perhaps he regretted his own failure to do so as a young man, considering the
horrible consequences of his actions. He certainly understood that young people would not always agree with the
older generation. Timothy had some older church members
who didn't respect him as a leader, and they were causing
him a lot of trouble. Timothy must have been tempted to
put them in their place. Paul's advice, however, was to show
them respect. Paul didn't say they were right, but he did say
to treat them respectfully.

The Bible gives young people no liberty to show disrespect
to their elders. This may be hard sometimes. Regardless of
who is right and who is wrong, you are called to honor the
older generation. Sometimes they may not earn your
respect, but God calls you to treat others the way you would
like to be treated. It may seem a long way off, but one day
you will be the senior citizen, so treat people today the way
you will want to be treated when that day comes.

Paul's Advice

April 13

Widows

Give proper recognition to those widows who are really in need.

1 Timothy 5:3

Paul's world was a man's world. Women had few rights. They could not vote. Few women had jobs. Their identity was wrapped up in the men they married. Their testimony was not even accepted in court. In light of the way women were looked upon back then, it speaks volumes about Jesus that he treated women so respectfully. Because they were so dependent upon their husbands, women who became widows had a hard time surviving. Their best hope was to find another husband to care for them.

Some widows were cared for by their families, and a few had wealth of their own. But Paul mentions other widows who needed their church to care for them. Since Timothy was a young man, he may not have given much thought to the care of widows. Paul reminded him that it is the church's duty to care for any member who is weak, elderly, or in need.

When you're young, strong, and busy, it's easy to overlook the needs of people like widows. Perhaps an elderly woman (or man) in your church needs a helping hand around the house or the yard. God may want you to be the one who helps out. Perhaps God wants you to befriend an elderly person who is lonely. You might be surprised to find that the person you help out has a lot to offer you as well! Is there an elderly person whom you regularly spend time with right now? If not, ask God to guide you to someone. It will enrich your life far more than you realize.

Taking Care of Your Family

If anyone does not provide for his relatives, and especially for his immediate family, he has denied the faith and is worse than an unbeliever.

1 Timothy 5:8

Young people are used to having their parents take care of them. When there is a need, the child calls on the parent. Parents are always there for the child. Yet it's important that each family member be sensitive to the needs of the rest of the family. This is especially true for Christians, who have the love of Christ to share. Of all people, we should know how to care for our families.

Take a few minutes to think about your own family. Do you have grandparents? How could you minister to them to show how much you love them? What about your father? He may seem strong and in control, but could it be that he's carrying a heavy load? Is he under stress? Has he suffered a loss? Do you find yourself only seeking him out when you have a need? When was the last time you prayed for him, encouraged him, or thanked him?

Think about your mother. Is there something you could say or do that would show your appreciation for all she does for you? Have you told her you love her? Do you pray for her? What about your brothers and sisters? Do you find yourself competing with them instead of showing genuine concern for them? Are you aware of when they are going through difficulties? Could they find encouragement in a kind word from you? Sometimes, the people we overlook the most are those closest to us. Today, be especially sensitive to the needs of your family members, including your extended family (aunts, uncles, cousins). Ask God to open your eyes to the concerns of those who mean so much to you.

April 15

Good Deeds

The sins of some men are obvious, reaching the place of judgment ahead of them; the sins of others trail behind them. In the same way, good deeds are obvious, and even those that are not cannot be hidden.

1 Timothy 5:24-25

Every day we keep hearing the same old lie: "You can do something wrong, and nobody will ever know." News reports parade an endless string of scandals before our eyes—scandals involving people who thought they could sin and never be found out. If they had known they would be found out, they might not have sinned, but somehow they convinced themselves they would never get caught. Most sin begins with this lie.

Paul told Timothy that good deeds will eventually be made known as well. Even when we try to do good deeds secretly, people eventually find out. Sometimes, very soon. Sometimes it is not until a person's death that his kindness and generosity are revealed. Ultimately, everything we have done, whether good or bad, will be announced before the throne of the Lord of the universe (2 Corinthians 5:10). What a humbling thought!

Have you been under the misconception that you can sin and not be discovered? Remember these verses! God says you will be found out. Have you been performing good deeds but feeling a little hurt that no one seems to notice? Don't worry. A time will come when every good thing you've done will be duly recognized for what it was. God is perfectly just. He will reward you for your goodness. Remember that God sees everything. Nothing is hidden from him. Knowing this should be all the incentive you need to live a holy life.

Contentment   April 16

But godliness with contentment is great gain.

1 Timothy 6:6

"What's in it for me?" Whether we admit it or not, this question is at the root of most of what we do. The bigger the payback, the more time, energy, or money we're likely to invest in a pursuit. We as Christians may believe ourselves to be an unselfish lot, far less "me-oriented" than the rest of the world. But let's take a closer look at our own motives. What we see might surprise us!

Selfishness was the very reason many of us embraced Christianity in the first place. We saw the options: everlasting life with Christ in heaven versus eternal separation from him in hell. We chose what was obviously most beneficial for us. Some of us joined the church we attend based on what it could give us: there were lots of people our age; this church offered the best programs; it seemed like a good place to find a husband or wife. Let's consider our actions: We do lots of good things, but would we do as many good deeds if God were the only one who saw them? It seems that we look out for ourselves no less than our nonbelieving friends!

Some members in Timothy's church had a rather selfish agenda. They became Christians in the hopes of becoming wealthy. They assumed that, if they were Christians, God would bless them financially. Paul's word to them is helpful for us as well. He said if they would pursue a godly life, and simply be satisfied with what God gave them, they would enjoy wealth that far exceeds what any amount of money could give them. Contentment—the ability to be happy with what we have—is worth more than all the rewards this world has to offer.

Flee and Pursue

For the love of money is a root of all kinds of evil. Some people, eager for money, have wandered from the faith and pierced themselves with many griefs.

But you, man of God, flee from all this, and pursue righteousness, godliness, faith, love, endurance and gentleness.

1 Timothy 6:10-11

"Money is the root of all evil." Although this is one of the most misquoted passages of Scripture, it is true that becoming consumed with the quest for material luxuries can sidetrack even the most well-meaning Christian. Paul adamantly warns his friends not to allow greed to distract them from the things that are really worth going after: righteousness, godliness, faith, love, endurance, and gentleness.

So how do you acquire all these great things? You ask God to build them into your life. Then be ready for the way he does so! For example, is God allowing you to go through hard times? Now is a great time to learn endurance! Don't quit. Don't give up hope. Endurance is learned by enduring, not by avoiding hardship at all costs. What about pursuing love? Maybe God has linked you in some way with a person who's very hard to love. Love that person anyway! Pray for her. Do something kind for him. Love grows the most when it's the hardest, and the person who is hardest to love probably needs love the most.

Pursuing riches takes a lot of effort. So does pursuing godliness. Each will take you in a different direction. One leads to grief; the other, to joy. So choose your path wisely.

Fight!

Fight the good fight of the faith. Take hold of the eternal life to which you were called when you made your good confession in the presence of many witnesses.

1 Timothy 6:12

Some people are gentle by nature. They avoid conflict of any sort. They are the peacemakers who will always find a way around controversy. Timothy was one of those people. He was so mild natured that Paul feared he would compromise his faith rather than fight for it. Paul urged him to fight the good fight, even when it was not easy. When others belittled Timothy or challenged his faith, Paul encouraged him to be strong.

You may know some people who gave in rather than holding on to their faith.

They began their Christian life enthusiastically; perhaps they were even leaders in their church. Then, along the way, things got tough. People disappointed them. Their prayers weren't answered in the way they'd hoped, so their faith was shaken. They were criticized and ridiculed for following Christ. Finally, they became disillusioned and turned away from Jesus. Paul was not about to stand by and let this happen to his young friend. Knowing Timothy's gentle nature, Paul gave him a spiritual pep talk. He urged him to take hold of God's calling and to hold on to it for all he was worth. When Satan sought to prevent him from serving God, Timothy was to resist. When circumstances seemed to go against him, he was to stand firm. When people tried to derail his ministry, he was to stay on track. Paul was not telling Timothy to be disagreeable or argumentative. Timothy should simply protect his faith, even if it meant standing up to those who intimidated him.

The Christian life is not for the fainthearted. There will be lots of resistance out there! That's why it's important for each of us to heed Paul's advice. We must be prepared to stand against any force that tries to dissuade us from following Christ!

April 19

Stand Guard

Timothy, guard what has been entrusted to your care. Turn away from godless chatter and the opposing ideas of what is falsely called knowledge, which some have professed and in so doing have wandered from the faith. Grace be with you.

1 Timothy 6:20-21

God gives each person unique gifts and opportunities. Timothy was blessed with a Christian mother and grandmother who introduced him to Christ at a young age. Then God brought the veteran apostle Paul alongside him as his role model to teach him to follow Christ. Further, God granted young Timothy the opportunity to serve him as a leader in his church. Paul reminded Timothy of the many ways God had blessed him. He didn't want Timothy to squander his gifts. For a young man of his day, Timothy had unusual Bible knowledge and experience in the Christian life. The danger was that he might get caught up in meaningless debates about theology and miss out on what God really wanted for his life.

Are you aware that God has blessed you as well? Are you a gifted communicator? A talented musician? A good teacher? Do you have a special tenderness toward children? Are you a natural leader? Be careful that you don't waste the blessings God has given you. Many Christians who had incredible potential for serving the Lord got sidetracked by the very abilities they could have used for God's kingdom. They did not make the connection between the things God had built into their lives and the way they could be used to share the gospel, to teach others, or to serve in the church. Instead, they wasted their gifts by using them for selfish ends rather than as tools for ministry the way God intended.

Paul advises you to guard everything God has built into your life. God has given you skills, talents, experiences, and relationships for a reason. He does not want you to receive his gifts only to throw them away on frivolous or selfish accomplishments. God plans for you to use your unique gifts to enrich his kingdom.

No Fear!

For God did not give us a spirit of timidity, but a spirit of power, of love and of self-discipline.

2 Timothy 1:7

Don't confuse gentleness with weakness. Gentleness, one of the fruits of the Spirit (Galatians 5:23), should characterize every Christian. Gentleness does not imply a lack of strength; it involves a strong person choosing to treat another person kindly. It's like the three-hundred-pound body builder who tenderly cradles his newborn baby in his powerful arms.

Some people, however, think being gentle means being timid. They assume that gentle Christians are wimps. Even some Christians are under this delusion. They think Christians are called to be doormats, so they allow anyone with a stronger personality to walk all over them. They are easily intimidated by loud, aggressive, and opinionated people. When someone challenges their faith, they quickly lose their confidence. When God asks them to do something, they are haunted by their own inadequacy.

Timothy didn't have to work at being gentle. That was his nature. His problem was fear and timidity. He struggled to find the confidence to address the strong personalities who challenged what God was doing through him. Paul, on the other hand, was not threatened by anyone or anything! In his letter to his young apprentice, Paul reminded Timothy that there was no need for fear in the Christian's life. As a Christian, Timothy had the very Spirit of almighty, all-powerful God living within him. Those who encountered Timothy encountered God himself! Paul was not asking Timothy to be obnoxious or contentious. He was encouraging him to have the confidence to obey whatever God asked him to do.

Christians should be characterized by power, not by fear. We can face any situation with confidence because our God is not intimidated by our circumstances. If you are struggling with fear, turn it over to God. Ask the Holy Spirit to make you aware of the power of God!

No Shame

That is why I am suffering as I am. Yet I am not ashamed, because I know whom I have believed, and am convinced that he is able to guard what I have entrusted to him for that day.

2 Timothy 1:12

Are you ever embarrassed to admit that you're a Christian? How do you feel when someone makes fun of Christianity? Have you had a well-meaning friend who tried to point out all the reasons your faith is misguided? Most of us have times when we're tempted to pretend we don't know Christ. (Remember the apostle Peter?) It saves us from having to answer some tough questions. It helps us feel more accepted. And it works, for the moment. But deep down we're miserable because we know we've let Christ down. At times like these, we must remind ourselves of who it is that we serve.

Jesus loved us enough to go to the cross for us. He had every reason to turn his back on us as we mocked him and tortured him. Instead, he died for us. He proved his power when he overcame death itself. History testifies that Jesus is who he said he was. Now that he has saved us, he has called us to be witnesses to his power. He offers us the same strength that raised him from the dead. We can be totally confident, as Paul was, that whatever we trust into Christ's hands will be safe.

Faith is not about what you don't know. Faith is about what you do know. In light of all that you know about Christ and what he has done for you, you have no reason to be intimidated. Don't let friends, classmates, teachers, professors, or anyone else steal your confidence. You probably know far more about truth than they do. When your faith is shaky or when you're afraid to stand up for your faith, get closer to Jesus. Let him assure you that he is everything the Bible says he is.

Strong in Grace   April 22

You then, my son, be strong in the grace that is in Christ Jesus.

2 Timothy 2:1

God looks at us and sees what he wants to see. He's not blind to our sin, but he chooses to focus on what we *could* be. He looks beyond our faults and sees our potential. He knows we don't deserve to be treated with mercy, but he shows us mercy nonetheless. If it weren't for God's grace, we would all suffer the enormous consequences of our own rebellion.

The lie that millions have believed through the centuries is that God withholds his love until we prove we deserve it. People labor their entire lives to earn a place in God's heart, never certain they have achieved their goal. They've been either unaware or unwilling to accept that God wants to give them his grace. God knows that no one could ever be good enough to deserve what he has to offer, so he gives it freely. Trying to earn God's favor is exhausting. Accepting the grace he offers is life changing.

Paul urged Timothy to "be strong" in God's grace so it would permeate every area of Timothy's life. Like Timothy, we ought to trust in God's grace for every part of our life. Grace changes our character. We are weak and unable to do God's will, but God has given us the power to do whatever he asks. If he wants us to love someone who is unlovable, his grace will enable us to do it. If he wants us to forgive when our heart has been broken, his grace will give us the strength to do it. If he asks us to share his gospel with others, he will graciously provide the courage we need to do it. Be strong in God's grace so you can share his grace with those around you.

April 23

A Workman

Do your best to present yourself to God as one approved, a workman who does not need to be ashamed and who correctly handles the word of truth.

2 Timothy 2:15

A Christian without the Bible is like a workman without tools. Ask a carpenter to build you a house with his bare hands, and you'll be a long time without shelter! Ask a Christian to serve God without the Scriptures, and you'll see a struggling believer with little to offer. God's Word is the Christian's most important tool.

The Bible holds the answer for every problem anyone will ever face. It gives the assurance of eternal life to all who will accept Christ. It encourages the downhearted, comforts the grieving, uplifts the sorrowful, and strengthens the fearful. But how will God's Word help those who don't know it? That's where you come in.

You are God's workman. You are the one he will send to those who need to hear from him. He has given you every tool you need to do what he asks. Many people are hurting, unaware of God's answer for their problems. They will continue to hurt unless you open up God's Word to them. Do you know what your Bible says? If a friend is struggling with guilt, do you know what God's Word has to say about forgiveness? If your friend wrestles with fear, do you know promises of God that can help him? It's crucial that you, as God's workman, have the tools you need to help those in need. If you do not know God's Word as you should, begin studying it immediately. It will give you the confidence you need to share a helpful word with the people you meet.

Evil Desires

Flee the evil desires of youth, and pursue righteousness, faith, love and peace, along with those who call on the Lord out of a pure heart.

2 Timothy 2:22

What tempted you when you were a child? Telling lies, stealing cookies, staying up past bedtime? What are the temptations you face now? Drugs, sex, vandalism, crime, cheating? Along with the bigger temptations come bigger consequences: addiction, pregnancy, disease, a criminal record, and broken relationships. The stakes are higher now, so you must make your choices carefully.

Being a Christian doesn't bring immunity from temptation. Timothy was a devout Christian and a leader in his church, yet Paul felt compelled to warn him about the dangers of temptation. Paul offered Timothy three ways to handle the temptation that he, like any young person, would face. First, Timothy should flee from temptation. He might not always be able to avoid temptation, but he should always flee from it. The best defense against temptation is understanding how dangerous it is and getting away from it immediately. Second, Timothy should spend his time striving to be like Christ. As long as Timothy was spending his energies on pursuing godliness, he'd be less tempted to sin. Third, Timothy should spend his time with others who were taking their Christianity seriously. There is strength in numbers; it's far easier to resist temptation when you are surrounded by Christian friends encouraging you to be faithful.

As you face the temptations that are common to everyone your age, keep Paul's wise words in mind. Flee temptation, pursue godliness, and surround yourself with Christian friends. Then when the evil desires come, you'll have the strength you need to resist them.

Don't Argue!

Don't have anything to do with foolish and stupid arguments, because you know they produce quarrels. And the Lord's servant must not quarrel; instead, he must be kind to everyone, able to teach, not resentful. Those who oppose him he must gently instruct, in the hope that God will grant them repentance leading them to a knowledge of the truth.

2 Timothy 2:23-25

Some people love to argue! They'll argue about anything, even if they don't believe the point they're arguing! These people feel it's their duty to present the other side to every point. They sometimes get so caught up in the debate that they'll say anything just to win the argument. In the process, they stir up anger and hurt people's feelings.

Paul warned Timothy not to be dragged into this habit. Christians can be deluded into thinking Christ wants us to argue his point with anyone who questions the gospel. We may think it is our duty to make others see the truth of the gospel. In our enthusiasm to win people over to Christ, we may behave in an un-Christian manner. We must treat others with kindness and gentleness, never with hostility. Truth can take care of itself; it does not need us to prop it up with our arguments. When we become angry or defensive, we show that we don't have total confidence in what we are saying. If what we say is true, God will see to it that time proves his Word to be right. If we get caught up in argument, we become more concerned with how we look than with bringing out the truth. Winning the argument becomes a matter of pride.

If you find yourself constantly arguing, something is wrong. Perhaps you have a pride problem. Perhaps you don't know how to get along with others. Maybe your heart is filled with anger and you're looking for an outlet. Maybe you're not as confident in the truth you express as you let on. Whatever it is that causes you to be quarrelsome, turn it over to Christ. Ask him to fill you with the love that is more concerned with truth than with being right.

Persecution

In fact, everyone who wants to live a godly life in Christ Jesus will be persecuted.

2 Timothy 3:12

Timothy didn't have the best character traits to be living in an age of persecution! His timid, sickly nature was a liability in a day when people were thrown to the lions for their faith in Christ. Paul tried to prepare him for the dangers he would face by warning that anyone who practiced Christianity would be persecuted. The only way to avoid persecution was to deny Christ.

Some Christians take suffering as a sign that they are out of God's will. They reason like this: *God wants me to be happy, but this is making me unhappy. God must want me to abandon it.* They spend their entire Christian life avoiding anything that causes them discomfort, even when it could be that God wants them to endure some discomfort for his sake. If God were only concerned that we be happy 100 percent of the time, Jesus would never have gone to the cross. John the Baptist would never have been beheaded. Paul would never have been imprisoned. God is more concerned with our obedience than with our comfort.

What does this mean for you? You will probably never be thrown to the lions for your faith, or beheaded, but you may have to accept some difficult things. You may be mocked for your faith at school or at work. You may be excluded from certain parties. You may not be as popular as you might have been. It could bring criticism from your parents or your siblings. Persecution comes in many forms, but as Paul pointed out, if you seek to live a godly life, be assured that persecution will come. Nevertheless, when you overcome it, you will share in the same glorious reward as John the Baptist, Jesus, and Paul. The Bible assures us that no suffering in this life can match the wonder of being loved by God for eternity!

God-Breathed

All Scripture is God-breathed and is useful for teaching, rebuking, correcting and training in righteousness, so that the man of God may be thoroughly equipped for every good work.

2 Timothy 3:16-17

Isn't it interesting that in a society like ours where many people have rejected God's ways, the Bible outsells all other books year after year? What makes the Bible unique?

If you were to take a stroll through most bookstores, you'd find a mind-boggling array of subject matter. There would be poetry, fiction, romance, biography, self-help, science fiction, and much more. There is a significant difference between all of these written materials and the Bible. Poetry may move your emotions, but it will not radically change your life. Scientific theories may impress you, but what guarantees they won't be proven wrong next year? You can read self-help books on just about any habit or problem, but the books don't give you the willpower you need to make the necessary changes. You can read novels about the ideal society, but they will offer no realistic solutions to make this perfect world come about.

The difference between other books and God's Word is that the Bible is more than words on a page. It is alive and powerful. When you read the Bible, it will change your life! You can read it with the assurance that it is true, now and forever. When you need to make a change in your life, the Holy Spirit will take the Scriptures and work them out in your life. You can read your Bible with confidence that God has the power to do anything he wants in the lives of people.

This knowledge should make reading your Bible exciting! Within the pages of your Bible are God's answers for every problem you'll ever have. Your Bible holds the key to any changes you need to make in your character. The next time you open your Bible, understand that you are not reading a book; you are encountering the living and powerful Word of almighty God!

Be Sober

But you, keep your head in all situations, endure hardship, do the work of an evangelist, discharge all the duties of your ministry.

2 Timothy 4:5

The sign reads, "Be alert! The world needs more lerts." Why is it important for Christians to keep our heads, or to "be sober" as some translations put it? One reason is so we don't miss the opportunities God has for us to serve him. God is at work all around us; there's no question about that. The question is, are we alert enough to see what he's doing and join him? If we make our minds numb with drugs or drinking, or if we dull them with endless hours of television and meaningless activity, we may be right in the middle of God's activity and miss it completely. Someone right next to us will desperately need to meet Christ, but we will be otherwise occupied. A friend will be hurting, but we will be caught off guard and have nothing to offer. We may even come to a crisis in our own lives and find ourselves unprepared to handle it.

When Paul encouraged Timothy to "do the work of an evangelist," he didn't mean Timothy should start his own television ministry or travel the highways preaching sermons. Paul was urging Timothy to be prepared for the opportunities God would bring directly across his path to share the good news of Christ. Often, we don't tell others how to know Christ in a personal way because we're so disoriented about what God is doing that we don't even recognize the opportunity! A friend can be under deep conviction by the Holy Spirit, but we're too preoccupied to be of any help. Another reason we fail to share God's truth is that we don't know it ourselves. We've neglected to pray or to spend time reading the Bible, so we're totally unprepared for what the day will bring.

God has many ways he wants to involve you in what he is doing. He knows what you will face today, and he wants to prepare you. Are you alert? Are you ready?

April 29

To the Pure

To the pure, all things are pure, but to those who are corrupted and do not believe, nothing is pure. In fact, both their minds and consciences are corrupted.

Titus 1:15

Do you usually trust people? Then you are probably trustworthy yourself. Do you suspect others of trying to take advantage of you? If so, you may be manipulative yourself. The way we look at others usually mirrors what's in our own heart. It's called perspective.

A chronic liar suspects that others are not telling the truth either. On the other hand, a truthful person takes people at their word. The skeptic calls the trusting person naïve just because the trustful person looks at life without cynicism. In reality, the skeptic may doubt people's motives because her own motives are questionable. The thief is constantly watching to see that no one takes advantage of him. The greedy person assumes everyone is motivated by a desire to gain money. No matter how we try to hide it, what's in our hearts eventually comes out—in our speech, our actions, or our reactions.

If there is anger or envy or bitterness in your heart, you'll know it by the way you suspect others of the same sins. God can change that. He can give you a new perspective by giving you a pure heart (Psalm 51:10). The world looks much better when viewed with a clean heart! If you don't like the way you are looking at the world around you, ask God to give you a pure heart. It will make all the difference!

To the Hypocrites

They claim to know God, but by their actions they deny him. They are detestable, disobedient and unfit for doing anything good.

Titus 1:16

Probably the number one reason people give for not going to church is that it's full of hypocrites. How many people have been turned off to Christianity by the numerous scandals involving high-profile Christians? Sometimes we comfort ourselves by saying, "Christians are not perfect—just forgiven." Or, "Of course there are hypocrites in church, but at least they're in church." Rationalizing may make us feel better, but God is even harder on hypocrites than our non-Christian friends are!

God hates hypocrisy. He looks past our words, even past our actions, to our hearts. What he wants to see is an attitude that matches every word and deed. The problem with hypocrites is that they do not really love Jesus. You may look at someone who claims to be a Christian yet whose life disgraces the name of Christ. You may ask yourself, *How can a Christian live like that?* The answer is simple: he can't. Jesus had no patience for those who claimed to be his followers yet did not love him. He predicted that on Judgment Day many would claim to have done great things in his name, but his reply to them would be, "I never knew you. Away from me, you evildoers!" (Matthew 7:23).

Paul had no tolerance for hypocrites either. He called them "detestable, disobedient, and unfit for anything good." So what can you do about all those hypocrites out there? Probably not much. God will deal with them. What you can do is examine your own heart. If you have been living the life of a hypocrite, saying all the right words, even doing all the right things, but without love in your heart for God, don't waste another minute offending God. Rush to him, repent of your sin, and pray that he will draw you near to him now.

Chapter 11

Lessons from the Life of Samuel

Samuel was one of the spiritual giants of the Old Testament. His entire life was dedicated to serving God. Even his birth was a result of the prayers of his mother. Samuel lived as someone who knew God had a purpose for his life. He learned at a young age how to hear God speaking to him. As a result, he had many years in which to walk intimately with God.

Samuel was also a person of integrity. He lived so blamelessly that no one could find fault with him. Samuel's walk with God was so close and powerful that even kings were afraid of him.

The encouraging thing about Samuel is that he was no different from us. He had no unusual intelligence or ability to hear from God. He simply started walking with God while he was a young person and gradually, over time, became one of the greatest saints of the Bible. Read carefully how Samuel learned to walk with God. If you follow his example, there is no reason you cannot have a walk with God that is equally powerful.

Answered Prayer

And she made a vow, saying, "O LORD Almighty, if you will only look upon your servant's misery and remember me, and not forget your servant but give her a son, then I will give him to the LORD for all the days of his life, and no razor will ever be used on his head."

1 Samuel 1:11

Samuel grew up knowing he was born for a unique purpose. His birth was an answer to Hannah's impassioned prayers. Even before Samuel existed, his faithful mother promised to dedicate him to God. It wasn't as though Samuel had no choice in how he lived, but he wisely chose to follow the path that God set out for him. Samuel never had to worry about an identity crisis; he lived his entire life secure in the knowledge that God had created him for a purpose.

You can be sure that your life is equally meaningful. You were no accident. God created you intentionally, and he has a purpose for you too. You're probably unaware of how many prayers God has heard with your name attached to them. Long before you were born, godly ancestors may have been praying that their children and grandchildren would trust and follow God. Even if your parents are not Christians, you may have no idea how many others have prayed for you specifically.

Don't ever think your life is insignificant. God has had his hand on you from the very beginning. Others have prayed for you. God has reached out to you because you matter a great deal to him, and he has much that he wants to do through your life. Take time today to celebrate your uniqueness. God has plans for you that only you can accomplish. Thank him for the faithful people who have prayed for you over the years, and praise him for answering those prayers.

Learning to Hear from God

Now Samuel did not yet know the LORD: The word of the LORD had not yet been revealed to him.

The LORD called Samuel a third time, and Samuel got up and went to Eli and said, "Here I am; you called me."

Then Eli realized that the LORD was calling the boy.

1 Samuel 3:7-8

Samuel grew into one of the greatest spiritual leaders the Israelites ever had. He was a fearless spokesman for God. When the people needed direction, Samuel brought a word from God. When the king needed to hear from God, Samuel was his man. Samuel walked so closely with God that he never had to wonder what God wanted him to do; God gave him clear guidance every step of the way.

Perhaps you know a man or woman who, like Samuel, seems to have an inside track with God. Do you wish you knew God like that? The Christian life is such that everyone begins at the same place. Think of the most godly Christians you know. They started out just like everyone else—as strangers to God. Every Christian starts out completely disoriented to God. Samuel was no exception. When God first called out to him, Samuel didn't even recognize who was speaking! He assumed it was the priest Eli. Samuel had to learn how to recognize God's voice and to understand what God was saying to him, just like everyone else. After years of spending time with God, Samuel came to recognize his voice instantly.

There is no other way to learn how to identify God's voice than to spend time talking with him. The exciting thing is that you have the same opportunity as the greatest spiritual giants you know. God will speak to you just as he speaks to them. Samuel took advantage of every opportunity he had to get to know God. As a result, God did great things through Samuel's life. You may not always recognize God's voice now, but continue spending time with him. The day will come when you won't have to wonder if it's God speaking. You'll know who it is.

Not Failing to Pray
May 3

"As for me, far be it from me that I should sin against the LORD by failing to pray for you. And I will teach you the way that is good and right."

1 Samuel 12:23

Rejection is never easy to take, but everyone faces it at some point. Samuel was rejected by an entire nation. God appointed Samuel as Israel's spiritual guide because he didn't want his people to have a secular king like other nations had. God wanted them to trust in him and to listen to his spokesmen, people like Samuel. But the Israelites had other ideas. They whined. They pleaded. They begged for a king. Samuel warned that they were asking for trouble, but they persisted in their demands. Finally, God gave them what they wanted. Poor Samuel had to anoint the person for whom he'd been rejected. Once the people got what they wanted, they realized their mistake. They turned back to Samuel and begged him to continue ministering to them. If there was ever a time for an I-told-you-so, this was it!

Fortunately for Israel, Samuel was more mature than that. He knew that if he gave up on God's people they would be in even worse trouble, so he swallowed his pride and stuck with them.

Your friends will not always thank you for warning them when they are headed into dangerous territory. They may reject your advice; they may even reject you. Even though it hurts, resist the temptation to abandon them to their own foolishness. Continue to pray for them, and be ready to forgive them when they realize their mistake. Wouldn't you want them to do the same for you?

May 4

What Is This Bleating?

When Samuel reached him, Saul said, "The LORD bless you! I have carried out the LORD's instructions."

But Samuel said, "What then is this bleating of sheep in my ears? What is this lowing of cattle that I hear?"

1 Samuel 15:13-14

Nice try, Saul! God's instructions had been clear: take no possessions from the enemy, but destroy everything and everyone as an act of judgment on the wicked people. Still, Saul couldn't resist pilfering some of the enemy's best animals. What a shame to waste perfectly good livestock! He also spared the wicked king's life. Then Saul made things worse; he lied to Samuel, boasting in front of the people about how he followed God's instructions. Samuel was no fool; he knew the truth. But Saul was still the king. You don't help your career by embarrassing the king in front of his subjects.

Sometimes it's a lot less trouble to look the other way than it is to confront sin. It's tempting to rationalize that your friends are just having some fun or that what they do really isn't your business. You don't want to look like a prude; besides, you know that you're not perfect yourself. Yet God expects you to do as Samuel did and see sin for what it is. Samuel didn't go around looking to see how many faults he could find in others. On the other hand, he was not about to stand there and let Saul insult God's name with his blatant disobedience. In fact, Saul was actually calling his sin obedience! When you are in a situation where others try to disguise their sin as obedience, pray for the courage to resist compromising with the truth.

Chapter 12

A Walk through Proverbs with a Wise Man

For someone who ended up as a wealthy and powerful king, Solomon had a rather inauspicious beginning. His mother was Bathsheba, the woman King David lured into an adulterous relationship. In a futile attempt to cover up their affair, David went so far as to have Bathsheba's husband murdered. Besides the shame their scandalous relationship brought them, David and Bathsheba were punished by God as well. Their first child died. Their second child was Solomon. Though David was a famous soldier, Solomon was not known for his valor. In fact, he seemed an unlikely choice to replace the greatest warrior king in Israel's history. Some considered Solomon unfit to be king and even conspired to keep him from gaining the throne.

Imagine you were Solomon, facing these challenges. When God came to you with an open invitation—you could ask for whatever you wished—what would be your answer? "Make me a valiant warrior like my father"? "Destroy my enemies"? "Bring peace to Israel"? "Grant me health and a long life"? "Give me wealth and every pleasure known to man"? Solomon asked for none of these things. He asked for wisdom. He decided that with all the temptations and decisions he faced, the best thing he could ask for was wisdom. His request pleased God so much that he gave him wisdom, along with everything else he could have requested.

Wisdom is the ability to apply head knowledge to the problems of everyday life. The Book of Proverbs, largely written by Solomon, contains some of the finest, most practical insights found anywhere in literature. Walk through these pages with a man who received his wisdom directly from God.

May 5

Wisdom

Let the wise listen and add to their learning,
and let the discerning get guidance.

Proverbs 1:5

Most of us want all we can get out of life. After all, we only have one life to live! Unless we are wise in our decision making, however, we could waste the one life we have.

Solomon said that a wise person is continually learning more. The more he learns, the more a wise person realizes how much is left to discover. The more knowledge she gains, the more a wise person understands her potential and the more she has to give to others. On the other hand, there are some who try to get by with the least amount of learning possible. In school, they put in only enough effort to get by. They never read or study anything they don't have to. They rarely ask questions. They are indifferent to what is happening around them. Solomon called these people fools.

A wise person seeks out the company of wise people (Proverbs 13:20). She reads, asks questions, and seizes opportunities to learn more about the wonders of life. Make it a habit while you are young to spend time with the wisest people you know. Observe their lives and ask them lots of questions. Be sure to spend time listening and not doing all the talking yourself. The knowledge you gain will enable you to live your life to the maximum. Don't live life as a fool. Life is far too important to live carelessly.

Fear

The fear of the LORD is the beginning of knowledge,
  but fools despise wisdom and discipline.

Proverbs 1:7

We often read in the Bible the phrase "do not be afraid," yet here Solomon is saying that fear is a good thing; fear is where knowledge begins. How can that be? Since all truth ultimately comes from God, the only way to understand the great truths of life is for God to show them to you. God chooses to give his wisdom to those who fear, or have reverence, for him. Reverence for God comes when you realize who you are compared to who he is.

Spend a few minutes thinking about what God is like. He is powerful: he created an entire universe from nothing! He is all-knowing: he is aware of your every action, your every mood, your hopes and dreams, your every thought. He is timeless: he has always existed, and he always will. He created time: he is not bound by it as we are. It's really too amazing to grasp, isn't it? Equally as incredible is the knowledge that God loves us more than we could ever understand. So complete is his love for us that he gave up his only Son to be humiliated, tortured, and murdered to pay for our sin. It seems inconceivable that he longs for a close personal relationship with each of us—the very creatures who sent Jesus to the cross. This knowledge ought to make us tremble, not in the fear that God would hurt us, but in reverence of his magnificence.

When we begin to understand who God is, what he has done for us, and what he is really like, we have started on the path to wisdom. Solomon said it best: only a fool would refuse such an opportunity, for to be wise is to know God.

May 7

Enticed

My son, if sinners entice you,
do not give in to them.

Proverbs 1:10

When you read this proverb, do you think, *Oh, sinners won't entice me; I don't even hang out with sinners.* In the Bible, *sinners* refers to anyone who is not actively obeying God. That means the enticing may not come from the drug dealer in the alley or the prostitute on the street corner; it may come through an invitation from your best friend. These invitations can be exciting and tempting, but be careful! They may also lead to great harm. Others may make choices without considering God's standards; that holds potential for disaster! Proverbs warns that the end for people who ignore God in their decisions is destruction. If you allow yourself to be lured into sin strictly for the thrill of the moment, you will also suffer the consequences. Don't be fooled! Mistakes made in your youth can haunt you for the rest of your life. You may ask for and receive forgiveness, but the consequences of your choices could last a lifetime.

So what should you do? God holds the perspective of eternity, not just the present. He knows what's in your best interest. Trust his Holy Spirit to alert you to dangerous invitations. Ask God daily for the strength to say no, even to your best friend. A final caution: if you have friends who constantly seek to persuade you into activities that don't honor God, these are not friends at all. The Bible calls them sinners. Don't give in to them, and don't spend time with them.

Understanding

Trust in the Lord with all your heart
and lean not on your own understanding;
in all your ways acknowledge him,
and he will make your paths straight.

Proverbs 3:5-6

It's one thing to trust God with your mind; it is quite another to trust him with your whole heart. You may be convinced in your mind that God is powerful and able to take care of people's needs. But when problems come, nagging doubts creep in, and you wonder if he really is trustworthy with *your* needs. Will he really do what he said he would do?

A common trap Christians fall into is trusting in our own instincts. We face a decision or a problem, and we feel quite capable of handling it in our own way. That's when we are in danger! Proverbs urges us not to trust our own understanding of our circumstances. We deceive ourselves if we think we're smart enough to make the right choices apart from God. You've probably heard someone say: "God gave us brains, didn't he? He must want us to figure this out for ourselves." Actually, God gave us his Holy Spirit to guide and teach us in every decision, in every direction we take. He also gave us the Bible, other Christians, and access to him through prayer. Considering these provisions, there is no need to live without his guidance.

God wants you, every day, in all things, to rely on his wisdom, not just when you are stumped and can't figure things out on your own. He wants you to trust him above your own best reasoning. Live each day with an attitude of complete trust and obedience, and God will lead you in the right direction every time.

A walk th   ise man

May 9

First Fruits

Honor the LORD with your wealth,
with the firstfruits of all your crops;
then your barns will be filled to overflowing,
and your vats will brim over with new wine.

Proverbs 3:9-10

How can you tell what is important to someone? Let's say your best friend is really into basketball. He spends a fair amount of time studying the sport, reading up on the best players, their statistics, and so on. He puts in a lot of time on the court himself, honing his skills and enjoying the game. He loves to talk about the sport, happily sharing his knowledge with the less informed. He goes to see a professional basketball game every time he gets a chance. Would he begrudge the cost of the ticket? Probably not.

Isn't that the way we all are? The things that top our priority list are the things we love to talk about. These are the things we read about, and they determine the way we spend our time. We are glad to open our wallets for something important to us—not because we have to, but because we want to.

Solomon understood that a good test of our love for God is how we honor him, not just with our words and our Bible reading, but also with our money. Some people give to God from whatever they have left over at the end of their paycheck. They pay their bills, pursue their hobbies, and shell out for entertainment. Then, if there's anything left, they give a token offering to God. *It's not much,* they rationalize, *but I'm giving all I have left.*

Solomon explained that there is another way to give. On payday, the person who loves God above everything else thinks first about what she can give to God's work. This person honors God. She does not begrudge her hard-earned money because she understands that it came from God in the first place. God provides for her needs and then blesses beyond that. Solomon knew a thing or two about God's generosity. No matter how extravagantly Solomon gave offerings to God, he received even more blessings in return. In fact, he became the wealthiest king ever to rule Israel. This proverb was his personal testimony about the blessings that come from honoring God with your possessions.

Is God honored by the way you handle your finances? If others examined the way you spend your money, would they understand how devoted you are to God?

Discipline

My son, do not despise the LORD's discipline
  and do not resent his rebuke,
because the LORD disciplines those he loves,
  as a father the son he delights in.

Proverbs 3:11-12

Do you know that God loves you? Do you really know it? You no doubt enjoy God's expressions of love, such as his forgiveness and his blessings. There are times, though, when God demonstrates his love by disciplining you. He may do this by allowing you to go through a tough time. Don't get angry when God does this. Don't assume he doesn't love you. The fact that he is disciplining you is actually proof of his love.

A loving father would not allow you to do something that would harm you. Likewise, your heavenly Father has perfect knowledge of the future. He knows the dangers you face. He wants to build a strong character in you that will benefit you your entire life. Perhaps you are spending time with the wrong kind of friends. You may be unaware of the effect they are having on you, but God knows the potential for pain and suffering that those friendships hold. He will warn you to seek out better friendships. If you ignore his warnings, he will discipline you. His discipline may not be severe at first. But if you refuse to change, his discipline can become increasingly painful.

There are many areas in your life where you might experience God's discipline, such as your habits, your attitudes, your relationships, or the entertainment you pursue. Whatever it is that he is cautioning you about, pay attention! He is disciplining you because he loves you and because he will settle for nothing less than his best for your life.

May 11

Get Wisdom!

Get wisdom, get understanding;
  do not forget my words or swerve from them. . . .
Wisdom is supreme; therefore get wisdom.
  Though it cost all you have, get understanding.

Proverbs 4:5, 7

Wisdom is the ability to see truth the way God sees it. Becoming wise is a choice; it doesn't come automatically. Some people assume that by the time the gray hair comes, wisdom will have just happened. That is a myth. Some older people are wise, but that is because they spent their years walking closely with God. Wisdom is something you actively pursue; it's not simply the result of spending a lot of years eating, sleeping, and breathing. There is a price to be paid for wisdom. It includes building God's standards into your life so you honor him in everything you do.

Wisdom involves learning to love others the way Jesus did, no matter how they treat you. Wisdom includes pursuing the goals that God pursues. Wisdom involves sharing God's value system.

How, then, can you obtain wisdom? First, you do just what you are doing right now; you study God's Word. The Book of Proverbs is a great place to start, but the entire Bible teaches you about godly wisdom. Read your Bible; learn from the successes (and the mistakes) of those you read about in the Scriptures. Second, ask questions. God is not intimidated by your questions; he welcomes them if they are asked in humility, out of a desire to know him. Third, be teachable. Don't be overly sensitive when someone shares a concern they have about you. Listen to their feedback to see if God is teaching you a valuable life lesson through their words. We all like praise; no one enjoys being criticized, but the end result—wisdom—is worth the pain. As Solomon said, "Though it cost all you have, get understanding."

The direction your life takes will be a result of the choices you make. Choose to go after wisdom; pursue it with all your energy, and hold on to it. It will enrich your life!

On Guard

Above all else, guard your heart,
for it is the wellspring of life.

Proverbs 4:23

The Bible describes the heart as the place where decisions are made. We may think that it is our mind that makes the decisions, but the values we hold in our heart determine our choices. The world encourages us to develop our minds, the center of our intellect. Some people train their brains to do amazing things. They may memorize volumes and grasp profound concepts, but sadly, people often neglect their hearts. Some people have high IQs but do not have good hearts.

According to the Bible, the heart includes emotions and will. Your heart represents who you really are. Some of the world's smartest people have destroyed themselves by their own bad decisions. Although they had intelligence, they never cultivated God's values. Smart people without morals or integrity are dangerous people.

The world values intelligence, but intelligence comes much more easily than good character. If you want your life to be filled with the good things God wants for you, don't neglect your heart. In your heart is where the great battles and decisions of life are won or lost. Your problem may not be that you don't have enough knowledge; it may be that your heart is not inclined to do what you already know to do! Guard your heart so you are always ready to do what you know is right. Be sure to spend at least as much time developing your heart as you spend developing your mind.

May 13

In Full View

For a man's ways are in full view of the LORD,
and he examines all his paths.

Proverbs 5:21

There's no point in pretending with God! There are no secrets kept from him. He knows everything you think, say, and do. You can keep things from your teachers, your parents, and your friends. They can't read your thoughts, and you can hide your actions from them. You may be putting on an act that fools everyone you meet (or at least you think it does). At times, you may comfort yourself with the thought, *Thank goodness no one knows what I'm really like. What a relief no one knows what I am thinking or feeling.* Don't count on it!

If you're holding on to secret sin, God sees it. It's no use trying to rationalize why you're doing it: he knows your motives as well. It can be comforting to know God is always watching over you to protect and guide you. But it can also be troubling to know that he clearly sees everything you are doing at all times. The next time you're considering something that you know isn't right, remember that you have an audience. Before you do something that you suspect is not right, ask yourself, Do I want God to watch me as I do that? For he is watching.

Other People's Debts

My son, if you have put up security for your neighbor,
if you have struck hands in pledge for another,
if you have been trapped by what you said,
ensnared by the words of your mouth,
then do this, my son, to free yourself,
since you have fallen into your neighbor's hands:
Go and humble yourself;
press your plea with your neighbor!
Allow no sleep to your eyes,
no slumber to your eyelids.
Free yourself, like a gazelle from the hand of the hunter,
like a bird from the snare of the fowler.

Proverbs 6:1-5

Are there times when friends pressure you to fulfill obligations they have made? Don't do it. When someone makes a promise, they must carry it out. Don't commit yourself to do it for them. Be a person who keeps your own promises but not those of someone else. For example, if a friend asks you to bail her out of a financial commitment she's made, graciously decline. Or, if a classmate or coworker agrees to a large project, then tries to pass it off onto you, kindly but firmly refuse. Be careful in the way you commit yourself or you'll find yourself so busy meeting the obligations of others that you have no time, energy, or money to keep your own commitments.

This may sound like an unkind way to treat others, but it is actually biblical and wise. Many young lives have been severely restricted because of overcommitment. Rather than being free to obey whatever God asked them to do, they were shackled by the careless debts of others. The Bible says it is foolish to link your life with the decisions of a fool.

This is not to say you're not to be helpful to others, only that you must allow them to face the responsibility for their own actions. Even the closest of friendships have been destroyed because of bad debts and foolish commitments. Don't allow yourself to be pressured into doing something out of guilt, for guilt is not the basis for true friendship.

May 15

A Little Sleep

A little sleep, a little slumber,
  a little folding of the hands to rest—
and poverty will come on you like a bandit
  and scarcity like an armed man.

Proverbs 6:10-11

Sleep is a good thing, right? To a point, that is. Rest is good, but too much of it robs you of the time for accomplishing anything. God designed people to need rest to remain healthy, but some people take this to the extreme! There is a great temptation to find a comfort zone and snuggle down into it. This attitude says: "I will not take risks. I won't exert myself. I'll avoid things that make me uncomfortable. I'll shoot for the minimum rather than the maximum. I'll try to get by with as little work as possible." God calls this laziness.

Habits formed now will be hard to break later. If you set a pattern of always taking the easy road, you'll wake up one day to discover your life is empty and you have accomplished nothing of significance. On the other hand, if you begin investing your efforts into what is worthwhile, your life will be full and productive.

Shortcuts will always be available. Lots of people will encourage you to take the easiest way. Don't do it. Nothing of lasting significance was ever accomplished by those always looking for a free ride. The world is filled with people who are unwilling to pay the price necessary for greatness with God. Great accomplishments take great sacrifice. Strive for excellence in everything you do, for you are doing it for God. Don't be overly concerned with protecting yourself. The world has been greatly influenced, not by people trying to protect themselves, but by those who strive to do all God had laid out for them to do.

Seven Things God Hates

There are six things the Lord hates,
seven that are detestable to him;
haughty eyes,
a lying tongue,
hands that shed innocent blood,
a heart that devises wicked schemes,
feet that are quick to rush into evil,
a false witness who pours out lies
and a man who stirs up dissension among brothers.

Proverbs 6:16-19

We like to think of God as a loving God and, indeed, he is. But there are several character traits that he detests. All of them are things that harm us as well as others. God makes it absolutely clear that there are several sinful practices he will not tolerate.

- Pride is putting yourself above others and above God. This is in complete contrast to the humility Jesus showed.

- God despises dishonesty because it damages relationships. God is truth; he hates falsehood.

- God is the defender of the helpless and the innocent; those who try to hurt them are his enemies.

- God scorns the heart that continually comes up with wicked things to do, for it loves sin more than God.

- He forbids us from indulging in sinful practices, for these practices reveal that we love evil more than we love him.

- When we gossip about others or seek to destroy their reputation, we bring God's anger on ourselves. The Bible has much to say about how much God loathes it when we hurt others by our words.

- God is a God of peace. He detests it when we purposely seek conflict with others. Some people are always in the midst of controversy. They aren't happy unless they're stirring things up. A child of God will be a peacemaker, not a troublemaker.

Take time to reflect on your personality. Are you a liar? A gossip? A troublemaker? There are some things in you that God wants to put to death because they are not befitting a child of his. Ask God to tell you what he hates about your character, and seek to change those things so your life is entirely pleasing to him.

A walk th

May 17

A Good Parent's Influence

My son, observe the commandment of your father
And do not forsake the teaching of your mother;
Bind them continually on your heart;
Tie them around your neck.
When you walk about, they will guide you;
When you sleep, they will watch over you;
And when you awake, they will talk to you.

Proverbs 6:20-22 (NASB)

If you are like most young people, you'll reach a point in life when parental advice is the last thing you want to hear! After all, your parents grew up in a different world. They didn't face the same problems young people face today; times have changed. Some of that is undoubtedly true. Nevertheless, some things don't change. It was God's idea that wisdom gained by one generation be passed down to the next.

Each generation faces new opportunities and new challenges, yet the truths found in Scripture remain relevant through the centuries. The Bible provides the answer for any problem you, your children, or your grandchildren will ever encounter. God instructs the young person to heed the wisdom found in his Word and passed down from those more mature in their faith. Perhaps your parents are not Christians. Even if they are, perhaps they have not lived out the teaching of the Scriptures as a model for you. This does not excuse you from being teachable and learning from Christians who are older and more familiar with God's Word than you are.

If you're smart, you'll take seriously the wise advice you receive from godly adults. You may not even understand it at the time, or you may think it doesn't apply to you. Listen to it anyway and remember it. There will come a time when you face an unexpected situation, and you'll be able to draw on the wisdom that a parent, grandparent, or older Christian shared with you. You will realize then that their words were for such a time as now!

Light and Life

For the commandment is a lamp and the teaching is light;
And reproofs for discipline are the way of life. . . .
My son, keep my words
And treasure my commandments within you.
Keep my commandments and live,
And my teaching as the apple of your eye.
Bind them on your fingers;
Write them on the tablet of your heart.
Say to wisdom, "You are my sister,"
And call understanding your intimate friend.

Proverbs 6:23; 7:1-4 (NASB)

Have you ever noticed how different things seem in the dark than in the light? When you were a child, were you frightened by shadows and night noises that seemed to disappear when the light came on? Life is like that. Sometimes it seems shrouded by darkness. Worries and uncertainties loom large, like monsters in the closet. Problems pop up, and we can't see our way around them. For a non-Christian, this is the reality of life, but Christians don't have to live in the dark. God has given us a lamp. His Word lights the way and shows us where he wants us to go. God has placed his eternal wisdom in the Bible, making it available to anyone who wants to know it.

Jesus often quoted Scripture when he needed wisdom or when he faced temptation. He relied on the truths in the Scriptures to guide him when he was facing difficult experiences (Mark 14:27). God wants you to rely on his Word even as Jesus did. His Word is not useful to you, however, if it sits on a shelf in your room. When you read your Bible and memorize verses of Scripture, you are doing as the Bible says; you're "writing them on the tablet of your heart." Later, when you face temptation, or when you are making an important decision, the Holy Spirit will remind you of Scriptures that apply to your situation.

Don't just scan your Bible quickly each day and then put it away until the next. As you read, ask God to show you a verse that will be important for you to remember. Mark it in your Bible. You may want to write it down and memorize it. Filling your mind with God's Word will prepare you for whatever dark place your life comes to next.

A walk through Proverbs with a wise man

May 19

Correcting Fools Can Be Hazardous!

He who corrects a scoffer gets dishonor for himself,
And he who reproves a wicked man gets insults for himself.
Do not reprove a scoffer, or he will hate you,
Reprove a wise man and he will love you.
Give instruction to a wise man and he will be still wiser,
Teach a righteous man and he will increase his learning.

Proverbs 9:7-9 (NASB)

According to Proverbs, you are either a wise person or a fool. There are several ways to tell the difference. One is the way you respond to advice. Fools don't want to learn. They have no desire to gain wisdom. Wise people, however, treasure good advice, even when it hurts.

Suppose you have a friend who is making some bad choices that you know will lead to trouble. If you point out his sin and try to help him, he will react in one of two ways. A fool will be more upset at you for pointing out his failings than at himself for having behaved like a fool. Rather than thank you for your concern, he will resent you and lash out at you. He would rather end his friendship with you than accept your correction. That's why it takes wisdom to recognize when you should *not* give advice to someone. Wisdom will sometimes guide you to say nothing rather than offend a fool.

A wise person, on the other hand, will welcome your input and thank you for having the courage to correct him. Wise people readily accept good counsel. A wise person has a teachable spirit because he wants to become wiser still. Be discerning. Know the difference between a wise person and a fool. Give advice to wise people; avoid fools. In the long run, it will save you a lot of grief, and it will win you the friendship of wise people.

Righteous Lips

When there are many words, transgression is unavoidable,
But he who restrains his lips is wise.
The tongue of the righteous is as choice silver,
The heart of the wicked is worth little.
The lips of the righteous feed many,
But fools die for lack of understanding.

Proverbs 10:19-21 (NASB)

Every time you speak, your words have the potential either to bring joy to others or to cause great pain. Not all words are the same. How you say something can be as important as what you say. For instance, you could say, "Time stands still when I look at you." Or you could say, "You have a face that would stop a clock!" You would be essentially saying the same thing, but one would be received far better than the other!

A wise person knows the power in well-chosen words, so she thinks before she speaks. Words of encouragement do not always come easily. Building up others requires us first to think about what they need to hear and to allow the Holy Spirit time to give us the words he wants us to say. Wise people stop talking long enough to listen to what the other person is saying. This requires setting aside the desire to do all the talking and focusing attention on the other person. It requires resisting the urge to interrupt every time we think of something to say.

A fool, on the other hand, does not think before speaking. A fool never considers the importance of saying the right thing at the right time. Opportunities to say an encouraging word are often lost because the fool is unprepared and preoccupied with selfish thoughts. Some of the deepest hurts people carry have come from careless words spoken by a fool.

Have you missed opportunities to bless others because you were too busy talking to listen to them? Are you in the habit of blurting out comments without thinking of the potential damage your words could cause? Commit yourself to become a wise person whose words bring comfort and encouragement. Begin by asking questions, listening more, and talking less. You'll be pleased with the results, and so will those around you.

A walk th ise man

May 21

A Wise Son

The proverbs of Solomon.
A wise son makes a father glad,
But a foolish son is a grief to his mother.

Proverbs 10:1 (NASB)

It has been said that those who refuse to learn from history are doomed to repeat it. Some people resist learning anything from those who have gone before them. They are determined to make their own mistakes. They reject the wisdom that experience has given their parents and foolishly rush toward danger. They recklessly ignore the cautions that come from those who know better. The Bible refers to these as "foolish" children.

The sad thing about rebellious children is that they cause so much sorrow to the very people who have pleaded with them to be wise. Sin, by its nature, brings heartache not only to the sinner but also to many other people. The consequences of sin are seldom limited to the one who does the sinning. The young woman who is determined to give her body away ends up with an unwanted pregnancy that becomes her parents' burden also. The young man who gets expelled from school or ends up with a criminal record stains the reputation of his family. The reason these children are called foolish is that they are blind to the grief and pain they cause to those who love them. Only a fool would reject wise advice from those who love him and resolve to do things his own way, regardless of the consequences for himself and others.

Some children bring joy to their parents. They show wisdom by listening to their parents even if they disagree with them. The wise daughter understands that her parents are motivated by love for her when they caution her to treat her body with respect. The wise son accepts the hard-earned wisdom of his parents and successfully steers his life through difficult choices. Wise children bring honor to their family by the choices they make.

Under which category do you fall? Do you bring joy to your parents? Do you realize the pain you cause them? Perhaps you need to ask your family's forgiveness and begin honoring them today.

The Secret to Being Rich

Poor is he who works with a negligent hand,
But the hand of the diligent makes rich.
He who gathers in summer is a son who acts wisely,
But he who sleeps in harvest is a son who acts shamefully.

Proverbs 10:4-5 (NASB)

Does it seem out of place for the Bible to be teaching us to pursue riches? It's true, as this proverb states, that "diligent hands bring wealth," but there is also more to this passage than meets the eye. It's not just about money; it's about hard work, about diligence and honesty. This proverb speaks more about character than money. Working hard pays off, not just financially but also by building good character. Staying with a job, rather than taking shortcuts, produces perseverance. It teaches us to be unselfish. We learn to take pride in a job well done. It also means that we can find satisfaction in looking back over the day, or the week, or the year, or even over a lifetime, and seeing how much we accomplished.

God abhors laziness. Lazy people are always trying to avoid work. They sometimes spend more energy avoiding work than they would spend if they just did the job in the first place! They have the misguided attitude that the world owes them something, so they allow others to do their work for them. They are always being cared for and rescued by others. They are takers rather than givers. They aren't bothered by the fact that others are working hard so that they can take it easy.

It's not complicated: Hard work pays off. If you're trying to figure out shortcuts to get where you want to go, stop your daydreaming and get to work. You stand to gain much more by putting in the necessary effort than by looking for a free ride.

May 23

Remembered

The memory of the righteous is blessed,
But the name of the wicked will rot.

Proverbs 10:7 (NASB)

How would you like to be remembered? When people hear your name, what mental image would you like them to have?

If you live a righteous life—choosing to honor God with what you say and do—you will create a legacy of blessing others. People will know they can trust you. They will have fond memories of times spent with you. They will be better people because of their friendship with you. If God leads you to live somewhere else, those you leave behind will remember you fondly as someone whom God used to bless them. Over a lifetime there will be many whose lives were richer because you were a part of it.

On the other hand, if you are not careful with sin in your life, you will leave a far different impression on people. If you are selfish, or egotistical, or vindictive, or unreliable in your relationships, a day will come when you discover you have a reputation. When your name is mentioned, people will immediately have negative thoughts come to mind. People will not want to be around you. They will warn others about you. You will not be trusted.

Sadly, some people never realize that the reason others avoid them or don't trust them is that they have allowed sinful behavior to tarnish their reputation. Now is a good time to decide how you'd like to be remembered and to make a conscious choice to develop a good reputation.

A Safe Life

May 24

He who walks in integrity walks securely,
But he who perverts his ways will be found out.

Proverbs 10:9 (NASB)

Life is extremely unpredictable! It is full of surprises. We can never be absolutely sure what awaits us around the corner. Yet God says we can be secure. He says the key to security is our integrity.

Integrity means having no flaws, being blameless, having no hypocrisy, being honest in every aspect of life, and being genuine all the time. Integrity is doing the right thing, even when no one is watching. Your integrity is revealed when you respond spontaneously to something without having time to plan your actions in advance. Integrity is when the way you live lines up with what you say you believe. God says that the person who lives a life of integrity will be secure.

It's like driving a car. You'll be more secure when you obey traffic laws than when you break them. If you exceed the speed limit, you won't feel secure because you'll be on the lookout for flashing lights. You'll know that much is at stake if you're caught. What's more, your life will be in danger because you don't control how you drive.

There is far more peace of mind when you do not have to worry about being found out. You never have to worry about people discovering what you have done because you have nothing to hide. This gives you tremendous freedom! Living with integrity means you have nothing for which you're ashamed. God's advice to you is to live with integrity and enjoy the freedom that comes with having a life that pleases God.

A walk through Proverbs with a wise man

May 25

Refreshing Others

The mouth of the righteous is a fountain of life,
But the mouth of the wicked conceals violence.

Proverbs 10:11 (NASB)

Some people are so easy to be around! They are happy and positive about life. They don't become angry easily. They make you feel good about yourself. They don't criticize you or offend you with careless comments. They don't gossip or say false things about you or others. You feel safe being around them because you know they care about you. When you are with them, they give you life.

Others seem to have an angry or violent streak in them. They hurt you with their words. There is a harshness about them. They are often negative and use their words as weapons. They take pleasure in ridiculing others. They laugh at people you know when you are with them, and you suspect they make fun of you when you're not there. When you are around people like this, you feel life draining from you.

What kind of person are you? Do you bring out the best in others? Do people seem drawn to you, or do they avoid spending time with you? You have the opportunity to be a source of life to those around you. Strive to be an encouragement to others. There are far too few people like that in the world, and most people are desperately looking to be refreshed.

Love and Sin

Hatred stirs up strife,
But love covers all transgressions.

Proverbs 10:12 (NASB)

Nothing can bring healing to someone who has sinned like love can. God chose to redeem a sinful world, not by punishing us, but by loving us and sending his Son to die for us (John 3:16). Don't underestimate how much your love can help someone who is carrying a burden of sin. When a friend is caught in sin, don't withdraw and tell everyone what your friend has done. Instead, find ways to restore him. Help him be reconciled with those he has offended. Encourage him to lean on the incredible love of God.

Has someone sinned against you? How are you going to respond? Will you refuse to forgive? Will you strike back in anger? Will you break off your friendship? Will you continue to bring up the offense? Love doesn't do that. Love forgives. Love doesn't hold on to a grudge or continue to make the person feel guilty. Love gives the person another chance. Love assumes the best of those who sin against you. Genuine love forgives many sins, not just the first one. When asked how often we should forgive someone who offends us, Jesus replied, "Seventy times seven." In other words, there should be no limit to your forgiveness.

If you have friends who are suffering from the consequences of their sins, why not reach out in love today to help bring them healing? Leave the judging to God. He asks you simply to love the people around you.

May 27

An Anxious Heart

An anxious heart weighs a man down,
but a kind word cheers him up.

Proverbs 12:25

How well do you know your friends? Can you tell something is bothering them without their having to tell you? If they are discouraged about something, does their face give them away? If you know your friends well enough, you should be able to tell by their behavior when their heart is heavy, because their anxiety will affect the way they view everything. They won't enjoy the good things that are happening around them. Everything will look dark to them. They might act moody or critical.

When this happens, don't jump to conclusions. They might not even be aware that their anxiety is affecting the way they treat you. Rather than striking back, ask God to help you show kindness toward your friend. It could be that God has chosen you to deliver a message of encouragement exactly when your friend needs it most. If this is so, the Holy Spirit will prompt you to know what to say. He may give you a specific Bible verse to share, or he may lead you just to listen so your friend can talk about what's worrying her. The important thing is that you are sensitive to what is happening in your friend's life and you are prepared to be God's instrument of encouragement.

In the same way, when *your* heart is anxious about something, listen carefully for God's special message for you. Your problems are never too small for him to notice or too personal for him to become involved. When your heart is hurting, he will give you the words of encouragement you need. Those words may come through a caring friend, or while you pray, or during your Bible reading, but be assured that they will come.

Laziness

The lazy man does not roast his game,
  but the diligent man prizes his possessions.
In the way of righteousness there is life;
  along that path is immortality.

Proverbs 12:27-28

Do you know what this verse is really saying? The lazy person doesn't even bother to cook his meat; he eats it raw! Disgusting, isn't it? Sometimes we think of laziness more as a personality trait than as a sin, but according to the Bible, laziness is a sin. Nothing less.

Some things in life only come through hard work. God has so much he wants to do in your life and through your life. He doesn't want you to miss any of it. Some opportunities come only once, but if you are too slow to respond or too careless with how you conduct your life, you will miss out. God has placed people around you who need you to be purposeful in the way you live. There are those younger than you who don't know how to live as Christ desires. You can be their model. There are people your age who are desperate for a word of encouragement. You can be their friend. There are people of all ages who need to experience the love of Christ. You can give it to them. You cannot allow God to use your life to the maximum and be lazy at the same time. It's impossible.

Jesus said he came to give you life to the fullest. Laziness is a trap that will rob you of the best that life has to offer. Diligently go after righteousness, and you'll experience life the way God intends for you to experience it.

A walk through ... wise man

May 29

Guard Your Mouth

He who guards his lips guards his soul,
but he who speaks rashly will come to ruin.

Proverbs 13:3

A Japanese proverb says, "The silent man is the best to listen to." George Bernard Shaw, the Irish playwright, once said, "I believe in the discipline of silence and could talk for hours about it." Shaw was also a critic. He wryly observed, "She had lost the art of conversation, but not, unfortunately, the power of speech."

Our generation can't tolerate silence. We'd rather fill the air with foolishness than endure an awkward silence. Far too often, we speak first and think later. Sometimes we assume that the only words worth listening to are the ones coming out of our own mouths! Rather than really listening to our friends, we use their words as springboards from which to launch our own opinions. Even our best intentions can be sabotaged if we speak up too quickly. For example, a friend shares a problem, and we blurt out bad advice without even thinking about the implications. Rarely do we regret taking the time to think before speaking, but how often do we long to take back something we said on the spur of the moment?

Careless words, tossed out without thinking, have more power than we might think. They have the power to hurt others or to embarrass them. Our foolish words are equally capable of hurting and embarrassing us! They are like the feathers of a pillow shaken into the wind: It's impossible to retrieve all the feathers once the wind carries them away. It is just as impossible to recover every hurtful word once it has left our mouth.

You do have protection from regretting what you say. It's called silence. When you are tempted to speak without thinking or to say something unkind, it's better to say nothing at all. Silence is never as awkward as rashly spoken words.

Hope Delayed

Hope deferred makes the heart sick,
  but a longing fulfilled is a tree of life.

Proverbs 13:12

Everyone faces the disappointment of realizing that something they fondly hoped for will never happen. If you are counting on people to fulfill your dreams, you're setting yourself up for disappointment. People make lots of promises, but not all of them will come to pass. Even those with the best intentions can't always come through when it counts. But God will.

You have certain things you hope for. You may spend great amounts of time thinking about and wishing for something. Maybe it is a relationship you hope will improve. Perhaps it is a job you desire. The possibilities are limitless for what you might be anticipating. It's vitally important that you put your hope in the right place. Don't expect your parents, or your friends, or your husband or wife to satisfy your inner longing for contentment. They can't do it. Neither can money. Neither can your dog, although some might argue that point! There is only one person who will never fail you when you place your hope in him—that's God. Your only guarantee against disappointment is to put your hope in God.

If you've been quick to take your longings to other people and slow to take them to God, you've been shortchanging yourself. Don't ask others to try to fill the gaps in your soul that only God can fill. Go ahead and put your hope in God. He delivers on every promise he makes.

A walk th... ...ise man

May 31

Constructive Criticism

He who ignores discipline comes to poverty and shame,
but whoever heeds correction is honored.

Proverbs 13:18

It's safe to assume that you're not perfect. In fact, it's probably safe to say that you're far from perfect. Having established that, let's conclude that you need all the help you can get! Don't be discouraged: we're all far from perfect; we all need help; and the sooner we realize our need for help, the better off we'll be.

God is not satisfied that we remain spiritual babies. God wants each of us to become spiritually mature (Matthew 5:48). To bring this maturity about, he gives us lots of opportunities to grow. The question is: will we take advantage of the opportunities? Often our pride, or our insecurity, prevents us from learning the lessons we need to learn. Refusing to take correction is as foolish as an athlete's refusing to listen to her coach or a student's refusing to listen to his teacher.

God has placed people in your life who are wiser than you are, people who care about you. If you reject the wise counsel of these people because you feel your self-worth is in jeopardy, you'll never mature as God desires. But if you're smart, you'll not only listen to good advice; you'll seek out constructive criticism from people you respect. Spending even a few minutes listening to wise counsel could save you years of future grief. The choice is yours: you can try to figure things out on your own, or you can trust that God knows what's best for you.

Choosing Your Friends

He who walks with the wise grows wise,
  but a companion of fools suffers harm.

Proverbs 13:20

Have you ever noticed how people and their dogs grow to look alike over the years? It's a good thing to keep in mind next time you're shopping for a dog! Well, maybe that's a myth, but it is true that you are shaped by the company you keep. If you spend time with wise people, you'll grow in wisdom. If you stick around fools, their foolishness will rub off on you.

Choosing your friends shouldn't be a haphazard venture, for they have a tremendous influence on your life. If you spend a lot of time with a gossip, it will be hard to resist falling into the same habit. If your friend has a critical spirit, you may find yourself growing judgmental as well. This is not to say you need to eliminate all imperfect people from your social circle; you would end up friendless! (In fact, you won't make the cut yourself!) It does mean you should choose friends who are striving to honor God with their lives. If your friend has no concern for Christian values, it will be an uphill battle to stay in the friendship and maintain your own integrity.

There are really two decisions to make here: the kind of friend you'll choose and the kind of friend you'll be. Actively seek out friends who will affect your character in positive ways. These people will challenge you to grow as a Christian, and you will enjoy being around them. At the same time, be sure you're a good influence on your friends. They should be better people because they know you. Take a few minutes to evaluate your friendships. Are they affecting you in ways you don't want?

June 2

The Power of Sin

Fools mock at making amends for sin,
but good will is found among the upright.

Proverbs 14:9

The biggest mistake Christians make is to underestimate the power of sin. We don't like to admit it when we sin because then we'll have to make amends for it or change our behavior. So, we rationalize that we haven't really sinned at all. The first thing we do is find a better name for it. Sin sounds so old-fashioned. So harsh. Let's call it a "mistake," or a "habit," or a "lapse in judgment." That sounds better. Next, we make a case to explain why we did it: "Everyone else was doing it." "I didn't think anyone would get hurt." "It wasn't my fault; I have an addiction." Finally, we de-emphasize the results: "People are too uptight these days." "They need to stop being so sensitive."

It comes down to a control issue: we don't like being told what to do. We want the freedom to make our own choices. But we fail to understand one thing: we don't control sin; sin controls us. Sin is any attitude or behavior that goes against God's desires. God's Word sets a clear standard for how he wants us to live. The Bible also warns us of the consequences for disobedience. Why? Because sin is serious. Sin destroys. Sin kills (Romans 6:23). That's not what God wants for us. He wants us to have life. He wants us to be free from the guilt, shame, and consequences of sin. As long as we refuse to take sin seriously, we'll never experience life the way God desires. That's the power sin has over us.

Don't be afraid to see sin for what it is. Don't allow a distorted view of sin to rob you of the life God intends for you. Ask God to tell you how you can make amends for your sin.

Rededication or Repentance?

The faithless will be fully repaid for their ways,
  and the good man rewarded for his.

Proverbs 14:14

We Christians have a language all our own, don't we? We *witness* so we can *lead someone to the Lord*. Once he's *saved* we can have *sweet fellowship* with him. Then we *disciple* the new *convert* so he doesn't *backslide* and have to *go forward* to *rededicate* his life. It's no wonder nonbelievers sometimes miss our message!

If you've been a Christian for a while, here's a challenge for you: see if you can go a whole day without speaking *Christianese*. OK, we're having a little fun, but it's a real challenge. While most of the terms we use are taken from the Bible, not everything we say necessarily reflects what the Bible teaches. For example, Christians are delighted when someone *rededicates* her life to God. (If you're uninitiated to the lingo, this means to make a fresh commitment to God.) People regularly rededicate themselves to be better Christians. Over and over, someone will stand before the church and share a renewed resolve to start living for Christ, and we all smile and nod our approval. So what's the problem?

Promises are easily made and easily broken. God isn't satisfied with promises; he's satisfied with obedience. Disobeying God is a serious matter. When someone realizes he has been living in sin, it's time for grieving, not for rejoicing. It's a time for brokenness, not celebration. It's time for *repentance*, not rededication. God isn't looking for another promise; he's looking for repentance—and the evidence of repentance is a changed life. Sometimes we feel if we make enough promises in front of enough people, we're living an obedient life. We dismiss our sin with a promise to do better next time. We're in such a hurry to get on with it that we never stop to consider what we've done and to ask God's forgiveness. The more we see sin for what it is, the less need we'll have to make new commitments because we'll be motivated to keep the commitments we've already made.

Don't be fooled into believing God is pleased with the promises you make. He's only pleased with the ones you keep.

June 4

Watch Your Temper

A quick-tempered man does foolish things.

Proverbs 14:17

It's a mark of maturity when you don't allow your feelings to control your actions. That's not to say self-control comes automatically with age. Many adults live with deep regret for things they've said and done in the heat of emotion. Self-control is a spiritual thing, not an age thing. It's a sign of spiritual maturity, not physical maturity.

Life is full of emotionally charged events; things happen every day that could send you over the edge if you let them. In fact, you have little control over much of what happens to you. Unless you find yourself a nice little cabin in the woods and become a hermit, people and circumstances can and will affect your life. The question is, how are you going to respond? That's something you *can* control. Jesus had every reason in the world to strike back in anger at those who hurt him. He chose to forgive them instead.

Never make excuses for a quick temper. Eliminate phrases like these from your vocabulary: "I was tired." "I was hurt." "I was under a lot of stress." "You pushed me too far." "I have red hair; we're *supposed* to be hotheads!" "I'm just a passionate person!" Self-control is one of the fruits of the Spirit; in other words, it's a sign of the Holy Spirit's working in your life. Since Christ lives within you, you have the ability to respond in love rather than reacting in anger. Ask God to show you how.

Why Did You Do That?　　　June 5

All a man's ways seem innocent to him,
but motives are weighed by the LORD.

Proverbs 16:2

Is the right thing still the right thing if it's done for the wrong reason? What if you go to church to please your parents instead of going in order to please God? What if you share a prayer request about your friend's problem, but what you're really doing is spreading gossip? What if you do good things for others, but only when you're being watched? It's possible to do all the right things, but with all the wrong motives.

When police try to solve a crime, one of the most important pieces of the puzzle is finding a motive. What benefit would the suspect have hoped to achieve by committing this crime? Not surprisingly, the million-dollar beneficiary in the will, who's suddenly jetted off to the Caribbean, is one of the first persons questioned after a suspicious death occurs. A person's motive says a lot! It's amazing, but often we are the worst judge of our own motives. We live our Christian life the way we think we should without ever examining why we do what we do. We go through the motions, but our heart is far from God. God wants us to live out our faith purposefully. That is, he wants us to do what we do for the right reason—because we love him.

Do you want to grow as a Christian? Invite God to probe deeply into your character and show you why you do what you do. If you don't like what you see, that's your opportunity for growth. Ask God to help you do the right thing for the right reason, and your faith will become much more meaningful to you!

June 6

Things That Destroy You

Wine is a mocker and beer a brawler;
whoever is led astray by them is not wise.

Proverbs 20:1

If all the advice in the Book of Proverbs could be boiled down to one sentence, it might read something like this: Don't believe everything you hear.

Our society has one message: tolerance. If you take a stand against anything, you're being intolerant, and that makes you a bad person. The problem is, you're not being told the whole story. The things you're being asked to tolerate can destroy you. Alcohol is one of those things. If you're to believe the world, drinking actually enhances your life. It relaxes you and loosens you up so you can have a good time. The commercials show you all the great things that will happen to you as long as you choose the right logo on your beer: cars, sports, travel, romance, adventure, excitement, good friends, good times, great music—whatever you need to make you happy.

But have you heard the rest of the story? Alcohol will play you for a fool. It will destroy your perspective. It will dull your senses, causing you to do foolish and dangerous things. It will remove your inhibitions so you say and do things you'll regret. Alcohol has caused more heartache than the world is willing to admit: broken hearts and broken homes, lost dreams and lost hope, despair and death.

The world says, "Go ahead; it won't hurt you." But when all is said and done and your self-respect has vanished, the writer of Proverbs says alcohol stands back and laughs at you. The commercials forget to mention that part. Don't be fooled just because those around you say something is good. If you're trusting the world to tell you where to find joy, you're heading for disappointment. Go to God; he'll tell you the whole story.

Fools Who Fight

It is to a man's honor to avoid strife,
  but every fool is quick to quarrel.

Proverbs 20:3

Conflict has been part of the human condition since Cain killed Abel in a fit of jealousy. Whether it's on a grand scale, like a world war, or a smaller scale, like an argument between siblings, conflict has been a part of life throughout human history. Besides, without conflict, what would we watch on TV? Some people just seem to have a knack for making us angry. They know exactly which buttons to push to get us to lose our cool. It's not as though we're looking for trouble; these people just seem to stir up anger from deep within us. The Bible calls people like this fools. But guess what? The Bible says we're fools too if we quarrel with them.

Any fool can pick a fight, but it takes a lot more character to avoid one, or better yet, to resolve one. It's ingrained in us to fight back when someone hurts us or to get revenge when someone wrongs us. We even get involved in fights that don't concern us because we can't stand to see wrongs go unpunished. God says he honors the peacemaker (Matthew 5:9), not the person who rights all the world's wrongs.

It takes far more courage to stop a conflict than it does to start one. As you go about your business today, remember that God has called you to a ministry of reconciliation (2 Corinthians 5:18). He hasn't asked you to prove how right you are; he's asked you to bring peace, even if it means backing down when you are right. The sign of true wisdom is the ability to end an argument, not the ability to win one.

June 8

Deep Waters

The purposes of a man's heart are deep waters,
but a man of understanding draws them out.

Proverbs 20:5

Discernment is the ability to see past the surface. If you are a discerning person, you have sharp insight that allows you to see through people who are trying to deceive you or mislead you.

It won't benefit you to be hardhearted and cynical, suspecting that everyone is out to get you. At the same time it's vitally important that you're not so gullible as to be taken in by the schemes of cunning people. If you believe everything you hear, you'll be, as Paul warned, "tossed to and fro, . . . with every wind of doctrine" (Ephesians 4:14, KJV). If someone is asking you to do something that you know is wrong, don't be swayed, no matter how convincing the argument or how winsome the person is. Always weigh what others tell you against God's Word, and match their arguments up with biblical principles that you know are true. When in doubt, seek the advice of a Christian whom you respect. Above all, trust God to guide you. God sees what people plot in their hearts, and he can protect you. He has given you his Holy Spirit to alert you to things that are false. If you have any doubt at all about someone's motives, guard your heart and take your concerns to God.

It is unfortunate that there are people out there who will take advantage of you. Fortunately, God knows what is in every person's heart, and he will give you discernment to know how to respond to the people around you. Are there people asking you to do something you are not sure about? Don't proceed until God has given you the assurance that it is OK.

Get-Rich-Quick Schemes

An inheritance quickly gained at the beginning
  will not be blessed at the end.

Proverbs 20:21

What motivates people to gamble or to buy lottery tickets? Some will tell you it's the thrill of the game. Others will say it's just a hobby. The ones who are really honest will tell you the truth: it's an opportunity to get a big return for a little investment. It's almost as good as getting something for nothing.

The chance for a shortcut to success holds tremendous appeal for some people. In fact, some folks spend more energy on doomed get-rich-quick schemes than they would if they simply resigned themselves to working for a living. They're always looking for their big break, their opportunity of a lifetime! Someone has said, "Opportunities are usually disguised as hard work, so most people don't recognize them!"

The prodigal son in the story Jesus told was one of those who looked for instant gratification (Luke 15:11–31). He coerced his father into giving him his inheritance early, but he had neither the wisdom nor the character to handle it. In the end, he lost it all.

It's time for some hard questions: Are you obsessed with getting things for nothing? Do you find it hard to be patient until you can afford something? Do you have a tendency to use other people for your own gain? Can you persevere with hard work over a long period of time? Here's a fact of life: things bought without a cost are usually worth exactly what you pay for them. Don't waste your energy looking for shortcuts. Trust God's timing; he'll see that you get what you need when you're ready for it.

June 10

God's Spotlight

The lamp of the LORD searches the spirit of a man;
it searches out his inmost being.

Proverbs 20:27

Oxford University in England sells T-shirts that bear its logo along with this saying:

> *The more I study, the more I learn,*
> *The more I learn, the more I know,*
> *The more I know, the more I forget,*
> *The more I forget, the less I know,*
> *So why study?*

If you're a student, you probably agree! Let's try another one:

> *The older you get, the more you realize how little you know.*

This one is definitely true, especially regarding your own character. Believe it or not, as you grow older, you'll realize more and more that you don't really know yourself the way you thought you did. You may have always thought of yourself as a forgiving person. Then someone hurts you, and you discover you're not as forgiving as you thought. It's like the person who calls herself a noninterventionist (one who doesn't believe in taking medication) and remains true to her convictions until she gets a big headache; then she heads straight for the medicine cabinet!

We don't really know our hearts the way we might think. We need to ask God to show us what we're really like so that we can grow and change. God knows everything there is to know about us, the good and the bad. King David wanted so much to please God that he opened himself up completely to God's scrutiny. Here's what he prayed:

Search me, O God, and know my heart;
test me and know my anxious thoughts,
See if there is any offensive way in me,
and lead me in the way everlasting (Psalm 139:23–24).

David knew that he might not like everything God had to say about his character, but he knew it was important to hear from God all the same. David had the right attitude. Why not make his prayer yours as well?

A Good Name

A good name is more desirable than great riches;
to be esteemed is better than silver or gold.

Proverbs 22:1

A good reputation is a priceless treasure. A good name may eventually lead to riches, but riches don't necessarily lead to a good name. You can't buy a good reputation. You can't even inherit one from your parents, though you can damage their good name. You earn a good reputation by living your life well, over time.

When the writer of Proverbs talked about a good name, he wasn't speaking of fame, or wealth, or power. He was talking about integrity—who you are, not what you've got. A good reputation takes time to build. If you want others to trust you, you must prove, over time, that you are trustworthy. If you want others to respect you, you must first earn their respect. If you want to have friends, you have to prove you know how to be a friend.

You are, right now, in the process of establishing your reputation. Even as you're getting your education or building your career, you're also making a name for yourself. Everything you say or do is creating in people's mind an image of what you are like. People are watching you, listening to you, and making up their minds about what kind of person you are. Once you have a reputation, it is hard to change. Keep in mind that as a Christian you have attached Christ's name to yours. Be sure you represent both names well.

June 12

Stay Out of Debt

Do not be a man who strikes hands in pledge
  or puts up security for debts;
if you lack the means to pay,
  your very bed will be snatched from under you.

Proverbs 22:26-27

It's foolish to make promises we know we can't keep. That was true when this proverb was written, and it's still true today. Yet we can be in such a hurry to get what we want that we find ourselves over our heads in debt. We can't stand to wait, so we sign on the dotted line and get what we want now with a promise to pay later. Then, we cross our fingers and hope our ship comes in before the bill does!

Even though the Book of Proverbs was written thousands of years ago, the advice is still relevant: if you don't have the money up front, don't buy it! Agreeing to make a regular payment, such as a car payment or a house payment, is not foolish as long as your income ensures you have the ability to make the payments. But agreeing to pay for something when you don't have the means to honor the loan is dishonest and irresponsible. Agreeing to guarantee someone else's debts is even more foolish! Proverbs warns you never to bind your life with the foolish choices others have made.

Be careful, especially now while you're young, that you don't saddle yourself with debt. Get sound financial advice from your parents or from a good financial counselor. Keep yourself free to respond to God's leading. Wouldn't it be tragic if God called you to seminary or to the mission field and you were too shackled with unnecessary debt to obey?

Honoring Your Heritage   June 13

Do not move an ancient boundary stone
set up by your forefathers.

Proverbs 22:28

In the ancient Middle East, land was a precious commodity. In those times there were no fences to distinguish where one person's property ended and someone else's property began. Instead, families would mark the boundaries with stone markers. Though ownership of the property would be passed down from one generation to the next, the boundaries would remain the same because Jewish law specified that land should remain within the family of the original owner. If someone wanted to rob his neighbor, he might try to move the ancient landmark, giving himself more land. This was a demonstration of gross disrespect for his neighbor, as well as his neighbor's ancestors.

When you are tempted to do something foolish with your life, keep in mind that your actions will affect other people besides yourself. It could be that your parents have spent a lifetime establishing a good reputation in your community. Will you tarnish their good name with one careless decision? While you're young, you won't always understand why your parents or grandparents considered some things important. But it's important to respect their traditions. Think very carefully about what's at stake before you move a boundary stone. You don't live in a vacuum. Be careful that your decisions don't lead you to steal what belongs to someone else. Understand that there may be very good reasons why certain values and traditions have been passed down from generation to generation. Realize that some boundaries need to be kept where they are.

June 14

Skilled at Work

Do you see a man skilled in his work?
  He will serve before kings;
  he will not serve before obscure men.

Proverbs 22:29

What kind of mental image does the word *work* conjure up for you? Do you think of work in a negative sense? If that's your view, you'll work just until you've met the minimum requirement or until you've earned enough money to do what you really want to do. You'll see work as a necessary evil merely to be endured until it's time to play. You'll always try to get the most return for the least effort. If that's your opinion of work, you still have some growing to do.

The Bible presents work as a positive thing. Regardless of the pay, or whether there is any compensation at all, work is a good thing in itself. When you do your best at a job, whatever job it is, it does something good for *you*. But if you put in just enough effort to get by, you will never become the best person you can be.

You may be thinking, *But what about workaholics? They work too much, and they neglect their health and their families.* That's true. It's a question of quality, not quantity. You can definitely do too much work, but you can never do too good a job of your work. No matter what God calls you to do, give it your best effort. Never settle for mediocrity; establish excellence as your standard. You don't have to work all the time, but never settle for anything less than giving a job your best.

Giving It All to God

My son, give me your heart
  and let your eyes keep to my way.

Proverbs 23:26

When we talk about the heart, we're usually referring to our emotions. Romantically, we speak as though we have little control over what happens to our heart. We can lose it or give it away accidentally; others can break it or take it from us against our will, as is made clear in that illustrious country tune: "You Done Tore Out My Heart and Stomped That Sucker Flat."

When the Bible refers to the heart, it's talking about your whole being, not just your emotions. Your heart includes the whole package: your mind, your soul, and your will. Proverbs 4:23 refers to your heart as the wellspring, or source, of life. When God asks for your heart, he's asking for *everything*. When God controls your heart, he has control of everything. He wants your entire life: your hopes and dreams, your thoughts and fears, your priorities and values, your wisdom, your knowledge, all of it. Why? Because it's safest with him.

When the Bible talks about relating to other people, it always cautions you to guard your heart carefully, but it says the opposite when it talks about relating to God. Don't be afraid to trust God with every ounce of your being. When it comes to relating to God, you harm yourself by withholding something from God rather than when you hand over every part of your life to him. If you've been holding back any part of your life from God, understand that whatever you give him, it's safe with him.

June 16

Don't Envy Evil Men

Do not envy wicked men,
*   do not desire their company;*
for their hearts plot violence,
*   and their lips talk about making trouble.*

Proverbs 24:1-2

What do wicked people look like? Do they dress in black? Do they have shifty eyes? Are they ugly or covered with warts? What do they act like? Do they prowl around at night? Do they have a sinister laugh? If only they were so easy to recognize! The truth is, evil people are often attractive and pleasant, on the outside at least. The Bible says that even Satan appears as an angel of light (2 Corinthians 11:14). Obviously, appearances can be deceiving. No matter how they look or act outwardly, wicked people hide sin and violence in their hearts. Their goal is to cause you harm.

Be careful that you never envy a wicked person. You might admire someone because he or she appears successful by the world's standards, but don't be fooled by worldly success. Sometimes, success comes at the expense of truth and goodness. The Bible teaches that, sooner or later, evil people will be exposed for who they are. In the meantime, don't let anyone who is motivated by sin set the direction for your life.

Ask God for the wisdom to discern whether someone is living for God or living for his own desires. If you know God well, it shouldn't be hard to tell the difference. If a friend or acquaintance tries to get you to go against what you know God wants for you, stay away from her!

You might conclude that this proverb doesn't apply to you, because you don't know anyone who is wicked. Hopefully, you are right, but ask God to open your eyes, just to be sure.

Preparing for Adversity

If you falter in times of trouble,
  how small is your strength!

Proverbs 24:10

If you're hoping for a trouble-free life, you're heading for disappointment. No matter who you are, how nice you are, how wealthy you are, or how attractive you are, you'll not escape problems in this life. Now is the time to prepare your character so you'll be able to handle adversity when it comes.

God knows what awaits you in your life, and he can prepare you so you won't crumble when the trials come. The most important thing you can do is spend time with him. The more you grow in your relationship with God, the stronger your character will be, because you'll be more like Christ. The better you know God, the more you will trust him and increase your faith in him. As God consistently helps you every time you experience trouble, you'll expect that he will be there for you the next time you have a problem as well.

What if you've just come through a difficult experience and you collapsed because you weren't strong enough to handle the load? Did you become discouraged? Did you turn your back on your faith? Were you trying to handle the problem on your own strength? Learn from your mistake. Like a ship captain who realizes the ship has drifted off its path, make a midcourse correction. Get back into your regular times with God. Ask him to strengthen you for the next trial so you'll be able to experience victory in spite of your circumstances.

A walk th   ise man

June 18

Getting Involved

Rescue those being led away to death;
  hold back those staggering toward slaughter.
If you say, "But we knew nothing about this,"
  does not he who weighs the heart perceive it?
Does not he who guards your life know it?
  Will he not repay each person according to what he has done?

Proverbs 24:11-12

The difference between your life and the life of a non-Christian is enormous. Beyond treating others in a basically moral way, non-Christians really only have one responsibility—themselves. Unless they choose otherwise, their purpose in life needn't go past simply getting through it as best they can.

Christians, on the other hand, have a much bigger obligation to those around us. Jesus said our purpose is to share the love of Christ with others (Matthew 5:16). That's not always an easy thing to do. Sometimes we're so busy with our own concerns that we don't take time for other people's needs. It's possible to become so preoccupied with ourselves that we don't even notice the hurting person right next to us. According to this proverb, that excuse doesn't hold weight with God. If we open our eyes, we'll see struggling people all around us, headed for disaster unless someone tells them where to find salvation. We might like to think it's none of our business, but God says it is. He has placed us in the midst of a hurting world so we can share Christ's love with those who desperately need it.

Let God lead you out of your comfort zone so you can help someone else. Ask the Holy Spirit to open your ears and your eyes so you can hear God's prompting and see the needs all around you. In other words, make the effort to get involved.

Don't Gloat

Do not gloat when your enemy falls;
  when he stumbles, do not let your heart rejoice,
or the LORD will see and disapprove
  and turn his wrath away from him.

Proverbs 24:17-18

What does it mean to gloat? The dictionary says it means to "gaze in malicious pleasure" at someone else's misfortune. Sounds pretty coldhearted, doesn't it? It takes a low character to find pleasure in someone else's pain. But what if the hurting person had it coming? What if he's been a source of pain and grief in your life? What if he deliberately set out to hurt you, and it backfired? Isn't it natural to find just a little satisfaction when your enemies are getting what they deserve?

Jesus set the standard for the way we should treat those who hurt us, and it doesn't involve gloating. Jesus knew that God would see that justice was done, so we don't have to. Therefore, Jesus commands us to respond with love, prayer, and forgiveness to those who hurt us (Matthew 5:43–45). A hard-hearted response toward our enemy reveals that we, too, have evil in our hearts. It shows that we are no better than the person who injured us. Today's proverb warns that our sinful response when another person is under God's discipline may cause God to release our enemy and turn his discipline on us.

If you find yourself taking pleasure in someone else's pain, recognize that you are sinning. Hurry to seek God's forgiveness, and ask him to help you see your enemy through Christ's loving eyes. When you see someone as God does, you won't feel like gloating.

A walk through Proverbs with a wise man

June 20

Breaking the Cycle

Do not say, "I'll do to him as he has done to me;
I'll pay that man back for what he did."

Proverbs 24:29

There are two ways to live your life: proactively or reactively. Living proactively involves setting a high standard for your behavior and not letting the sinful influence of others drag you down. Your guide for this way of life is the Bible. That's where you'll learn how God wants you to treat yourself and how he wants you to relate to others. Living proactively doesn't mean you look down on everyone else or that you think of yourself as perfect. It does mean you consciously follow a pattern of behavior that honors God, rather than living your life in response to what everyone else is doing. Living proactively requires a strong character. It can only be done by keeping your eyes on God.

If you live reactively, you'll be constantly taking your cue from other people. If people gossip about you, you'll take that as permission to gossip about them. If a friend treats you poorly, you'll consider it an invitation to treat your friend poorly. The problem with living reactively is that you lose control over your own life. You spend so much time responding to real or perceived injustices that you have no energy left to live as God wants you to live. Living reactively is the sign of a weak character. It happens when you take your eyes off God.

Instead of acting the way everyone else acts, or treating people exactly as they treat you, seek to raise the standard of behavior by your example. Break the cycle of sin by acting with integrity, regardless of what others are doing.

Words of Gold

A word aptly spoken
  is like apples of gold in settings of silver.

Proverbs 25:11

It's not only what you say but when you say it and how you say it that matters. Anyone can dish up compliments, especially if he's trying to get something in return for the praise: that's called flattery. Anyone can criticize under the pretense of "just being honest." That's judging. These words are more like apples of aluminum in settings of tin—not worth a whole lot. But the truth spoken in love at the appropriate time—that takes wisdom. It's genuine—like golden apples in silver settings—and much more valuable.

The key word in today's verse is *aptly*. It means "appropriately." The words you speak might be pleasant, but false. For instance, your friend might come to you under deep conviction for his sin; you want to spare his feelings, so you try to convince him he hasn't really sinned at all. You're saying nice words, but you're not doing your friend any favors. Yes, he needs your kindness; but if the Holy Spirit is making him uncomfortable with his sin, don't you try to make him comfortable with it.

On the other hand, you might speak the truth, but with the wrong motives. When a friend is suffering, even if it's because of her own choices, that's not the time to point out all the shortcomings that got her into her predicament. What she needs more than criticism is kindness. Don't use her vulnerability as a springboard to launch into sharing all her imperfections.

The difference is subtle; that's why it takes wisdom. But there is a way to be sure you use your words properly: always put your listener's best interests first. Will your friend be helped or harmed because of what you have to say? God wants to use you to encourage those around you. Be sensitive to what he wants to say through you, and you'll deliver a blessing to someone who really needs one.

Don't Boast About Tomorrow

Do not boast about tomorrow,
for you do not know what a day may bring forth.

Proverbs 27:1

Some people love to live as if there's no tomorrow, but that's not what this proverb is talking about. Only a fool lives without regard for the future. A fool lives for the present only; he doesn't figure out that if he spends all his money today, he'll have none for tomorrow's bills. A fool lives recklessly because it hasn't occurred to her that there'll be consequences for her actions later. A fool doesn't bother with school because he thinks a career will happen automatically.

The Bible doesn't advise us to live as if tomorrow will never come. It does caution us against worrying about the future (Matthew 6:25) and about making our own plans without regard for what God might ask of us (James 4:13–15).

God has far too much for you to experience of him today for you to waste even a moment worrying about tomorrow. It is also a waste of your time to make extensive plans for your future when you have not consulted with God first. God is in control of tomorrow, just as he is in control of today. The main question to ask yourself is: "What does God want me to do today?" That will keep you busy enough; you won't have time to worry about what might happen tomorrow. If you spend each day in God's will, you'll be well prepared for every tomorrow. God is not a God of disorder, but of order. He has a plan for your future, and if you follow him step by step, your future will unfold as it should.

Real Friendship

The kisses of an enemy may be profuse,
  but faithful are the wounds of a friend.

Proverbs 27:6

A friend you can trust is a priceless treasure. If you have a trustworthy friend, consider yourself wealthy, and never take the friendship for granted.

What is a real friend like? A genuine friend is not afraid to be honest with you. He'll be kind, but he won't dish out flattery in order to hold on to the friendship. In turn, a real friend will listen to truth, spoken in love, and accept constructive criticism, even when it hurts. A true friend will be reliable. She'll not stab you in the back or spread gossip about you. The sign of an authentic friend is that she puts your interests ahead of her own. She doesn't act out of selfish motives but out of genuine concern for your well-being. Wouldn't it be great to have a friend like that? Wouldn't it be great to *be* a friend like that?

There are others who only appear to be your friend. They spend time with you for what they receive instead of what they give. They tell you what they think you want to hear instead of what you need to hear. They have ulterior motives for being your friend, motives you can't trust. These are the kinds of friends to avoid!

In all of your friendships, strive to treat the other person the way you'd like to be treated. Be the best friend you can be, and let God worry about what you'll get in return for your kindness.

June 24

Iron

As iron sharpens iron,
so one man sharpens another.

Proverbs 27:17

All the self-help books in the world can't do for you what a true friend can do. Just as the wrong kind of friends can do you immeasurable harm, a good friend can do you incredible good. Two pieces of iron left on the ground to rust are useless. But if those pieces are used to sharpen each other, both become valuable.

The Christian life is a journey that God doesn't expect you to make on your own. He'll bring friends alongside you to help you become the best person you can be. A good friend sometimes walks ahead of you, showing you by example. Sometimes he walks beside you, helping you when the path is rough. At other times she walks behind you, encouraging you to keep moving in the right direction. If you have a friendship like this, thank God for it, because it's a gift from him.

As you strive to be all that God wants you to be, open yourself up to your friends so they can help you along the way. Seek to be the kind of person who is always sensitive to the concerns of your friends. Search for friends who will be a positive influence on your life. Make the effort to be the kind of friend who helps others reach their potential. Ask yourself if your friends are better off with or without your influence. If you don't have a friendship that is mutually uplifting, ask God to help you develop one.

Does Your Reputation Reflect Your Character?

The crucible for silver and the furnace for gold,
but man is tested by the praise he receives.

Proverbs 27:21

Precious metals are subjected to intense heat in order to burn away the impurities. Once everything else has melted away, what's left is the substance that's truly valuable. Your character is, or should be, a highly valuable treasure to you. For this reason, God will refine your character to remove the impurities. His goal: a righteous, or Christlike, character.

Be careful that you don't draw your conclusions about your character from what others say about you. They only see the part of you that you present to them; that's your personality, or your reputation. What others see on the outside and what is really there on the inside can sometimes be two different things! For example, you could acquire the reputation of being a generous person by making sure others often see you in the act of giving. But, in reality, you might only give when someone is watching. You may, in fact, have a selfish character, but you do your taking in private and your giving in public.

We all want to present the best possible picture to the world, and we need to remember that we are representing Christ by our behavior. But God's opinion of us is far more important than man's. Be sure you get your feedback about your character from God, not from the praises of people. While your friends may praise you for your self-control, God knows if you're actually prone to angry fits of rage at home, when the curtains are closed. Never be lulled into complacency by the high opinions of others. They only see what you show them. God sees your heart. Remember, God is more interested in your character than in your reputation. Allow him to refine your character and burn away all the impurities until you are truly like Christ. You may think you have a pretty good handle on what your character is like, but if you listen carefully to what God says about you, what you hear may surprise you!

ʌ ʍalɐ tɥ   uɩƨɘ nɐn

June 26

Confession

He who conceals his sins does not prosper,
   but whoever confesses and renounces them finds mercy.

Proverbs 28:13

Unconfessed sin is the most needless form of self-punishment there is. When we refuse to acknowledge that we have disobeyed God, we voluntarily take on an extraordinary load of shame and deceit. The sad thing is, it's unnecessary. God already knows that we've sinned. He doesn't need us to confess it for his benefit. He needs us to confess it for our own good.

Unconfessed sin will eat away at you like a disease. You'll be plagued by worries: *Do others know what I've done? When will the truth come out?* You'll be weighed down by guilt and shame: *How could I have been so stupid? Can the one I offended ever forgive me? Can God ever forgive me?* You'll be dragged down into deception: *If I tell just one more lie, my secret will still be safe.*

When you've sinned, the last place you may want to be is the first place you should go, and that's straight to God. Go to him and let him show you your sin for what it is. Let him help you see the damage your sin has done so you won't be tempted to do it again. Let him give you the strength to turn your back on your sin. Let him give you the courage to seek forgiveness from whomever you've sinned against. Let him love you, and forgive you, and cleanse you, and give you a new start. As long as you hold on to your sin and try to conceal it, it has mastery over you. But when you confess your sin to God and seek restoration, you'll find mercy and freedom.

The Condition of Your Heart

Blessed is the man who always fears the LORD,
but he who hardens his heart falls into trouble.

Proverbs 28:14

Why is it that some people can go through life's dark valleys and never lose their faith in God, while others turn their backs on God at the first sign of hardship? It's the same reason some people can run a marathon, while others can't climb a flight of stairs without stopping to catch their breath. It all depends on the condition they're in.

A marathon runner doesn't start out as a marathon runner. She works her way up to it, training her body little by little until she can endure the grueling intensity of a twenty-six-mile race. If she tried to run the race with no training, her body wouldn't know how to handle it, and it would shut down.

The reason some people can trust in God when the big problems come is that they've been trusting him all along in the little things. They've conditioned their hearts by spending regular time with God. They've watched him at work all around them, and they've listened for his voice, even when there was no crisis. Others may have gradually turned away from God, possibly without even realizing it. They found it more comfortable to stay in bed than to get up and spend time with God. Their nonbelieving friends ridiculed them for their involvement with Christians, so they gradually pulled out of church. Before they knew it, their hearts were no longer sensitive to God's leading, and they no longer heard his voice. When a crisis hit, they found themselves alone and in trouble.

Take an honest look at your own heart's condition. Is your heart tender toward God, or are you pulling away from him? If you sense cynicism creeping into your life, spend some quality time in God's Word. Pray that God will soften your heart so you can stay with him for the whole race.

June 28

Fearing Others

Fear of man will prove to be a snare,
*   but whoever trusts in the LORD is kept safe.*

Proverbs 29:25

Christians often talk about looking for God's will, trying to discover what it is that God wants us to do. We act as if God were playing hide-and-seek with us, trying to make his desires as obscure as possible. That's nonsense. Most often, we know exactly what he wants us to do, but fear prevents us from doing it! We fear a lot of things: we fear failure; we fear the unknown; we fear what others will think of us.

Fearing other people is a common trap for Christians. We want to obey God, but we don't want to ruffle anyone's feathers in the process. Therefore we don't speak up against something we know is wrong, or we stay in an unhealthy friendship even though God tells us it's wrong for us. Sometimes when God tells us to do something, the fear of embarrassment stops us from doing it. For example, we know God wants us to be baptized, but we wouldn't be caught dead in front of our congregation with a wet head! We want others to like us, so we may be tempted to compromise our faith for the sake of popularity. It can get even closer to home than that: our parents may disapprove of our Christianity, so in an attempt to please them, we dishonor God. In our quest to please everybody around us, we can do the very opposite of what we know God wants.

Consider David's prayer: "In God I trust; I will not be afraid. What can mortal man do to me?" (Psalm 56:4). It's not always possible to fear God and fear man at the same time. You're far better off to trust in God. His love for you far surpasses anything you might fear from man.

Chapter 13

Lessons from the Life of Daniel

Daniel was born into nobility. He should have enjoyed all the advantages, pleasures, and opportunities that came with life in the upper class. However, when Daniel was a teenager in Jerusalem, his nation was invaded by Babylon, the world superpower of that day. Nebuchadnezzar, Babylon's ruler, stripped Israel of most of its wealth. In 605 B.C. Nebuchadnezzar had Israel's finest young people arrested and brought to Babylon. His goal was to brainwash them into forgetting their heritage and their belief in God so they would adopt the pagan religion of the Babylonians. The king's steward, Ashpenaz, was given the task of turning the Israelite youth into Babylonians.

Daniel's Hebrew name meant "God is my judge." He was given the Babylonian name Belteshazzar, meaning "protect his life." He was offered every luxury the king could provide in an attempt to coerce him into giving up his religion. Daniel refused. He committed himself to remain true to God, even if he were the only one to do so. As a result, Daniel ended up in some pretty frightening situations.

Ultimately, God honored Daniel's commitment. He granted him unusual wisdom and gave him a prominent place in world affairs. When conniving men grew jealous and sought to destroy Daniel, God saved his life. Daniel lived a long, productive, and honorable life. He steadfastly refused to compromise his faith in God, even for the most powerful person in the world. In return, God blessed him.

Daniel stands out as a young person who remained true to God, even in the face of great danger. Let's spend the next few days getting to know this faithful young man.

June 29

Far from Home

*And the Lord delivered Jehoiakim king of Judah into his hand,
along with some of the articles from the temple of God. These he
carried off to the temple of his god in Babylonia and put in the
treasure house of his god.*

*Then the king ordered Ashpenaz, chief of his court officials, to bring
in some of the Israelites from the royal family and the nobility.*

Daniel 1:2-3

How do you handle change? If you were to move to a new
country with a strange language, different customs, and foreign foods, how do you think you would adjust? Daniel had
no choice about moving. Nebuchadnezzar, the powerful
Babylonian king, had conquered Jerusalem. He had forcibly
taken young people from the wealthiest families and
brought them to the distant city of Babylon. Daniel had
been taken from his family, his home, and his country to
live in a hostile land filled with idol worshipers.

Everything changed for Daniel. The language was different.
The religion was different. The laws were different.
Everything was different except one thing—God. Daniel
found that God was just as real to him in Babylon as he had
been in Jerusalem. Daniel's enemies could remove his parents and his friends, but they could not take God away.
Daniel would face his new life with God by his side. As a
result, instead of letting the change in surroundings beat
him, Daniel actually thrived and experienced a full, rich
life.

God's presence made all the difference to Daniel. He was
able to approach his new life with confidence rather than
fear. God stood by Daniel and blessed his efforts. If you are
experiencing troublesome changes right now, remember
that one thing hasn't changed: God is still with you. You
may feel all alone, but God loves you, and he's ready to help
you, no matter what you face next. You may not always
have your parents or friends nearby to help you, but God
has promised that he will always be with you, wherever you
are (Isaiah 41:10).

But Daniel . . .

But Daniel resolved not to defile himself with the royal food and wine, and he asked the chief official for permission not to defile himself this way.

Daniel 1:8

If Daniel were strictly to examine the facts, they would look something like this:

- Fact: He was far from home, facing the temptation to do things he knew were wrong.

- Fact: His parents would never find out if he gave in to the temptation.

- Fact: Most of his friends were sinning and encouraging him to join them.

- Fact: The most powerful king on earth wanted him to give up his beliefs in return for wealth and power. That would be a welcome change from his current status as a foreigner in a hostile land.

The facts seemed to indicate that it was in Daniel's best interest to abandon his faith and take up this foreign religion. Then comes the word *but*. "But Daniel" made a commitment in his heart not to compromise his faith in God, no matter how tempting it was and no matter what the price he would have to pay for his obedience to God.

It's something to think about, isn't it? *Others seem to be doing whatever they please. . . . Mom and Dad will never find out. . . . There are certain rewards for following the crowd. . . . But . . . I've made a commitment not to compromise my Christianity no matter what others are doing. No matter what the cost, no matter what others think or say, no matter what it takes, I will be faithful to God.* You must decide whether you will be faithful to God regardless of what even your best friends are doing. God will bless you for your faithfulness, just as he blessed Daniel for his.

But Even If He Does Not . . .

If we are thrown into the blazing furnace, the God we serve is able to save us from it, and he will rescue us from your hand, O king. But even if he does not, we want you to know, O king, that we will not serve your gods or worship the image of gold you have set up.

Daniel 3:17-18

Would you continue to trust God . . . if? If you asked him for something and his answer was no? If your sister died of a terminal disease? If your parents divorced? Is your faith only strong when things are going your way, or do you continue to trust him when things seem to be falling apart?

Daniel had three friends named Shadrach, Meshach, and Abed-nego. The three of them had a couple of things in common: First, they all had strange names. Second, they had each made a commitment to God that regardless of what everyone else did, they would remain faithful to him. They didn't make deals with God: "Lord, if you keep us safe . . ." or, "Lord, if you let us see our parents, we will follow you." Rather, they promised to obey God, regardless of the consequences.

They soon had an opportunity to prove their faithfulness. The king issued an order that every person in the nation must bow down to a golden idol. In essence, he was asking them to forsake their God and to worship his god instead. The instant the king's musicians began to play, the massive crowd dropped collectively to the ground in deference to the king's god. To Nebuchadnezzar's displeasure, Daniel's three friends remained standing. The king summoned the infidels and gave them one last chance to comply with his order by renouncing their faith. They stood firm. Nebuchadnezzar was furious!

For their treason they were to be thrown into a gigantic furnace. As the king's slaves stoked the fire to seven times its normal temperature, the king had the rebels bound. He was determined to get rid of these stubborn foreigners. Then came perhaps the greatest statement of faith found in the Bible: "We know God is able to save us if he chooses. But whether or not he saves us, we still trust him!" That's real faith. Faith is not based upon getting what you want but on knowing who God is and trusting in his love regardless of what is happening to you.

Scrutinized

At this, the administrators and the satraps tried to find grounds for charges against Daniel in his conduct of government affairs, but they were unable to do so. They could find no corruption in him, because he was trustworthy and neither corrupt nor negligent.

Daniel 6:4

What would happen if your enemies set out to find every damaging piece of information they could about you? What if they followed you to see where you spent your time? What if they tapped your phone and eavesdropped on your conversations? What if they checked your bank account to see where you spend your money? What if they interviewed your classmates or coworkers, looking for someone with some dirt on you? Would they come up with embarrassing information?

That's what Daniel's enemies tried to do. They desperately wanted to dig up some incriminating evidence on him to make him lose his job. But Daniel had nothing to fear. They could find nothing because there was nothing to find. The worst thing they could come up with was that he prayed a lot!

There is incredible freedom in living a clean life. It eliminates the need to keep secrets or to worry about what might be exposed. It removes the vice grip that guilt can hold on your conscience. Perhaps you have already done things that, if revealed, would cause you shame. Although you cannot change the past, you can start fresh today. Ask God to forgive your past sins and help you to begin a life of absolute integrity. Each time you face a questionable decision, ask yourself this question: "Would I be ashamed if what I'm about to do were made public?" If you choose to live a pure life, you will enjoy the tremendous freedom that comes with it.

Answered Prayers

As soon as you began to pray, an answer was given, which I have come to tell you, for you are highly esteemed. Therefore, consider the message and understand the vision.

Daniel 9:23

Can you imagine hearing these words directly from heaven? "As soon as you began to pray, an answer was given . . . for you are highly esteemed." After all Daniel had been through, the angel's comforting words must have been extremely welcome!

This was not the first time God heard Daniel pray. Daniel prayed when things were going well for him, not just when he was having problems. He prayed because he enjoyed talking with God. Daniel's faithfulness and his love for God earned him high regard in heaven. God quickly sent an angel to minister to Daniel as soon as he began to pray.

Sometimes we neglect to pray for long periods of time. When everything is going our way, we forget to thank God. We get busy and don't really see the need to spend time talking with him. Then a problem pops up and we need help—*now*! We pray fervently and want God's answer immediately. We feel frustrated if our prayer isn't answered promptly! We need to follow Daniel's example. God responded to Daniel's need even before Daniel finished his prayer. Their relationship was that close. The best part for Daniel wasn't even the speediness of God's answer but the security Daniel had in knowing he was highly respected by God.

How would you characterize your relationship with God? Do you pray because you enjoy talking with God, or do you just pray when you need something? Strive to be like Daniel, and enjoy spending time with God in prayer no matter what your situation.

Chapter 14

Advice for Sinners: Paul's Letters to the Corinthians

Sometimes we think following Christ was somehow easier in Bible times than it is today. Have you ever assumed it was easier to live a holy life in the first century than it is to be godly today, in our evil society?

If Hollywood ever made a movie about the church in Corinth, it would receive the strictest of ratings! There was gross immorality in that church. There was pride, selfishness, and divisiveness. You name a sin—they were dealing with it. Why did the church struggle so much? Because it was located in an ungodly city. Corinth was a famous city on the sea coast with sailors from all over the world coming ashore to find diversion and excitement. The city was wealthy, offering every form of entertainment and temptation imaginable. Even the Greek temples were immoral. They would actually have prostitutes plying their trade in the temple buildings as a form of worship. Things were as bad as you could possibly imagine. Yet the Christians of Corinth were trying to live faithfully for Christ.

The Bible never tells only the good things while glossing over the bad. The Bible tells things the way they are. Paul's two letters to the believers in Corinth were painfully honest about the changes necessary if the Christians were going to honor Christ surrounded by vulgarity. Can you identify with the Corinthian Christians? Does your environment pressure you to abandon your Christian values and join the crowd? As you read Paul's straightforward advice to the Corinthian church, remember that these words were written to Christians like you, Christians who were trying to honor God in an environment that was as ungodly and immoral as any place you will find today.

July 4

Power

For the message of the cross is foolishness to those who are perishing, but to us who are being saved it is the power of God.

1 Corinthians 1:18

Don't be surprised when not everyone is as excited about the gospel as you are! As you enjoy the thrill of walking with Jesus, you may be surprised when others choose not to experience God in the same exciting way that you do. Paul understood that those who approach Christianity with skepticism will not find any power in it. Such people consider the gospel foolishness. On the other hand, those who believe the good news know firsthand the power of God that changes lives.

Why is it some people never experience God's activity in their lives? Their lack of faith prevents them from seeing him at work. Ultimately, their rejection of the Truth costs them their lives. However, those who approach God with faith see him at work, and they experience his mighty power.

The Bible says some people will refuse to accept the truth of the cross. To nonbelievers, the Christian message is nonsense; therefore it holds no power for them. They won't understand how anyone could accept it. They may even ridicule you for believing it. The Bible says these people are doomed to perish. Don't ever stop sharing the good news simply because some reject it. There will be those who accept the truth of Christ, and you will see them experience God at work in their lives in the same powerful way he has worked in yours.

Free Gifts   July 5

We have not received the spirit of the world but the Spirit who is from God, that we may understand what God has freely given us.

1 Corinthians 2:12

Part of the fun of receiving gifts is wondering what's inside the package, and part of the fun in giving gifts is *knowing* what's inside! At Christmastime, do you enjoy thinking of just the right thing for those who are close to you? Do you like to picture the look on each person's face as he or she receives a token of your love?

God enjoys giving gifts too. In fact, each Christian has a storehouse brimming with good things that God wants to give us. Along with eternal life, the first gift we receive when we become a Christian is God's Holy Spirit. If it were not for the presence of God's Spirit within us, we would never even know about or experience the many blessings God wants to give us. The Spirit knows the invaluable difference that God's gifts will make in our lives, and he prompts us to seek out God's best, rather than relying on our own resources. It is not God's intention that we struggle in our own power or settle for less than his best for us. He has treasures that will meet every need we have if we will just ask. He wants to give us courage to calm our fears, peace to erase our anger, joy in place of sadness, forgiveness to remove our bitterness, and much more.

Are you now enjoying the good gifts your Father has for you? Are you living in your own strength, unaware that God has a much better plan? Listen to the Holy Spirit within you. He will make you aware of all the blessings God has available for you. Find out what's inside the package.

July 6

Revealed by Fire

His work will be shown for what it is, because the Day will bring it to light. It will be revealed with fire, and the fire will test the quality of each man's work.

1 Corinthians 3:13

As you read this page, you are making an investment. Life holds for each of us a certain number of days. As every new day arrives, we begin to spend it hour by hour, minute by minute. We have no choice about spending the time; the clock ticks away second by second whether we want it to or not. The choice we have is in how we will spend our time.

There is a way to live that is intentional. It means putting your energy into things that help you grow as a Christian: Bible study, prayer, your church, etc. It also includes time spent helping others to know God. Living this way involves some choices. It takes effort. It means investing time—getting involved. Or you can choose to live your life unintentionally, squandering the days on meaningless activity. The person who lives unintentionally gives no thought to his spiritual life. He cares only for things that have earthly value. Her concern is for temporary satisfaction. Her goal is not to have a goal.

The Bible tells us that on the day of judgment, God will test our lives with fire. Just as fire burns away impurities from precious minerals, God's judgment will strip away everything from our lives that has no eternal significance. Business success will be removed. Earthly honor will evaporate. Sports accomplishments will disappear. Material wealth will be gone. All that will remain will be spiritual things: our love for God, those who are in God's kingdom because of our involvement in prayer and in sharing the gospel, and the relationship we developed with Christ. These are God's priorities. These things will last. These are things worth pursuing.

God's Temple   July 7

Don't you know that you yourselves are God's temple and that God's Spirit lives in you?

1 Corinthians 3:16

If you've ever been to a royal palace, you probably noticed how perfectly everything is kept. The lawns are neatly manicured. The furniture is in place. The floors gleam; in fact, the whole place is immaculate. An entire team of housekeepers and gardeners works full time to make sure everything is groomed and in perfect working order for the monarch. Every room is decorated with exquisite art and costly furnishings because kings and queens don't live in run-down shacks; they inhabit palaces.

God, the King of the universe, has chosen you as his dwelling place. He wants to make your body a place of residence for his Holy Spirit. That makes your body holy. Do you treat it that way? Is everything in order for the King? Or have you abused the temple of God by allowing impure thoughts to flood your mind? Have you insulted the King by dulling your senses with drugs and alcohol? Have you taken your body to places where it will be tempted by the enticements of this world?

As a Christian, you take God's Spirit with you everywhere you go. Since it is God's dwelling place, your body is a holy and special place. Don't think less of your body than God does. Treat your body as the holy temple that it is, and use it to bring glory to God in all that you do.

July 8

Judging Others

Therefore judge nothing before the appointed time; wait till the Lord comes. He will bring to light what is hidden in darkness and will expose the motives of men's hearts. At that time each will receive his praise from God.

1 Corinthians 4:5

When people hurt you or offend you, do you review their behavior over and over in your mind, analyzing what would make them do such a thing? It's a natural response to wonder what's behind someone else's actions, especially when their conduct causes pain in our lives. It's easy to ascribe motives and assume the worst: *She's just jealous . . . uncaring . . . selfish . . . cruel, etc.* We often want to see our offender receive just punishment for offending us. Although it's tempting to judge other people this way, it's not biblical. Only God knows what is in people's hearts. He alone understands what motivates people to do what they do. And he tells us to leave the analyzing to him.

We can spend a lot of time figuring out the imperfections in those around us, or we can do as Paul says and "wait till the Lord comes." It's much wiser to focus on our own character, working on the things we need to change, than it is to waste time worrying about others getting what they deserve.

A day is coming when God will judge every person for what he or she has done. On that day, justice will be done in perfect measure. In the meantime, don't waste time or energy worrying about the sins of others. Concentrate on keeping your own life pure before God. One day your motives will be exposed before God just like everyone else's. If they are pure, you will enjoy God's praise.

Power, Not Talk   July 9

For the kingdom of God is not a matter of talk but of power.

1 Corinthians 4:20

Christians often talk and sing about the powerful God we serve. Yet when we come up against challenges to our faith, we start to backpedal furiously: "Of course, God can do anything he wants, but not in my life. I'm no spiritual giant. I'm just an average run-of-the-mill person." We need to reread the Bible! It's filled with accounts of ordinary men and women whom God empowered to do great things! Joshua was an ex-slave who defeated every army he faced. Esther showed incredible bravery, putting her life on the line for her people. Elijah challenged the queen and her army of hostile pagan priests by calling down fire from heaven. Paul was stoned almost to death; then he got up, brushed himself off, and headed right back into town!

Were these all unusually rugged people, gifted with supernatural bravery and endurance? Not at all. They were ordinary men and woman whose strength came from God. God is not intimidated by anyone or anything. His power is more than enough to handle any problem you will ever face. So, if this same God who defeated menacing armies and destroyed entire cities now lives within you, there is no reason your life should not also reflect his awesome power. You don't need to be intimidated by those who oppose your Christianity. Don't let anyone or anything frighten you out of obeying God. When God calls you to follow him, he empowers you to accomplish his desires.

Walk closely with almighty God, and let his power shine through your life. Don't trust in your strength, but in the infinite power of the one who lives within you. Don't just talk about the power of God; *experience* it!

July 10

Freedom!

"Everything is permissible for me"—but not everything is beneficial.
"Everything is permissible for me"—but I will not be mastered by
anything.

1 Corinthians 6:12

Not everyone in the world is free. Some are in bondage to
dictatorships, restricted from doing anything that goes
against their government's wishes. Others live out their
days in prison, paying their penalty for breaking the law.
There is another kind of bondage, however, that doesn't
involve being enslaved by others. This bondage involves
the restrictions people place on themselves by their own
choices.

Addictions, for example, are a form of bondage. The more
a life becomes enslaved to a chemical, or to a habit, the less
the addicted person is able to make choices. Some people
allow themselves to be taken captive by sin. They do not
guard their minds and hearts from temptation, so sin slowly gains a stronghold over them that they cannot break.

Paul said he had once been a prisoner of sin. Sin had such
a grip on his life that he didn't even realize how enslaved
he was. Once he became a Christian, he experienced true
freedom for the first time. There were some in Paul's day
who, once they became Christians, used their new freedom
only to become slaves again. Their thinking was: *Now that
I know God loves me and has a place for me in heaven, I am
free to indulge in any sin I want and still have the assurance of
eternal life.* Paul called this attitude foolishness. Why would
someone who had been freed from a terrible taskmaster
turn around and walk right back into captivity?

Having experienced both slavery and freedom, Paul was
determined never again to be entrapped by sin's lies. Even
though he was free to make his own choices, he would only
choose those things that honored God. Freedom is a wonderful thing, and there is no one who has more freedom
than a Christian. Don't ever take lightly the freedom that
Christ bought for you on the cross. Use it wisely.

Falling Brothers

Therefore, if what I eat causes my brother to fall into sin, I will never eat meat again, so that I will not cause him to fall.

1 Corinthians 8:13

Some Christians are stronger than others. Don't become frustrated with those who are weaker in their faith than you are. Maybe they are new Christians, or perhaps they struggle with areas of temptation that you don't. You may be tempted to judge them, but they don't need your criticism. They need your encouragement.

In Paul's time, animals were sacrificed to idols in pagan temples. After they had been offered to the gods, the temple priests would sell the meat in the local market. Some Christians would buy the meat for food, while others refused to have anything to do with meat that had been a part of idol worship. The nonmeat eaters claimed that a Christian who was truly devout would never eat something that had been dedicated to false gods. The controversy over unclean meat was causing division in the early church.

Paul was not troubled by where the meat had come from. He knew that the idols were merely pieces of stone or wood and not gods at all, and he considered the meat nothing more than a good bargain. Yet he knew that eating the meat would scandalize Christians who disagreed with him. He could have said, "Well, that's their problem," and dismissed their viewpoint, but he considered unity more important than who was right or wrong, so he chose not to eat the meat. Though his own conscience freed him to do so, he chose to refrain so he didn't cause another Christian to be offended.

Paul's behavior is a good model to follow. Is there something you are doing that other Christians find objectionable? Are you causing another believer to stumble in his faith? Are you mature enough to give up some of your freedom in order to live in harmony with your fellow Christians?

July 12

Weak Like the Weak

To the weak I became weak, to win the weak. I have become all things to all men so that by all possible means I might save some.

1 Corinthians 9:22

What are you willing to do to help someone know Christ? Are you willing to establish a friendship? What if the other person is totally different from you? What if the two of you have nothing in common, and you don't identify with the person at all? Maybe you assume God wants you to befriend only those people with whom you feel comfortable. If he wants to reach someone you don't understand, surely he will work through someone else!

Isn't it a good thing Jesus didn't make that assumption about us? What did God's Son, seated on his throne in heaven, have in common with us? Yet, when he saw our need, the holy and perfect Son of God became human, like us, so he could communicate the good news of salvation with weak and sinful humanity.

Paul was determined to find a way to identify with whomever he could, if it meant he could tell them about salvation. Paul was as comfortable telling kings about Jesus as he was telling beggars. Could you begin a friendship with others, even though they are different from you, so you can tell them about God? Who knows, you might even discover there aren't as many differences as you thought!

Run for the Prize   July 13

Do you not know that in a race all the runners run, but only one gets the prize? Run in such a way as to get the prize. Everyone who competes in the games goes into strict training. They do it to get a crown that will not last; but we do it to get a crown that will last forever.

1 Corinthians 9:24-25

No Olympic medalist will ever tell you the prize came easily. Successful athletes spend years of extensive training, preparing for the day they will match themselves against other competitors to see who is the fastest, strongest, or steadiest. To the athlete, the prize is well worth the many hours spent in training. It's true, good things seldom come without a cost.

This truth applies in the spiritual world as well. When you read about the spiritual giants in Christian history, or when you admire the strong faith of your pastor, don't assume that the same walk with God they have is not available to you also. You have just as much opportunity to walk closely and powerfully with God as they have. The question is this: Are you willing to pay the same price they were in order to be filled with God's powerful presence? Spiritual strength doesn't come without exercise. You cannot be spiritually lazy and vibrant at the same time. It's not possible to neglect reading your Bible and ignore the place of prayer and still become a strong Christian. There is a price to pay for having an intimate walk with God. Paul says if we are willing to do whatever is necessary in order to run the race of the Christian life well, the prize will be more than worth our effort.

July 14

No Temptation

No temptation has seized you except what is common to man. And God is faithful; he will not let you be tempted beyond what you can bear. But when you are tempted, he will also provide a way out so that you can stand up under it.

1 Corinthians 10:13

You're going to be tempted. There's no way around it. You can go to church regularly, read your Bible faithfully, and pray diligently, but you will be tempted to sin just the same. The question is: When temptation comes, will you be ready?

Temptation catches some people by surprise when it shouldn't. They find themselves in a compromising situation, and they don't know what to do. Before they know it, they have given in to sin. They may try to excuse their actions, pleading that they were caught off guard. They may claim they were overtaken by the one sin they are powerless to resist. That is nonsense.

The Bible says that we will never face a temptation that we are powerless to resist. No matter what it is, God will provide a way for us to escape without sinning. The problem is that we don't want to resist some temptations. We ignore the warning signals and walk right past the escapes God provides for us. Then we find ourselves in the clutches of a powerful temptation and cry out at the last minute, "God, save me!" But it is too late. How much wiser it is to listen to God at the outset, when he first cautions us of the danger!

Don't ever take temptation lightly. Listen to the warnings of your friends, your family, or your pastor. Take the escape route that God provides. Don't rush headlong into sin, assuming that you are too weak to resist anyway. You can live a victorious life if you will listen to the one who can give you victory.

All for the Glory

July 15

So whether you eat or drink or whatever you do, do it all for the glory of God.

1 Corinthians 10:31

You don't have to be a missionary or a martyr to glorify God. Nor does God need you to glorify him. You bring God glory by living a transformed life—a life that demonstrates the unmistakable presence of the Holy God who lives within you. When people see how you live and marvel at the goodness of your God, you are bringing glory to God. God doesn't need the glory your holy life brings him, but he delights in receiving it.

God is accustomed to receiving glory for his wonderful creation. The vast expanse of the universe, the majestic mountains, the peaceful lakes, the gigantic canyons . . . all of the wonders of his creation compel us to praise him for his marvelous works.

We, too, are God's creations that can bring him glory. When others watch us love people as Jesus did, and forgive as Jesus did, when they notice us serving rather than seeking to be served, when they see us at peace in the midst of turmoil, and when we give the glory for our righteousness to God, they will be moved to praise God for his transforming power. When people see how God can transform sinners like us into people who look like Christ, God will receive the glory.

God has given you much. You can give something back to him by living a life that brings him honor.

July 16

Role Models

Follow my example, as I follow the example of Christ.

1 Corinthians 11:1

Who are your role models? Are you aware of the effect that others have on you? We are all influenced by other people, sometimes for good and sometimes for bad. Those who claim to be their own person, boasting that no one influences them, are living in denial. The question is not, Will someone influence me? but, Who is going to influence me?

Paul understood that the ultimate role model is Christ. As he strove to be like Christ, he urged others to follow his example. Paul was not boasting; he understood fully that the only things in his life worth emulating were the things that were like Jesus. He was taking on the responsibility of mentor, and he took it seriously. He was motivated by love for those Christians less mature in their faith than he was. His desire was not that they be like him, but like Christ.

We often choose our role models unwisely. We idolize sports heroes or other celebrities, knowing very little about their character. Then we are crushed to discover that our heroes are not all that we thought. It is important to be smart about role models we choose. Take stock of who exerts the most influence in your life right now. Is it someone whose example you'd be better off not following? Consider ending an unhealthy relationship and seeking out those who, by their example, will show you how to be more like Jesus.

Parts of a Body   July 17

But in fact God has arranged the parts in the body, every one of them, just as he wanted them to be.

1 Corinthians 12:18

There are times in our lives when we wish we could spend time with Jesus, not just spiritually, but physically. We want to see him, touch him, hear his voice. We wish we were like those privileged few apostles who spent time with him, day in and day out. God's provision for this desire is the church.

When Jesus ascended physically to heaven, God established the church to be the body of Christ on earth. The church is now God's flesh-and-blood expression of his love. The church is not a haphazard group of people, thrown together with no purpose except to get together Sunday mornings. It is much more than that. God lovingly puts each church body together with a purpose. He brings to each church specific people who will help the body more accurately reflect the character of Jesus. Just as Jesus had compassion for sinners, the church today should have compassion for sinners. Just as Jesus brought salvation to people, so people should find salvation through the church. Just as Jesus fed and ministered to the poor, so the poor ought to have their needs met by the church. Everything Jesus did while he walked on the earth he chooses to do now through his body, the church.

If you're not presently part of a church body, seek the church God wants you to join. Then ask his direction for how to get involved. God has a reason for placing you in your church. Allow him to use your life to minister to others through your church.

Childish Things

When I was a child, I talked like a child, I thought like a child, I reasoned like a child. When I became a man, I put childish ways behind me.

1 Corinthians 13:11

For the most part, there are a number of advantages to being a child. Not a lot is required of you. You're not given much responsibility because, of course, you can't handle it. You're allowed to be more self-centered than adults; in fact adults are *expected* to cater to your wants and needs! Your job is to play and to make messes. All in all, it's a pretty good life. But, of course, no one remains a child. As we grow older and more mature, more is expected of us. Life brings responsibility, work, and sacrifice. Yet, growing up also brings many joys and pleasures! With maturity come new experiences, and life takes on new meaning.

When you became a Christian, you were a spiritual baby. Regardless of your age, you were a child in God's kingdom. Unlike your physical body, however, you do not mature spiritually simply through the passing of time. It's not automatic. You could be a Christian for thirty years and yet still be a spiritual baby. Spiritual maturity comes only through effort.

Some people are satisfied with being spiritually immature their entire life. They remain self-centered, interested only in their own happiness and pleasure. Others, like Paul, are not content to remain spiritual children. Paul wanted to grow up. He wanted to experience God as a spiritual adult. So, Paul made the effort.

How would you describe your spiritual maturity right now? Are you still a baby, or are you growing in your faith?

Bad Company

Do not be misled: "Bad company corrupts good character."

1 Corinthians 15:33

How strong do you think you are? Do you believe you can stand up against temptation? Do you think you can resist the opinions and attitudes of those who do not love or follow God as you do? If you think you can, the Bible has a warning for you. Paul claims that you *will* be influenced by the people with whom you spend your time. If you associate with wise people, you will become wise (Proverbs 13:20). If you hang around with fools, you will be influenced by them. It's pretty straightforward, isn't it?

But does this mean you should never associate with those who hold different beliefs than you do? Of course not. It does mean that you must maintain a real awareness that someone is going to have an influence on the other. Sometimes we argue that we are in a friendship in order to have a Christian influence on a person whose values differ from ours. Maybe we are. It's crucial, however, never to forget that influence goes both ways. At times we can be under someone's influence far more than we are influencing that person.

It is vital that you hold up each of your relationships to God and ask for his guidance. Be prepared to remove yourself from bad company as he leads, so that your own character is not harmed. At the same time, be looking for people to spend time with who will encourage you to become more like Christ.

Always Victory

But thanks be to God! He gives us the victory through our Lord Jesus Christ.

1 Corinthians 15:57

There are plenty of forces at work to defeat you in your Christian life. There are people who wouldn't think twice about causing you to stumble and fail your Lord. There are temptations that could easily destroy your life if given the opportunity. The Bible warns of the "spiritual forces of evil in the heavenly realms" (Ephesians 6:12). It's enough to discourage even the strongest Christian, but it shouldn't. Why not?

Christians should never fear what Satan or the world throws at us, for Jesus Christ is our Lord, and through *him* is our victory. Paul never said trials wouldn't come. Rather, he assured us that in spite of any obstacles, we can be victorious, thanks to Jesus Christ. Paul experienced this victory himself. When critics taunted him, God affirmed him. When his enemies arrested him, God ministered to him in prison and used him to share the gospel with his warden. Even Paul's execution did not defeat his life passion of telling others about Christ, for to this day millions of believers find inspiration in the letters he wrote to the early church.

If you're looking for a trouble-free life, Paul made no promises. But if you seek victory over God's enemies, it's yours for the asking. You need only trust God and do what he tells you. When you obey God no matter what the cost, you already have your victory.

Stand Firm   July 21

Therefore, my dear brothers, stand firm. Let nothing move you. Always give yourselves fully to the work of the Lord, because you know that your labor in the Lord is not in vain.

1 Corinthians 15:58

Whenever you sin, Satan is pleased. When you are lazy and waste your time, Satan is content. But when you commit yourself to do the work of the Lord, Satan is vehemently opposed to you. It may surprise you to discover that life becomes the most difficult when you are trying to do the right thing. When you make a commitment to obey what God is asking you to do, you might come up against a lot of opposition. Perhaps it will come from your friends, or maybe your finances will give you a challenge. Maybe your parents will try to discourage you from obeying what God is telling you to do. Whatever it is, you'll be tempted to ask, "Why me? I'm just trying to do what God told me to do!"

Paul has two things to say to you; the first is a word of advice and the second, a note of encouragement. First, he urges you to stand firm. Paul, of all people, knew that serving God isn't always easy. Satan will try to sabotage your efforts. Those around you may not understand what you are doing. But Paul advises you not to hold back. Obey your Lord with everything you've got, because there are eternal consequences at stake. Second, when you stay faithful to your commitment, your efforts are never in vain. Don't get frustrated and give up. When you are obeying God, victory is a given.

If you are facing some difficult times because of your desire to obey God, rest assured. Your efforts are not wasted. God sees your heart, and he will give you the victory (Romans 8:37).

July 22

A Great Door

Because a great door for effective work has opened to me, and there are many who oppose me.

1 Corinthians 16:9

Don't expect everyone to be pleased as you try to live a victorious Christian life. Likewise, don't be surprised if not everyone encourages you to keep the faith. Sometimes the number of people opposing you is in direct proportion to how much you are doing for God! When you serve God, you have to get used to being encouraged and oppressed at the same time. Just because you are doing God's will, it doesn't mean you will not have problems. Just the opposite may be true.

The apostle Paul rejoiced that a new and exciting opportunity had opened up for him to serve the Lord. At the same time, however, there were many who were opposing him. It seemed that there was always some bad that came with Paul's good. Paul chose to focus on the positive instead of the negative. If he had become sidetracked by those who criticized him, he would have missed some exciting things God wanted him to do.

Be careful never to let your critics rob you of the joy of serving God. There will always be some who stand by and evaluate your life. They will assume they know your motives. They'll be quick to point out your failures. If you let their opinions consume you, you'll lose sight of the good things God is doing in your life. Always weigh the opinions of others against God's Word. Concentrate on pleasing God, for his is the opinion that matters most.

A Fragrance
or a Stench?

But thanks be to God, who always leads us in triumphal procession in Christ and through us spreads everywhere the fragrance of the knowledge of him.

2 Corinthians 2:14

Back in the days of the Roman Empire, Roman generals would hold a victory parade whenever they defeated an enemy. The enemy prisoners would be marched through the streets as evidence of the Roman victory. This celebration was known as a "triumph." During the parade, sweet-smelling incense would be released into the air. The fragrance would signal to everyone in the area that their general had won a great victory.

Interestingly, the apostle Paul compares Christians not to the Roman conquerors, but to the captives. He explains that we have been captured by Christ, and now we are his prisoners of war to display to the world his victory over sin. Paul says that through our lives comes the victory fragrance that alerts others to the presence of Christ, the Conqueror. We are the fragrance of life to those who come to know Jesus through our witness. On the other hand, we are the smell of death to those who reject Christ (2 Corinthians 2:15–16).

When people meet you, do they have the unmistakable sense that you belong to God? It should be obvious to them that through you they can come to know Christ. The choice is theirs whether to accept God's love or to reject it, but there should be no doubt by your example that it is available to them. Ask God to use your life so that everywhere you go, you will fill that place with the knowledge of Christ.

July 24

Competence from God

Not that we are competent in ourselves to claim anything for ourselves, but our competence comes from God.

2 Corinthians 3:5

Do you sometimes lack the confidence that you can carry out what God is asking you to do? Do you look at yourself and conclude: *I'm not a gifted person or a Bible scholar. I don't have what it takes to do anything significant for God?* If you think this way, you are missing the point. You see, the ability to make a difference in God's kingdom never comes from us. It always comes from God.

Take Paul's life as an example. You might wonder how one man could have accomplished all that he did. How did he start new churches in so many places when he was up against such fierce opposition? How did he perform all those miracles? How did he find the strength to keep going in spite of beatings, shipwrecks, imprisonment, and constant danger? The answer, of course, is that his ability came from God. It wasn't that Paul was a supernatural being. His strength was not in himself, but in his relationship with the Lord.

Likewise, God will never ask you to do something difficult and then leave you to do it on your own. The reason you can have total confidence is that, no matter what Christ tells you to do, he will provide you with the ability to accomplish it. Is God leading you into a new area of ministry? Accept his assignment with boldness, for he will enable you to do whatever he asks.

Renewed Day by Day   July 25

Therefore we do not lose heart. Though outwardly we are wasting away, yet inwardly we are being renewed day by day.

2 Corinthians 4:16

Teenagers are often teased about how much time they spend in front of the mirror. The fact is, people of all ages will spend thousands of hours over a lifetime keeping their bodies presentable. Consider how much time will be used just taking showers! Add to that the time we spend getting haircuts, brushing our teeth, and all the other grooming tasks we do, and the total time spent is pretty substantial. Although we give our bodies the best of care, our bodies are only temporary and they will one day pass away. That is not to suggest you should give up and never comb your hair again, but it's important to keep the right perspective.

Paul was never one to mince his words. Here he gives it to us straight: "Outwardly we are wasting away." That would be a pretty depressing thought if this life were all we had. But as Christians, we know that our bodies are on temporary assignment. When we go to spend eternity with Christ, he'll give us a new body. Our souls, however, are eternal. The soul never grows old. When we feed our souls on God's Word and when we take time to pray, our efforts are never wasted. Rather than withering away, our souls become fresher and more vibrant each day as we renew our inner person. Our outer bodies are slowly moving toward death, but our inner selves are able to experience more and more of life as we grow in our relationship to Christ.

Think about how much time you spend caring for your body. Compare this to the amount of time spent nurturing your soul. Remember, your soul will be around long after your body is not. Be sure to take good care of it.

July 26

Judgment

So we make it our goal to please him, whether we are at home in the body or away from it. For we must all appear before the judgment seat of Christ, that each one may receive what is due him for the things done while in the body, whether good or bad.

2 Corinthians 5:9–10

Have you ever been caught in the act, doing something you shouldn't have? Do you remember the shame? Can you recall times when you did things you knew were wrong and you didn't get caught? Did you feel guilty? The apostle Paul warns that regardless of whether or not our sins are revealed in this life, no one escapes the scrutiny of the Lord Jesus. Jesus warned his disciples very clearly: "There is nothing concealed that will not be disclosed, or hidden that will not be made known. What you have said in the dark will be heard in the daylight" (Luke 12:2–3). Nothing escapes God's notice; he sees how we spend every minute of every day.

How should this affect the way we live? It caused the apostle Paul to live with a reverent fear of God. He determined to live a life so blameless that he would not have to dread facing Christ on judgment day. He was also quick to confess any sin in his life so that God would deal with it then, and not at the judgment. We, too, ought to live with the awareness that one day God will ask us to account for the things we have done, both good and bad.

Is there anything in your life right now that you need to settle with God? If you do not make things right with God now, you will have to do it later.

A New Creation   July 27

Therefore, if anyone is in Christ, he is a new creation; the old has gone, the new has come!

2 Corinthians 5:17

One of the many exciting things about the Christian life is that it gives all believers a completely new start. No matter how much sin haunts our past, or how deep the scars from old wounds, regardless of how many times we've failed, no matter how stained our reputation, Christ makes each of us an entirely new person. The Bible uses the term *born again* because, for the Christian, life starts all over again!

When you became a Christian, God didn't simply add some spirituality to your life to mix in with all of your sin. Nor did he lay down a set of rules to help you try to curb your sinful habits. He created something absolutely new! He gave you a new heart, a heart that desires to love and to serve God. Before giving your life to Christ, you couldn't live the Christian life, even if you wanted to. Now that your inner self is renewed, you are empowered to say no to temptation and yes to God. Have you known someone who met Christ and was so radically changed that you hardly knew it was the same person? Were you amazed at the transformation? The apostle Paul was like that. But not just Paul. The truth is that everyone who joins with Christ undergoes the same radical transformation, becoming a completely new creation!

Many Christians underestimate what happened when they became God's children. They assume they are still the same sinful, weak, unfaithful person they used to be, only now they must try to live the Christian life to the best of their ability. That is not true! Living under that misconception will lead only to frustration.

At the moment of your conversion, you become a totally new person embarking on a brand-new life. Past failures cannot hold you back. Earlier sins have no power over you today. Determine today *not* to believe the lie that Christ has not changed you; remember that in Christ you are "a new creation; the old has gone, the new has come!" Gladly embrace the good news of the Scriptures and live like the new creation that you are!

Christ's Ambassadors

We are therefore Christ's ambassadors, as though God were making his appeal through us. We implore you on Christ's behalf: Be reconciled to God.

2 Corinthians 5:20

Every time you go out the door, you represent Christ to those you meet. You may assume you are just going to school, to work, or to be with friends, but you are also on official business to represent your King. Scripture indicates that every Christian is God's ambassador to a searching world. Ambassadors represent their country while living in a foreign place. The ambassador speaks on behalf of his country. The ambassador tells others what his nation thinks about certain issues. If people want to know the customs of a particular nation, they watch the life of the ambassador.

It's incredible that God would appoint us to represent his kingdom. Yet he has chosen to do just that. If others wonder what God is like, they need only ask us. If they want to know how to contact the King of kings, we should be able to tell them. When those around us watch how we live, they should get a good idea of what God's kingdom is like. If someone we know is hurting, we should be God's messenger of healing. If those around us are rebelling against God, we should be willing to help them reconcile with him.

Just as Jesus showed people what God was like when he walked on the earth, now you are God's earthly representative to a world that does not know what God is like. People are watching your life. Take your job seriously and represent him well.

Light and Darkness

Do not be yoked together with unbelievers. For what do righteous-
ness and wickedness have in common? Or what fellowship can light
have with darkness?

2 Corinthians 6:14

Some things don't mix. Light and darkness can't coexist, for the mere presence of one eliminates the other. The Bible makes several references to both light and darkness. God the Father is often described as light (Isaiah 60:1–2). John's Gospel describes Jesus as "the true light that gives light to every man" (John 1:9). The term *darkness* is reserved for Satan and for references to sin (John 3:19). *Darkness* is also used to describe the person who does not know Christ (Ephesians 5:8).

The apostle Paul warns against trying to mix light and darkness together. A Christian and a non-Christian can never be as close as two Christians can be. That's because the Christian lives in the light. The Holy Spirit lives within believers, causing them to long for what God values and to despise the things God hates. Christians are no longer their own masters; they have willingly surrendered to Christ the authority over their lives.

Non-Christians live by a different standard. They have no love for Christ, nor any desire to follow God's ways. The Bible describes such people not only as living in darkness but also as enemies of God (Romans 5:10). Therefore, Paul warns, it is impossible for believers and unbelievers to be compatible. Christians want to please God; non-Christians are God's enemy. We Christians must be extremely careful how entwined we become with those who do not share our belief in God. This doesn't mean we don't love nonbeliev-ers, or that we avoid them completely. The exhortation is not to be *joined* with unbelievers. That is, Christians should not become so closely tied to nonbelievers that their deci-sions hinder our walk with God. If we marry unbelievers, their attitudes and practices can dramatically affect our Christianity. Christians must not be fooled into thinking a close relationship with a non-Christian will not affect our love for God. It's like adding cold water to hot water; it all becomes lukewarm and eventually grows cold.

Heed Paul's warning: don't link your life with anyone who will distract you from loving God.

July 30

Weak or Strong?

That is why, for Christ's sake, I delight in weaknesses, in insults, in hardships, in persecutions, in difficulties. For when I am weak, then I am strong.

2 Corinthians 12:10

The Scriptures are peppered with paradoxes—statements that appear at first glance to contradict themselves. The Bible says if you want to be first, you must be last. To live, you must die. To receive honor, humble yourself. Some statements don't even seem to make sense, like when Paul says, "For when I am weak, then I am strong."

Most people these days envy the strong. They admire the self-assured, those who are secure in their own ability to handle whatever comes along. Self-confidence is considered a sign of a strong character. Was Paul saying he had no strength? Not at all. His strength came from his faith in God, however, and not from relying on his own abilities. Paul knew the difference. He had already tried self-reliance. Before he met Christ, he oozed self-confidence. Why shouldn't he? He was a brilliant, powerful, and respected Pharisee. As he went about persecuting Christians, he had no doubt in his mind that his life was pleasing to God. Then God humbled him. After spending three days blind and totally dependent on others to guide him, he was ready to listen and to do things God's way.

You, too, may assume you are self-sufficient. You may think you can handle anything life throws at you. As long as your confidence comes from your own abilities, you will not rely on God for your strength. That's called pride. Paul learned the hard way where pride gets you. If you are presently experiencing hardships, it may be that God is revealing to you your weakness. Turn to him; allow him to demonstrate his power in your life. As you realize how absolutely weak you are without Christ, you are on the way to becoming strong. That's called faith.

Thoughts from James

Many Bible scholars believe that James was the half brother of Jesus. Whether he was or was not related to Jesus, he certainly knew him well. The Book of James is a treasure chest of practical, down-to-earth wisdom. James gets right to the heart of what it truly means to be Christ's disciples. James strips away everything about the Christian life that is false and pretentious and leaves no doubt about how Christians should live. The flavor of the Book of James is characterized in chapter 1, verse 22: "Do not merely listen to the word, and so deceive yourselves." Do what it says. That's the way James speaks. Directly. Clearly. He tackles the big subjects—obedience, temptation, wisdom, faithfulness, sin, and more—in a clear and precise way that leaves no doubt about what he's trying to say! The Book of James is a fascinating, easy-to-understand guide to living out your faith day by day. It's a short book, only five chapters; over the next couple of weeks we'll cover much of what James has to say. But be sure to take time to read the verses we don't cover, as the entire book is filled with practical, relevant advice that will help you know how to live a victorious Christian life.

thou ... nes

July 31

Consider It Joy!

Consider it pure joy, my brothers, whenever you face trials of many kinds.

James 1:2

No one enjoys pain. We would all prefer that our lives be carefree with no hardships. When we go through tough times, we experience a variety of emotions, but joy usually isn't one of them. When trials come, we become frustrated that things aren't going the way we would like. We get angry at others, at God, or at ourselves. We may feel profound sadness. Often, when we are in the middle of a difficult situation, we feel totally helpless, even fearful. Yet, according to James, we are not at the mercy of our circumstances. Incredibly, James says we should "consider it pure joy" when we go through adversity. He urges us to see the positive, even in distressing times.

What could be good about trials? James says that when your faith is tested, you learn to rely on God. If you never experience difficulties, you won't learn to trust God to the same degree as when you realize how much you need him. Tough times build endurance. They're like exercise; it can bring discomfort, but it strengthens your body. Likewise, misfortune can be painful, but it can make you a stronger Christian. When God carries you through a dark period, you experience him in a new dimension. You gain a fresh understanding of how much he loves you. Your faith is stronger, and you're more prepared to trust him next time. It isn't that you enjoy suffering, but you can find joy in the knowledge that even through your darkest moments God can bring about good things in your life and make you spiritually strong.

If things look gloomy for you right now, take heart. Don't become bitter. Allow God this opportunity to care for you. Let him show you the positive side. Let him strengthen you. He alone can give you joy—joy that no one or no circumstance can take away from you.

Asking for Wisdom

*If any of you lacks wisdom, he should ask God, who gives gener-
ously to all without finding fault, and it will be given to him.*

James 1:5

If there's anything we need to get along in this world, it's
wisdom. We can be fabulously wealthy, unbelievably good-
looking, incredibly intelligent, and amazingly talented, but
without wisdom we will make stupid choices, some that
could ruin us. We confront new problems and decisions
every day. We deal with all kinds of people and situations.
One wrong decision can hurt us for the rest of our lives. The
Bible is filled with warnings for the foolish person. Life is
too complicated to be foolish. We need wisdom.

Wisdom is not knowledge. You can read thousands of
books, earn a dozen degrees, and take a hundred classes—
what you'll gain is knowledge. Wisdom comes from God.
It's the ability to apply what you know to how you live. It's
making decisions with the understanding of which option
is from God and which is from the world. It's knowing when
a relationship is unhealthy, and having the courage to break
it off. It's being able to take what you read in the Bible and
apply it to your own circumstances.

You don't learn wisdom. It is a gift that God wants to give
you. Every morning, before you face what the day holds for
you, ask God for the wisdom to guide you through. James
assures you that God will give it generously.

August 2

Every Perfect Gift

Don't be deceived, my dear brothers. Every good and perfect gift is from above, coming down from the Father of the heavenly lights, who does not change like shifting shadows.

James 1:16-17

One of Satan's tricks is to try to convince us that we don't need God. That we can get along fine without him. That the good things in our life are the result of our own hard work or good luck. James warns us not to be deceived. We are in dangerous territory if we start to believe that we are responsible for what we have. God, who gave us life itself, is the one behind everything in our lives that is worthwhile.

Often, we neglect to notice gifts from God. For example, we are short of money; then, unexpectedly, we receive a check that exactly matches our need. We exclaim, "What luck! I can't believe how fortunate I am to receive this money right when I needed it most!" Or perhaps we are feeling discouraged, when suddenly a friend happens by to encourage us. We say, "What a coincidence that my friend would come along at that very moment!" Too often we don't make the connection between the good things that happen in our lives and God's provision for us.

Take some time to consider all the good things that have crossed your life recently. Review some of the things you have asked God to provide for you, both material and spiritual. Then begin writing down your prayer requests so you can take notice when God answers them! Make the connection between the many blessings in your life and the one to whom you owe thanks.

Do What It Says!

August 3

Do not merely listen to the word, and so deceive yourselves. Do what it says.

James 1:22

James had a knack for getting right to the heart of things. The great thing about the letter of James is its down-to-earth message. He gives sound, practical advice that is useful for living everyday life. Here, James warns us about something that we're probably all a little guilty of—that is, substituting good intentions in place of actually delivering the goods.

We often spend our time going to church, attending Bible studies, reading Christian books and magazines, and listening to Christian music. We may think that in doing those things we are living the Christian life. We are deceived! Although each of these activities is a worthy pursuit, they are all for nothing if we never put into practice the knowledge we gain. Our generation has access to more biblical information than ever before, but we're not necessarily the most skilled at living out the truths of that information.

We may very well understand what God wants us to do, yet choose to do something else. Many times what we need is not another conference teaching us more things; we simply need to put into practice what we've already learned. The fact is, just knowing the right things to do is not the same as doing them, and promising to do them is not the same thing as doing them. God is not interested in our knowledge or our intentions; he is interested in our obedience.

Today, consider if there is anything you know God wants you to do that you have been putting off until you've gained more knowledge. Then, be a doer of the word, not just a listener.

thoughts from James

August 4

Worthless Religion

If anyone considers himself religious and yet does not keep a tight rein on his tongue, he deceives himself and his religion is worthless.

James 1:26

James, in his typically straightforward way, warns us about living under false assumptions. Over and over, James urges us, "Do not be deceived!" He understood how easy it is to become self-satisfied in the way we're living the Christian life, when in reality there are some things that need to change radically. Here, James refers to the destructive power of our words. He comes on pretty strong; he's actually saying that with careless words we can discredit everything we claim to believe!

The tongue, according to James, is "a world of evil among the parts of the body." It is "a restless evil, full of deadly poison" (James 3:6, 8). That may sound pretty grim, but consider some of the ways that your words can be destructive. With one comment, you can devastate a friend. An angry outburst can destroy a relationship and betray a trust. It's absolutely crucial to keep guard over what comes out of your mouth. You can talk all you want about your Christian faith, but if you are known as a liar, a gossip, or a betrayer, or if you constantly offend others by what you say, your reputation will drown out your Christian witness. The sad thing is, in your heart, you may genuinely care about others. That's why James warns you so strongly not to live under any delusions.

There is a positive spin on James's warning: the words we say also have the potential for much good. Our words can encourage someone who is down, challenge others to grow in their faith, share the good news of Christ, and praise God. The important thing is never to let our guard down when it comes to what we say. The consequences of speaking carelessly can be devastating. The choice is up to us. We can use our words to build up or to tear down our Christian witness.

Dead Faith

If one of you says to him, "Go, I wish you well; keep warm and well fed," but does nothing about his physical needs, what good is it? In the same way, faith by itself, if it is not accompanied by action, is dead.

James 2:16-17

Suppose you were going through a really difficult time financially. You had no place to live for the winter and no food. A friend approached you and said, "I hear you're having a tough time of it. I certainly hope things get better for you. Call me if you need anything." Then your friend hurried off to an appointment. A second friend came along and listened to your troubles. This friend said, "I certainly hope things get better for you. Come and stay at my place and let me help get you through this." Obviously, you'd prefer the offer of the second friend over the first, though both wished you well. James said Christianity is like that. Faith is much more than just saying the right words. Faith is proven by actions.

Words are cheap. They cost us nothing but our breath. Deeds cost a lot more. God is not impressed if we talk about good things but never do them. We can become pleased with ourselves because we are learning so much in our Bible study about faith, but if the time comes to trust God and we refuse, our faith is no more real than it was before. Christianity is not just an academic pursuit. It applies to everyday, real life.

Today, consider doing something specific to help someone in distress. Is there someone close to you who needs more than just your words of comfort? Is there something you can do that will cost you something, but will meet a real need? If you show your faith by your actions, not just your words, both you and the one you help will receive the blessing.

thoughts from James

August 6

Trembling with Demons

You believe that there is one God. Good! Even the demons believe that—and shudder. You foolish man, do you want evidence that faith without deeds is useless?

James 2:19-20

Demons have pretty solid theology. They believe in God's existence: how could they not believe when they've seen him in heaven? They also believe that God sent his Son to the cross to die for the sins of humanity. They were there, fighting God's plan every step of the way. They were there to witness his resurrection from the dead and his triumphant return to his throne in heaven. They believe all the right things; the problem is what they do with their belief. Over and over, the Bible reminds us that "faith without deeds is useless."

It doesn't matter how many times we say "Jesus is Lord." What we really believe is shown by our actions. Christian faith is not head knowledge; it is life-changing belief in the Creator and Master of the universe. The problem with demons is that their theology has no impact on their lives. They know certain facts to be true. For example, they know Jesus is powerful because they experienced his power first-hand when he cast them out of the possessed man. But this knowledge did not lead them to trust in Jesus' power. The demons even claimed with their words that they knew Jesus (Acts 19:15). Obviously, claiming to believe is not faith; otherwise the demons would be pleasing to God.

The way to tell if someone trusts God is not whether she knows God is trustworthy, or even whether he says God can be trusted; it's whether they actually trust God. Examine your own life. Are you living with the assumption that your knowledge or even your words are evidence of your faith? Don't be fooled. What you really believe about God will be proven by what you do.

Wrong Praying

When you ask, you do not receive, because you ask with wrong motives, that you may spend what you get on your pleasures.

James 4:3

Is there such a thing as a bad prayer? Isn't God pleased with any prayer we offer him, just as long as we take time to pray? No. God doesn't see all prayers in the same light. He looks beyond the words we say to the condition of our hearts. In his letter, James addressed some believers who were apparently becoming frustrated as they prayed. They were not getting what they asked for, and they were beginning to doubt if prayer really worked. James pointed out the selfish motives behind their prayers. Their prayers consisted of long lists of things they wanted for themselves. Like spoiled children at Christmas, they would go before God with long wish lists of all the things they wanted. Then they watched impatiently for the parcels to arrive. James makes it clear; that isn't real prayer.

God does not reward selfishness. One benefit of praying is that it takes our attention away from ourselves and causes us to think more about others. Even more important, when we pray, we are to seek God's will above our own (Matthew 6:10). Then, our prayers will be pleasing to God, and he will answer them.

If you've been disappointed in the way God has been answering your prayers, perhaps it's time to examine the motives behind what you pray. The Bible says, "Delight yourself in the LORD and he will give you the desires of your heart" (Psalm 37:4).

Near to God

Come near to God and he will come near to you. Wash your hands, you sinners, and purify your hearts, you double-minded.

James 4:8

Do you sometimes feel that God is right there with you, and at other times he seems thousands of miles away? When you pray, is there close communion with God some days, and other days it's as though your prayers go unheard? Why does God seem so far away at times? Is he preoccupied with running the universe? Is he busy doing battle with Satan or tied up attending to the needs of more important people? Jesus promised that he would never leave you (Matthew 28:20), yet why are there times when you don't sense his presence?

James gives the answer to these questions: "Come near to God and he will come near to you." When we're separated from God, we're the ones who have strayed, not God. There may be sin in our lives that we need to confess and then ask for his forgiveness. Or we may have been distracted by other things, so we've neglected to spend time in prayer and Bible study. When we realize this has happened, we should immediately seek God with all our strength. We need to keep seeking after him until, once again, we enjoy close fellowship with him.

If your relationship with God is cold and distant, examine your life to see if there are sins or attitudes that you need to ask God to remove. Spend time in prayer and in God's Word; go to him with a humble heart and confess your sin. Always remember, God is not the one who changes (Malachi 3:6). It is you who wanders, and it's your responsibility to return to him. He stands ready to love you, to forgive you, and to restore your relationship.

Humble Yourself

Humble yourselves before the Lord, and he will lift you up.

James 4:10

Humility doesn't come naturally to most of us. We may consider ourselves quite modest, yet it's amazing how quickly we become proud of what we have done. We want people to admire us and envy us because of our talents or our accomplishments. The Bible warns us against setting ourselves up for disappointment by exaggerating our own importance, because in doing so we lose sight of our dependence upon God. Pride is deceiving ourselves into thinking that we, not God, are in control. Pride has caused the downfall of many a person, going back to the very beginning of time. It wasn't that Adam and Eve went around boasting about their capabilities. Their sin was in forgetting their place. They allowed the serpent to convince them that they should be as powerful as God himself.

The only defense against pride is humility. James urges us to keep ourselves in proper perspective. When we remember that we are but creatures and that we owe everything to God, it's hard to grow arrogant. That is not to say that we consider ourselves worthless. On the contrary, we are highly valuable to God, who paid for our salvation at an incredible price. But we must remember that without Christ, we can do nothing (John 15:5). We are treasured because of who God is, not because of anything we have done on our own.

How much better for us to choose humility, because God promises that those who seek to exalt themselves will be humbled! (Luke 14:11). For our own good, God will show us just how weak we are. The choice is ours. We can seek to build ourselves up before others, only to be brought back down. Or we can humble ourselves and allow God to honor us, for he takes delight in doing so (Psalm 84:11).

thoughts from James

August 10

Sins of Omission

Anyone, then, who knows the good he ought to do and doesn't do it, sins.

James 4:17

When we talk about sin, we usually refer to the bad things people do—lying, stealing, blasphemy, killing, etc. We sometimes forget that we can also sin by the things we don't do. These are sins of omission, and though they are more subtle, they are just as harmful. James reminds us that sin is not just doing the wrong things; it also includes not doing the right things.

God will lead you to share your faith, to help someone in need, or to forgive someone who has hurt you. If you refuse, you are sinning. If you delay, you are sinning. You may assume that you are living a blameless life because you don't steal, lie, or cheat others. But if you've neglected to do the things you know God has told you, you have sinned just the same.

God wants to use each of us to be a blessing to others. We'll never know, this side of heaven, how our obedience can benefit someone else. It's easier for us to see the harm done by blatant sins like gossip, stealing, or murder. Less obvious is knowing what could have been if only we had responded to God's prompting to get involved where he is at work. When we refuse to obey God, we rob someone else, as well as ourselves, of God's blessing.

Are you aware of some things God wants you to do? What is holding you back from obeying him today?

As Good as Your Word

Above all, my brothers, do not swear—not by heaven or by earth or by anything else. Let your "Yes" be yes, and your "No," no, or you will be condemned.

James 5:12

How reliable are you? When you give your word, do others consider it as good as done? When you make a vow, do your friends take you seriously, or laughingly dismiss your words as yet another empty promise? Your word is a great indicator of your character. If people don't take what you say seriously, you probably have an untrustworthy character.

In James's day, just as in ours, people wanted to be respected. When these people gave their opinion, they would quickly add, "I swear by heaven that it is so!" or something to that effect. Today, someone might say, "As God is my witness . . . ." They thought that if they brought in heaven, or God, as their witness, it would give their words more credibility.

James said your word ought to be enough. If you have to back up what you say with witnesses, then your word isn't worth much. How seriously do people take you when you tell them something? Does your life back up what you say? Does the Bible support you? You don't have to swear by anything when you consistently tell the truth. If you always keep your word, people will learn to trust you. On the other hand, if you make promises but then forget to keep them, you may need to rebuild your reputation.

thou James mes

August 12

Confess Your Sins

Therefore confess your sins to each other and pray for each other so that you may be healed. The prayer of a righteous man is powerful and effective.

James 5:16

One of the healthiest things Christians can do is to confess their sins to God and to fellow believers. We all sin. If we act as if we never sin, we fool no one but ourselves. When we sin against God, he wants us to admit our fault and seek his forgiveness. When we offend someone, it's foolish to pretend it never happened. James urges us to go to that person and seek to restore the broken relationship. Sin that is not dealt with does not just go away. Until we confess it, it stays with us and eats at our soul. Admitting our sin is the beginning of healing.

It's not always easy to confess a sin, but when we do so, a healing takes place that makes it worth the effort. The healing begins within our own heart, as a heavy burden is lifted. We are then free to approach God with a clean heart, and that relationship grows stronger. Even if the one we have offended refuses to forgive us, we are freed from the guilt of unconfessed sin that weighed us down.

Of course, our responsibility does not end with mere confession. The next step is to change our sinful behavior. We must learn from our mistake and strive never to commit that sin again. If someone still has something against us, we must keep trying to mend the broken relationship. But it all begins with confession and prayer.

A Man Like Us

Elijah was a man just like us. He prayed earnestly that it would not rain, and it did not rain on the land for three and a half years. Again he prayed, and the heavens gave rain, and the earth produced its crops.

James 5:17-18

Sometimes we can be tempted to think, *If only I were a spiritual giant, like my pastor, or my grandmother, or the people in the Bible, then my prayers would be answered like theirs were!* We assume we are too ordinary to see extraordinary things happen when we pray. James gives a very pointed challenge to that line of thought. Referring to Elijah, the man who saw God perform incredible miracles, James reminds us that he was an ordinary person. He had fears and doubts and mood swings just like we do. He had moments when he stood up bravely for God and other times when he ran and hid, fearing for his life! Yet, despite Elijah's weaknesses, God chose to answer his prayers in miraculous, spectacular ways.

Elijah was not a super saint. He didn't have a supernatural ability to trust God or to make miracles happen. He was a normal person, like us, who prayed that God's will would be done where he was, and it was. The power was not in Elijah, but in God.

Anyone can have faith. Faith is not based on intelligence or ability, but on our willingness to trust what God says. Faith is accepting that the promises God gives in the Bible are true. It is assuming that God can do anything he wants to do. You can believe God just like Elijah did. You can see God do great things through your prayers. Don't be afraid to trust God for fear that he won't answer the prayers of an ordinary person. When you pray within God's will, everything ordinary becomes extraordinary!

thou   mes

August 14

Saving Others

Whoever turns a sinner from his error will save him from death and cover over a multitude of sins.

James 5:20

We live in a world that teaches us to mind our own business. We try not to get involved in other people's problems. We tell ourselves it's not our place. This attitude is completely opposite to what the Bible teaches. As Christians, we are called to become involved in the lives of others, especially when we see someone headed for trouble.

It is actually our responsibility, when we see a fellow believer drifting toward sin, to warn that person of the dangers ahead. Sometimes we are reluctant to say anything to others because we don't want to offend them. We don't want to act "holier than thou." Besides, if we point out the sins of others, they might point back at us and begin naming *our* sins! So, often we say nothing and think that's the most Christian thing to do. James argues, however, that when we help someone avoid the danger of sin, we are saving that person from death!

We need to check to see what is happening in the lives of people around us. If our friends keep falling into sin and we keep minding our own business, we have failed as a Christian friend. Is there someone you need lovingly to warn of the danger ahead? Take courage. Regardless of the response you receive, speak up before it is too late. Do so out of genuine concern for the well-being of your friend.

Chapter 16

Lessons from the Life of David

David is one of the best-known Old Testament characters. Even people who don't know their Bible well can probably tell you about David's encounter with Goliath. In some ways David's life provides a strong role model for Christians. Other lessons can be learned from examining his mistakes and striving to avoid them. Either way, David is a fascinating character study because everyone can relate to his life in some way.

The youngest of Jesse's eight sons, David grew up in a home that was probably considered quite ordinary in his day. He started out tending sheep, but proved to be a talented musician and a brave warrior as well. God showed favor toward David, choosing him over all the obvious candidates to be king of Israel. But the crown did not come without a cost. David endured intense adversity on his way to the throne.

Like most of us, David had loyal friends. He also had enemies: people were sorely jealous of him for a variety of reasons. David could show remarkable wisdom at one point and incredible foolishness at another. He experienced tremendous joy in his life, yet he also suffered grievous heartache. He caused some of his own problems through poor choices, and some came in spite of his wise choices. David's name means "friend of God." Let's spend some time getting to know this fascinating person whom God considered worthy to be his friend.

August 15

What God Sees

But the LORD *said to Samuel, "Do not look at his appearance or at the height of his stature, because I have rejected him; for God sees not as man sees, for man looks at the outward appearance, but the* LORD *looks at the heart."*

1 Samuel 16:7 (NASB)

King Saul was a man's man. He was tall, good looking, and popular, and he came from an influential family (1 Samuel 9:1–2). It was not surprising, then, that God chose him to be the king Israel was begging to have. David, on the other hand, had a few things going against him. He was a shepherd, which was not a respected profession. Today we think of shepherds as kind and gentle, but back then they were considered thieves whose word could not be trusted. Furthermore, as the eighth son in his family, David was a long way removed from the coveted position of eldest son. In his time, the firstborn son received the greatest opportunities for success. David was considered so insignificant in his own home that when the prophet Samuel came to anoint a king, the older brothers were presented, but David was left out in the field watching the sheep! He was the Cinderella of the Old Testament.

Fortunately for David (and for us), God doesn't do things the way people do. We are dazzled by outward appearances. We assume that the strongest person, or the most attractive, or the smartest, is the one who deserves the most honor. God doesn't think that way; he is far more concerned with the condition of our hearts than with the persona we present to the world.

As it happened, for all of Saul's attributes, he turned out to have a shallow character. He was a selfish man, plagued by anger and jealousy. David would prove to be a far better king than Saul. What's even better, David would be known as a man after God's own heart. What an incredible honor for a lowly shepherd boy! But then, that's the way God does things.

Skill

Then one of the young men said, "Behold, I have seen a son of Jesse the Bethlehemite who is a skillful musician, a mighty man of valor, a warrior, one prudent in speech, and a handsome man; and the LORD *is with him."*

1 Samuel 16:18 (NASB)

In many ways we live in an age of mediocrity. We do only what we have to in order to get by. We try to get the most we can by doing the least we can. That's why sweepstakes and lotteries are so popular and why gambling is such a growing social problem. It's an attitude that says, "Give me something for nothing, or at least show me a shortcut!" The Bible warns against this kind of attitude.

When King Saul was looking for someone who could play an instrument, not just anyone would do. He was looking for someone with skill, someone who had practiced and perfected his ability. He found David. David was chosen because he could do things well. Later, David's son Solomon would write a proverb that affirmed this:

> *Do you see a man skilled in his work?*
> *He will stand before kings;*
> *He will not stand before obscure men (Proverbs 22:29*
>   *NASB).*

As a young person, you have incredible opportunities before you. You have the option to become skilled in many areas of life. You can work hard to develop your athletic or musical ability. You can study hard and make significant contributions to the world of medicine, law, or engineering. You can acquire a diversity of knowledge and skills so many doors will be open to you in the future.

Some young people accept this challenge to become the best they can be and make a difference in the world. Others look at the cost involved and decide it's not worth it. They'd rather find an easier, shorter path. They settle for mediocrity. Don't be one of those who seeks the path of least resistance. Work hard. Do your best. Take advantage of the numerous opportunities God will give you to be the best you can be. You will honor God by your effort, and he will bless you for it.

Lesson david

August 17

God's Record

And David said, "The LORD who delivered me from the paw of the lion and from the paw of the bear, He will deliver me from the hand of this Philistine." And Saul said to David, "Go, and may the LORD be with you."

1 Samuel 17:37 (NASB)

Most things in life are learned by experience. How do you know what pain is? You've experienced it. How do you know what cold feels like? You've felt it. It's the same way with relationships. If a friend lets you down again and again, you learn by experience not to trust her anymore. If you're taken in by a con artist, you learn to be more wary of his next scheme. This principle also applies to our relationship with God. We trust God with a problem today because he was there for us yesterday, and the day before that. We pray with confidence now because God has heard our prayers in the past.

If anyone had a track record with God, it was David. Of course it was terrifying to fight a giant. David had never faced a giant before! But he had faced a bear and a lion. God had saved him from death on both of those occasions, so David had no reason to believe God could not save him now.

You may not even be aware of it, but unless you are a brand-new Christian, you and God have a history together. Think back over the times when you trusted God to help you. How did he respond? When you faced new and challenging situations, and you called out to God to give you courage, what did he do? As long as you're living in obedience to God, there is never a reason to doubt that he will be there for you. His record speaks for itself.

Giants

August 18

Then David said to the Philistine, "You come to me with a sword, a spear, and a javelin, but I come to you in the name of the LORD of hosts, the God of the armies of Israel, whom you have taunted."

1 Samuel 17:45 (NASB)

Imagine you were a member of the Israelite army the day young David arrived to take on the Philistine giant. You would have considered David a fool to take on this menacing monster with no armor and only a slingshot for a weapon. No doubt the fight would be a short one!

David wasn't as naive as everyone thought. Nor was he blind. He could see Goliath towering over all the other soldiers. Even from a distance, he noticed his enemy's enormous weapons—his sword, his spear, and his javelin. He saw how huge the giant's shield was. Yet David could see other things that the rest of the crowd missed. He could see God's strength, which was far superior to any giant or his weapons. It's interesting that even David may have underestimated how quickly God would give him victory. He took five stones with him to hurl at Goliath; God needed only one.

For you, a giant is anything you are facing that seems beyond your power to handle. It may be a tuition payment, an illness, or a broken relationship you need to mend. What giant are you facing right now? Does it seem enormous? Unbeatable? Don't underestimate how powerful your God is! If you will trust him, as David did, you'll see that God is more powerful than any giant you'll ever face.

Signs of God's Presence

Now Saul was afraid of David, for the LORD was with him but had departed from Saul.

David was prospering in all his ways for the LORD was with him.

1 Samuel 18:12, 14 (NASB)

Why would God abandon Saul and bless David? Wasn't it God who chose Saul to be king in the first place? It looks as if God was playing favorites; why wouldn't he bless both men? The answer is in the verses that precede today's passage (1 Samuel 18:6–11). Saul had himself to thank for losing God's blessing. His downfall was assured when he became jealous of David. That led to anger, hatred, and bitterness. All of this came because Saul took his eyes off God and grew envious of the way God blessed David. Saul couldn't tolerate David being more successful than he was. After all, he was king; David was not. Ultimately, Saul completely lost perspective and became separated from God, and his misguided sense of entitlement cost him the very thing he coveted—the crown.

David, on the other hand, was busy doing what God asked him to do. He didn't assume it was his right to become king. Even Saul had to admit God took care of David. Saul could see the obvious difference in David's life because of God's blessings. When David went through hard times, as he often did, God took care of him. When Saul saw the way God blessed David's life, he should have learned his lesson, but pride prevented him from returning to God. Instead, he grew even more self-centered and fearful of David. David was not spared from experiencing hardship, but going through the hard times with God's presence made all the difference to him. David grew closer to God, even as Saul grew more distant.

Jealousy can start out as a small thing. You notice that your friend seems to have something you don't have (success, talent, possessions). You pay closer attention, looking for differences in the way God blesses your friend, compared to you. You have an increasing sense of entitlement—*Don't I deserve to have what my friend has?* Before you know it, you're headed down the same path Saul took; you grow angry, bitter, and suspicious of your friend, and you look for ways to even the score. In the end, though, the one who gets hurt is you. Learn from Saul's mistake. Saul had plenty of reasons to be thankful, but his jealousy blinded him to his own blessings. Don't take your eyes off God to compare your blessings with anyone else's. Choose the path David took—the path of thankfulness—and you'll enjoy God's blessings throughout your life.

What Have I Done?

August 20

Then David fled from Naioth in Ramah, and came and said to Jonathan, "What have I done? What is my iniquity? And what is my sin before your father, that he is seeking my life?"

1 Samuel 20:1 (NASB)

David's life was tragic in many ways. He did his best in every situation he was in, and he loved God with all his heart. He was literally minding his own business when he was plucked from the shepherd's field and made special assistant to the king. He served King Saul faithfully, but instead of enjoying the king's favor, he received only his wrath. King Saul noticed David's success and grew jealous. He envied David's popularity. Rather than appreciating David as a friend, Saul tried to murder him as an enemy.

David was bewildered. He had done nothing wrong. Why did King Saul hate him so much? It didn't make sense. David grew to recognize that jealousy and hatred never make sense. Bitterness isn't rational. When people are miserable with their own lives, they become angry and jealous of others' happiness. And, as the saying goes, "Hurt people, hurt people." Poor David was a victim of his own success. The more successful he became, the more Saul hated him.

Don't be surprised if this happens to you as well. If God honors you as you obey him, your life will stand in sharp contrast to those whom God is not blessing. They may grow envious of you. They may resent your holy life because it reveals their disobedience for what it is. They may seek to bring you down to their level. Don't be discouraged. Understand that anytime someone walks with God there will be those who will resent him. The religious leaders of Jesus' day resented his life so much they killed him. Yet it is better for you to walk with God and have integrity than to ever settle for lukewarm Christianity as some do.

Lesson David

david

August 21

Attractive People

Everyone who was in distress, and everyone who was in debt, and everyone who was discontented gathered to him; and he became captain over them. Now there were about four hundred men with him.

1 Samuel 22:2 (NASB)

The dictionary describes an attractive person as "pleasing, charming, having the power to attract others." Attractiveness goes much deeper than our physical features. We've all known some beautiful people who had personalities like rattlesnakes. They were either abrasive, obnoxious, self-centered, shallow, or all of the above. They may attract us initially with their good looks, but we are soon repelled by their personalities.

David was a handsome man, but that wasn't what attracted people to him. He had a large circle of close and loyal friends because of his personality. He was like a magnet for hurting people because he understood their situation. He had been mistreated and misunderstood enough himself that he was able to sympathize with others. He was kind and thoughtful of others, so they wanted to be around him. Hundreds of men followed his leadership willingly because they knew he cared about them. No doubt David could have been as ugly as a can of worms, and he would have attracted the same people.

Do you have a personality like David's? Do people know that if they are hurting you will listen to them and sympathize with them? Or are you unknowingly giving off the message that you have time only for those who can help you? If you've been more of a taker than a giver lately, ask God to soften your heart and make you aware of ways to be a friend to someone today. More than likely, you'll receive a blessing in the process!

Thanks a Lot!

August 22

Then David said, "Will the men of Keilah surrender me and my men into the hand of Saul?" And the LORD said, "They will sur-render you."

1 Samuel 23:12 (NASB)

Have you ever done something nice for someone and then had them turn against you? It hurts, doesn't it? It happened to David. As he was fleeing for his life, with King Saul's army in hot pursuit, he became aware of a city under attack by the Philistines. As if they didn't have enough to worry about, David and his army stopped long enough to help the town of Keilah repel its enemy. The problem was, Saul was still after him. David might have been safe within the walls of Keilah, but he received word from God that the people he had just risked his neck to help were going to betray him! So David was forced to escape again and try to make up for lost time.

How do you respond when people you have helped are hateful in return? Did you stand up for a friend who was being criticized or bullied? Then, when you were under attack and needed a friend, he turned on you! Maybe you've gone out of your way to be kind to someone, only to find out she's been gossiping about you behind your back. Have you ever made a big sacrifice to help out a friend, and your thoughtfulness was never even acknowledged? How do you respond in times like these? David just moved on. He didn't waste valuable time fretting over the ingratitude of others. He trusted that God knew about his kindness, and God did, indeed, reward him.

Don't be discouraged if people are not always thankful for what you do for them. All you need to be concerned about is what God wants to do in you. Let God deal with those who have not treated you as they should. The Father is working to produce a godly character in you, and he will see to it that your kindness is rewarded.

August 23

Enemies

So David and Abishai came to the people by night, and behold, Saul lay sleeping inside the circle of the camp with his spear stuck in the ground at his head; and Abner and the people were lying around him. Then Abishai said to David, "Today God has delivered your enemy into your hand; now therefore, please let me strike him with the spear to the ground with one stroke, and I will not strike him the second time."

But David said to Abishai, "Do not destroy him, for who can stretch out his hand against the LORD's anointed and be without guilt?" David also said, "As the LORD lives, surely the LORD will strike him, or his day will come that he dies, or he will go down into battle and perish. The LORD forbid that I should stretch out my hand against the LORD's anointed; but now please take the spear that is at his head and the jug of water, and let us go."

1 Samuel 26:7-11 (NASB)

Opportunities aren't always what they appear to be. Don't be too quick to assume an opportunity is from God just because it's in front of you. Christians talk a lot about God opening doors, and indeed he does. But we need to be discerning because not every open door is from God. David's experience is a case in point. King Saul had made his life miserable for years. David's days were spent on the run; his nights, hiding in caves. And all the while, David had to accept the fact that he, not Saul, was supposed to be the king.

Then it came! An incredible opportunity that would solve all David's problems. There was Saul, asleep and defenseless at David's feet! David's friend immediately assumed this chance must be from God. Who would ever blame David for killing Saul? His friend even offered to do the job for him. But David knew God better than that. He understood that God would take care of Saul himself, in his own time. David was a warrior; he had taken many lives before. But this was different. Even though Saul had been his enemy, David realized that God had called Saul and that God would deal with Saul in his own way. So David spared Saul's life. This would not be the last time he would do so. Ultimately, David did become king, and Saul did get what he deserved, but it wasn't because David took matters into his own hands.

We, too, must distinguish between temptation and opportunity. What seems to make perfect sense to us may be totally contrary to God's will. How can we know the difference? We must learn to know God's heart as David did, and God will give us the ability to discern the difference.

God's Directions

David inquired of the LORD, saying, "Shall I pursue this band? Shall I overtake them?" And He said to him, "Pursue, for you will surely overtake them, and you will surely rescue all."

1 Samuel 30:8 (NASB)

Then it came about afterwards that David inquired of the LORD, saying, "Shall I go up to one of the cities of Judah?" And the LORD said to him, "Go up." So David said, "Where shall I go up?" And He said, "To Hebron."

2 Samuel 2:1 (NASB)

David lived in dangerous times. One small mistake could cost him his life. So, whenever he needed to know what to do, he asked God. He didn't just ask in generalities; his questions were always specific. God's answers were equally direct.

There is a theory that God does not have a specific plan for our lives. This teaching suggests that God does not guide his people daily. Rather, he gives us a brain and leaves us to make our own choices. The problem with this approach is that it totally ignores what the Bible teaches. From Genesis to Revelation, the Bible shows that God has always given clear instructions to his people. When David needed a specific battle plan, God did not say, "David, you're a soldier. What do you think?" When David wasn't sure where to go next, God didn't say, "David, you know this area like the back of your hand. Just do what makes sense to you." No, God told him exactly what to do. David obeyed, and he experienced success.

Don't assume that God isn't interested in the everyday decisions of your life. Yes, he gave you a brain. He also gave you the Holy Spirit, the church, and his written Word. All of these are ways he communicates with you. He is vitally interested in the details of your life. Never hesitate to seek his direction in any decision.

Worshiping God

So David said to Michal, "It was before the LORD, who chose me above your father and above all his house, to appoint me ruler over the people of the LORD, over Israel; therefore I will celebrate before the LORD."

2 Samuel 6:21 (NASB)

There's one thing you can say about David: he wasn't ashamed to worship God! When David brought the ark, representing God's presence, into Jerusalem, he was so joyful that he shed his kingly robes and danced all the way down main street! Every person in the nation, from the youngest to the oldest, could see David praising God with all of his might! His public display of exuberance embarrassed his wife, who thought a king ought to show more dignity than that. She mocked him for revealing his emotions so openly.

David's explanation: He *had* to humble himself and worship God. He was under no delusions. He knew that he was king only because God had made him king. He understood that, compared to the King of the universe, he was small potatoes! David loved God so much he was trying to express, somehow, his love to God by the way he praised him.

Do you ever find it embarrassing to worship God? Do you feel awkward singing in church? Are you afraid to pray publicly? Do you dread being asked to share your salvation experience with a group of people? Are you embarrassed for others to see how deeply you feel about God? Take courage from David's example. He was not ashamed for anyone to see that he loved God. His only concern was that his behavior be pleasing to his King. When you love God with all your heart, you won't be hindered by what anyone else thinks.

Not Where You
Should Be

Then it happened in the spring, at the time when kings go out to battle, that David sent Joab and his servants with him and all Israel, and they destroyed the sons of Ammon and besieged Rabbah. But David stayed at Jerusalem.

Now when evening came David arose from his bed and walked around on the roof of the king's house, and from the roof he saw a woman bathing; and the woman was very beautiful in appearance. So David sent and inquired about the woman. And one said, "Is this not Bathsheba, the daughter of Eliam, the wife of Uriah the Hittite?" David sent messengers and took her, and when she came to him, he lay with her; and when she had purified herself from her uncleanness, she returned to her house.

2 Samuel 11:1-4 (NASB)

David learned the hard way that idleness can bring dangerous temptation. Kings traditionally led their armies into battle. The Bible doesn't tell us why David chose to stay home when he should have been leading his army. For whatever reason, he sent someone else in his place, and he remained at home with little to do. If only he had been where he should have been, doing his job, he would not have come across Bathsheba and committed the sin that would tear apart both their families. David, a man who loved God with all his heart, ended up doing something he would regret for the rest of his life.

You can learn from David's tragic mistake. No matter how strong you think your faith is, you are vulnerable just as David was. If David could commit a horrible sin, so could you. If you find yourself drifting away from the things you know you should be doing—Bible study, worship, prayer— understand that you are in great danger. You will fill your time by doing something. As you neglect your Christian life, you'll be tempted to fill the gaps with activity that could bring you enormous heartache. Far better to be where you're supposed to be than to sit idle, an easy target for temptation. Begin today to do the things you know you should be doing. It will save you from regret in the future.

Despising God's Word

Why have you despised the word of the LORD by doing evil in His sight? You have struck down Uriah the Hittite with the sword, have taken his wife to be your wife, and have killed him with the sword of the sons of Ammon.

2 Samuel 12:9 (NASB)

We Christians have lots of euphemisms for our sin: we call it backsliding, a bad habit, an error in judgment, or a moment of weakness. Sometimes we just don't want to face up to what we have done. But God always calls sin what it is—sin.

When David sinned against Uriah by committing adultery with Uriah's wife, God saw David's sin much differently than David did. Rather than repenting immediately, David tried to cover it up by having Uriah killed. Perhaps he thought God would let him get away with this one, since he'd been faithful in so many other ways. But God would not overlook David's sin. Even though David had been obedient time after time, his sin was an insult to God. David knew better. He knew what God thought about adultery—and about murder—yet he chose to satisfy his own selfish purposes.

We sometimes excuse ourselves for disobeying God's Word. We may assume God will just forgive us and treat us as if it never happened. We may think our disobedience is not a big deal. We may rationalize by telling ourselves, "Nobody's perfect!" The fact is—when we sin, we are despising God's Word. Perhaps if we really understood how God looks at our sin, we would take his Word far more seriously. Perhaps if we realized that we insult God and his Word when we sin, we would be more hesitant to do what we know is wrong.

Safe in God's Hands

And David spoke the words of this song to the LORD in the day that the LORD delivered him from the hand of all his enemies and from the hand of Saul. And he said,

"The LORD is my rock and my fortress and my deliverer;
My God, my rock, in whom I take refuge,
My shield and the horn of my salvation, my stronghold and my refuge;
My savior, You save me from violence.
"I call upon the LORD, who is worthy to be praised,
And I am saved from my enemies."

2 Samuel 22:1-4 (NASB)

People were not always kind to David. They mistrusted him and betrayed him. They lied about him and plotted against him. He should have enjoyed a carefree youth, but instead, he spent years hiding from a jealous man who was obsessed with murdering him. Where could he turn? Even his wife mocked him.

The more David suffered, the more he turned to God. God was all he had, and David discovered God was all he needed. God was the one constant in David's life. God was the only one he could really trust, so his Lord became his shelter. David had seen many fortresses in his day; he had even hidden in a few. But none could offer the safety he found in God. As long as he was close to God, he was secure.

David had only two choices: he could get angry and blame God for his troubles, or he could find refuge from those troubles in his relationship with God. David chose to trust God. He knew that as long as he stayed close to God, he was safe from his enemies. Therefore, instead of going down to defeat, David could sing his praises to God for giving him victory.

You will experience betrayal in your life. People will misjudge you. People will let you down; they will even attack you. It's crucial to understand that your security does not come from people. It comes from God. If you're hurting because you've been treated unfairly, don't turn away from God. Now is the time you need him most. Allow him to be for you all that he was for David: rock, fortress, deliverer, refuge, shield, salvation, stronghold, savior. There is no safer place in all the world than in God's hands.

August 29

Consider the Heavens

When I consider Your heavens, the work of Your fingers,
The moon and the stars, which You have ordained;
What is man that You take thought of him,
And the son of man that You care for him?
Yet You have made him a little lower than God,
And You crown him with glory and majesty!

Psalm 8:3-5 (NASB)

When David gazed at the starry night sky, he was admiring the same beauty that we enjoy now, centuries later. David was so moved by the enormity of creation that he wrote a praise song to its Creator. Yet David had no idea just how vast the heavens really are! He had no knowledge of galaxies beyond his own. He knew nothing of black holes or light-years or supernovas. But what David saw was enough to convince him that God is amazing!

Reflecting on God's greatness made David keenly aware of his own weakness. Looking at the stars in the sky helped put David and his importance in perspective! It astounded him, as it should astound us, that a being as powerful as God would bother with mere creatures like David. Even more incredible is that God would choose to "crown us with glory and honor."

We still have much to learn, but we know a lot more about the cosmos than David did. We have even more reason to be impressed! We have even more reason to ask God the same humble question that David asked: "What is man that you are mindful of him?" Take a walk this evening and study the night sky. Remember, the same God who put every star in its place wants to have a close, loving relationship with you. It's mind-boggling, isn't it?

The Honor Seat

I have set the LORD continually before me;
Because He is at my right hand, I will not be shaken.

Psalm 16:8 (NASB)

Have you ever been to a banquet or some other formal meal with a seating plan? You found the place card with your name on it, and that's where you sat. In early Near Eastern culture, seating plans held great significance. When someone held a feast, he would reserve the seat to his right for his most esteemed guest. This sometimes caused embarrassment for those who assumed they held this honored position, only to find themselves seated at the far end of the table while someone else enjoyed the host's attentions!

Usually a person's closest friend and advisor sat on his right-hand side (thus the term right-hand man). The Bible refers to Jesus, after his resurrection, as "sitting down at the right hand of the Father" (Hebrews 1:3). His Father was giving him the highest honor that exists in heaven or on earth. Therefore, when David acknowledged God's place at his right hand, he said a lot in a small phrase. He revealed that God occupied the most important position in his life. He declared that God had priority over everyone else and everything else. He called God his close friend and trusted advisor. David knew, from experience, that he would be nowhere without God's protection and guidance. For David, there was no question about where to put his trust. As long as God had his rightful place in David's life, David could take on anything life had to offer. Come what may, David was not afraid. His words overflow with confidence: "I will not be shaken!"

Are you aware that you can live with the same confidence that David did? Have you reserved the most important place in your life for God, or have you given the honor seat to someone (or something) else? Only one guest is to sit at your right hand. If you've not extended this honor to God, now is the time to do so.

LESSON

August 31

God's Way

As for God, His way is blameless;
The word of the LORD is tried;
He is a shield to all who take refuge in Him.

Psalm 18:30 (NASB)

Have you ever wondered if God really knows what he's doing? Come on, you can admit it! You know in your head that God is in control. After all, that's what your Sunday school teacher taught you. Your pastor preaches about it all the time. You've even read it for yourself in your Bible. Yet aren't there times when, deep down, you suspect God has forgotten you, or missed a few important details?

David certainly must have had a few doubts hidden in his heart. God promised that David would be king, yet he seemed to have overlooked a significant obstacle: Saul. Where was God when David had to flee to the hills to escape Saul's sword? Didn't God care that David was forced to live in caves, or that he had to fake insanity just to preserve his life? Surely God was otherwise occupied, and he simply forgot to remove Saul and clear David's way to the throne. If David did wonder about the reliability of God's word, he came to understand that his doubts were groundless. Through experience, David learned that God was indeed aware of every detail in his life. Even in the cold, damp caves, God was there. David discovered that he didn't have to understand God's ways in order to trust him. Everything God promised David did come to pass. David found that God is exactly who he says he is.

Don't be afraid to trust God, even when you can't figure out what he's doing. You don't have to figure him out in order to find refuge in him.

Loving and Faithful

All the paths of the LORD are lovingkindness and truth
To those who keep His covenant and His testimonies.

Psalm 25:10 (NASB)

At times you may be tempted to think God asks too much of you. You might feel that he expects you to be perfect and that he doesn't want you to have any fun. If that's how you view God, you need to get to know him better!

Through a variety of experiences, David grew to know God well. He concluded that God always relates to his people lovingly and faithfully. David found that, no matter what his circumstances were, God was not only there for him, but God also knew what was best for him. David came to realize that even God's most demanding commandments were merely another way of God expressing his love for him. Ultimately, God fulfilled every promise he made to David.

If you look at your own situation and doubt that God loves you, or if you question his willingness to keep his promises to you, remember David's words. The longer you walk with God, the more clearly you will see that everything God does in your life is done in perfect love. Even when he disciplines you or puts restrictions on you, it's because he loves you.

God's faithfulness to you is beyond question. But what about your faithfulness to him? Will God find you to be as faithful to him as he is to you? If you will trust him and keep his ways, you will experience life in a greater dimension than you can imagine.

September 2

Forgiven!

How blessed is he whose transgression is forgiven,
Whose sin is covered!
How blessed is the man to whom the LORD does not impute iniquity,
And in whose spirit there is no deceit!
When I kept silent about my sin, my body wasted away
Through my groaning all day long
For day and night Your hand was heavy upon me;
My vitality was drained away as with the fever heat of summer.
*   [Selah]*
I acknowledged my sin to You,
And my iniquity I did not hide;
I said, "I will confess my transgressions to the LORD";
And You forgave the guilt of my sin. [Selah]
Therefore, let everyone who is godly pray to You in a time when
*   You may be found;*
Surely in a flood of great waters they will not reach him.

Psalm 32:1-6 (NASB)

Guilt is a heavy load to carry. When you've done something horrible, and you know it, it really weighs you down. You can only carry your unconfessed sin around for so long before growing exhausted. You long for things to be as they were before your sin saddled you with the oppressive burden of shame. David felt that shame. He said that his sin sapped his strength the way an unbearably hot summer day drains your energy. He could not get his mind off his guilt, and it was too much for him to handle. It's too much for you to handle too.

When David could bear it no more, he confessed his sin to God and sought forgiveness. Immediately, the load was lifted. David felt renewed and energized. He enjoyed a sense of freedom that he hadn't known for a long time.

The irony of unconfessed sin is that God knows about it anyway. There is no hiding from God. God simply waits for you to acknowledge to him that you have sinned and to admit that you were wrong. If your sin is weighing you down, you're carrying a burden you don't have to bear. Confess your sin to God. Seek his forgiveness. Ask him to restore you so you can enjoy your relationship with him once again. Go ahead; you'll feel like a new person.

Praise

I will bless the LORD at all times;
His praise shall continually be in my mouth.

Psalm 34:1 (NASB)

It should not surprise us to read that David wanted to praise God his entire life. After all, it seems he was always writing psalms and singing praises to God. It is interesting, though, that David wrote the above words immediately after one of the most humiliating experiences of his life. As if he wasn't in enough danger already, trying to stay one step ahead of his old nemesis, King Saul, David had just experienced a close call with another enemy, the Philistine king of Gath. The only way out was to feign insanity so his enemy would see no need to kill him. Talk about a low point! Here was a man destined to be king, ranting and slobbering all over himself. Did obeying God really require such a loss of dignity? It didn't seem like the time to burst into songs of praise, yet that's exactly what David did. He understood that God had again spared his life and protected him. He was so grateful for this that he wanted to praise God right away.

Sometimes, we completely miss something good that God has just done in our lives. We concentrate on the negatives of the situation, rather than on the positive. For example, we're involved in a car accident, and we're so worried about the damage that we fail to see the miracle that God brought us through safely. At other times we do see God's goodness, but we're too busy to praise him. David was a very busy man, yet he made it a habit to praise God always, no matter where he was or how he felt. That's not a bad habit for us to copy.

LESSON david

September 4

Fear

I sought the LORD, and He answered me,
And delivered me from all my fears.

Psalm 34:4 (NASB)

People can be afraid of almost anything. There's agoraphobia, the fear of public places, or claustrophobia, the fear of closed-in spaces. The astraphobic is afraid of thunder, while the algophobic is afraid of pain. The hydrophobic is afraid of water, while the pyrophobic is afraid of fire. Those who don't suffer from any of these phobias have a number of things to fear. Some people are terrified of failure, so they never attempt anything. Others are afraid of what people will think, so they withdraw into their own world where it's safe. Some people would rather bathe in battery acid than give a speech. At some point, we all fear death or disease.

The things that strike terror in one person may not bother another, but the point is, we all know what fear feels like. It can consume us. It can cause us to do irrational things. If we let it, fear can cripple us emotionally so we no longer enjoy life the way God planned. Life isn't meant to be lived that way.

God wants to deliver us from our fears and give back the joy that fear takes away. David had lots of reasons for fear, but he took his fears to God. To his delight, God "delivered [him] from all [his] fears!" Does fear have control over you? Call out to God and let him free you from the fear that has captivated you.

Taste and See

O taste and see that the LORD is good;
How blessed is the man who takes refuge in Him!

Psalm 34:8 (NASB)

God is good! He loves you more than anyone else you will ever know. He has wonderful plans tailor-made for you. He is reserving a place in heaven for you that is indescribably exquisite. It's impossible to understand just how good God really is. Do you believe that?

Some people never come to know God as he is. They have a mental image of him that is totally distorted. Some see God as a heartless being who delights in condemning people to hell. Others consider him a cruel puppeteer, engineering natural disasters at whim. Many people don't view God in such a drastic way, but their view is distorted nonetheless. They may think of him as a legalistic ruler who puts restrictions on everything and demands that they be followed. Many people don't know what God is really like because they don't even acknowledge his existence. They simply consider him a nonentity. Sadly, many Christians don't really know what God is like. They view him warily, from a distance, as though he is just waiting for them to mess up so he can punish them. All of these are false images of God. God is *good!*

No one can tell you how good God is. You have to experience him for yourself. Don't accept someone else's distorted image of God. God is a person who wants you to get to know him. Spend time discovering what he is really like. You'll be delighted to discover just how wonderful he really is!

Lesson ... david

September 6

Enjoying God

Delight yourself in the LORD;
And He will give you the desires of your heart.
Commit your way to the LORD,
Trust also in Him, and He will do it.

Psalm 37:4-5 (NASB)

People often think about God in terms of the Ten Commandments: he lays down the rules, and we wear ourselves out trying to follow them. Even some Christians view God as a cosmic policeman. His job is to catch us breaking the rules, and our job is to avoid getting caught! We are sadly deceived. The truth is that knowing God is the most freeing experience we could ever have. Our relationship with God is primarily for our enjoyment. Spending time with God each day ought to be a delight.

Sometimes we get things backwards in our thinking. We assume that God will only give us good things if we beg and plead for them. We act like spoiled children, seeking the Father only when we want something. We throw tantrums when we don't get what we want. We may conclude that God must not love us. But the problem is not God. We are the problem. God delights in our company. He takes pleasure in answering our prayers.

The more time we spend getting to know God, the more we see just how much he loves us, and the more we see things the way God sees them. We grow to understand the difference between selfish whims and true prayer. We find ourselves praying the way God wants us to pray. We think less and less about what we have to do and more and more about who it is that we know. The difference between what we want and what God wants becomes smaller and smaller.

If your prayers seem to be going unanswered, pay attention to the way you pray. Are you reciting a wish list or getting to know a person? Getting to know God is far more important than getting what you want.

Never Forsaken

I have been young and now I am old,
Yet I have not seen the righteous forsaken
Or his descendants begging bread.

Psalm 37:25 (NASB)

David had walked with God for a long time. As a young boy herding sheep, David had played songs of praise to God on his harp. As a soldier going into battle, he put his trust in God. When his enemies were trying to destroy him, David relied on God to save him. David turned to God for guidance when he became king, the most powerful man in the country. Now David was an old man. He had trusted God throughout his long life. As he looked back over his experiences, David concluded that he had never seen God fail a righteous person.

If your heart is right before God, this is a promise for you. Throughout history God has never failed anyone who sought to obey him, so he's unlikely to start now! However, if you are choosing your own way, don't hold false assurance that God is obligated to meet your needs. Many Christians are confident that God will take care of them simply because they are Christians, even though they continue to live in disobedience to him. The only ones who can count on God's blessings are those who choose to live a righteous life. David was by no means perfect, but all his life he sought to nurture his relationship with God. At times this meant crying out in anguish for forgiveness. David always made his relationship with God the highest priority in his life.

Are you worried about whether God will take care of your needs? If you are living the way God wants you to, you have no reason to be concerned. God will be just as faithful with you as he was with David and with every other righteous person who ever lived.

September 8

A New Song

I waited patiently for the LORD;
And He inclined to me and heard my cry.
He brought me up out of the pit of destruction, out of the miry
*   clay,*
And He set my feet upon a rock making my footsteps firm.
He put a new song in my mouth, a song of praise to our God;
Many will see and fear
And will trust in the LORD.

Psalm 40:1-3 (NASB)

There's no question: at some time or other anyone can fall into the pit. You know the pit. It's the place where everything looks dark and gloomy. You feel all alone. Things look hopeless. Every time you try to climb out, you lose your footing and slide back down. You feel miserable about yourself and about life in general. It seems no one understands what you are going through, and if they did understand, they wouldn't care! The only song in your heart is off-key.

David had been in the pit. He knew from experience that there was only one way out, so he cried to God. Then he did the only thing that was within his power to do. He sat and waited patiently. Waiting on God can be difficult to do, but it is always the most effective way of getting out of the pit. Sure enough, God rescued him. God picked him up and put him on solid ground. God gave him renewed confidence. God even gave him a new song, a song of hope and joy instead of bitterness and despair. As hopeless as the pit had seemed to David only moments before, now it had no power over him.

Maybe you're in the pit of despair right now. Perhaps your current situation seems hopeless. You may feel as if no one cares. Have you called out to God? Wait patiently and trust him. He'll get you out and put you on your feet once more. You may be only a prayer away from a heart filled with joy!

In Broad Daylight

"'Indeed you did it secretly, but I will do this thing before all Israel, and under the sun.'" Then David said to Nathan, "I have sinned against the LORD." And Nathan said to David, "The LORD also has taken away your sin; you shall not die."

2 Samuel 12:12-13 (NASB)

Sin, by its very nature, is shrouded in darkness. Most of us want our good deeds to be made public and our sins to be kept private. When David sinned by taking another man's wife as his own, he went to great lengths to cover up his actions. He even had the man he had wronged murdered so he wouldn't have to face him! David used all his powers as king to escape the consequences of his sin. We may marvel at David's foolishness in trying to conceal both the adultery and the murder, but are we any smarter?

How often do we do things in secret that we never expect to be made public? How often do we see people in the news who are humiliated when their private lives are opened up for public viewing? David was the most powerful person in Israel, yet even he could not escape God's scrutiny when he sinned. We are only fooling ourselves if we think we can sin and never be found out.

The only way to live without fear of being found out is to live a clean life. Don't be fooled as David and countless other red-faced sinners have been. What you do in secret can, and most likely will, be proclaimed in broad daylight. Be sure it's something you don't mind the world knowing.

Chapter 17

The Ten Commandments

The Ten Commandments are the most famous rules ever given. Even non-Christians are aware of them. Most could even quote one or two. The most basic of God's laws were summarized long ago on those two slabs of stone. They are not an exhaustive list of every transgression possible but a summary of our most common sins.

As always, it is important to examine anything in the Old Testament in light of the further revelation of the New Testament. Jesus explained, in the Sermon on the Mount, that God was not merely giving us a set of rules: he was telling his people what our hearts should be like. It is possible to obey all ten commandments but not love God. Some people rest easy on the knowledge that they do not break these rules. Yet, if you look carefully at what lies behind each command, you will see that they are more difficult to keep than they first appear.

If you want to live a life that honors God, the Ten Commandments are a good place to start. If you are not keeping the Ten Commandments, you have not yet mastered the basic expectations of the Christian life. Keep in mind, however, that there is a truth behind each one of them that specifically addresses your attitudes as well as merely your actions. Turn to Exodus, chapter 20, and let's begin our study of the Ten Commandments.

No Other Gods

You shall have no other gods before me.

Exodus 20:3

We know there is only one God. But sometimes the way we live shows that our loyalty is divided. We treat something as if it were our god. We give it priority over everything else. We keep thinking about it. We spend our money on it. We let it determine what we do. We might not consider it a god, but it has mastery over us as only the one true God should have. Whenever anything or anyone takes first place in our hearts, God considers that an idol, a false god. The Bible says that God is a jealous God. He wants nothing else to take his rightful place in our lives. That's where we get the term *idolize*; it means to give something so much esteem that it is as if we were worshiping it.

Money is an idol for some who trust in their wealth to give them happiness and to see them through life's circumstances. Some people value the approval of their friends more than anything else. They would readily abandon God's will in order to gain popularity.

It's possible to elevate other people to god-status by giving their opinions priority over God's commands. By doing this, you can inadvertently allow those you respect, such as your parents or friends, to exercise more control over you than God does. It might surprise you to know that even honoring your parents must not prevent you from honoring your Lord. God established clearly in the first commandment that he will not tolerate anything displacing him as the one and only God. Watch over your heart that you allow *nothing* to become more important to you than pleasing God.

September 11

Idols

You shall not make for yourself an idol in the form of anything in heaven above or on the earth beneath or in the waters below. You shall not bow down to them or worship them; for I, the LORD your God, am a jealous God, punishing the children for the sin of the fathers to the third and fourth generation of those who hate me, but showing love to thousands who love me and keep my commandments.

Exodus 20:4-6

Our generation tries so hard to portray God as a tolerant, accepting, soft-spoken being. How wrong we are! The second commandment gives us a wake-up call! Our God is indeed just, loving, and long-suffering. But he is God! He will not tolerate sin, and he will not tolerate idols in our hearts. There is room for only one master in our lives, and God alone holds the rights to that position.

As ridiculous as it seems to us, people in Moses' generation actually carved idols from wood or stone, then prayed to them and offered sacrifices to them. These superstitious people hoped that these statues would bring them success. It's similar to people in our day relying on their horoscopes to guide them through each day or seeking the advice of so-called psychics. As we learned when we examined the first commandment, there are many ways we can fall into the trap of idolatry, some of which may seem innocent to us.

In case you missed it the first time, God gives another stern warning against turning to anyone or anything before seeking his will. The things that have priority in your life may seem like good things—a job, friends, money—but they are only good as long as they never take God's place in your heart. Give God first place in everything, and you will experience his love in the gentle, accepting way that you desire.

God's Name

You shall not misuse the name of the LORD your God, for the LORD will not hold anyone guiltless who misuses his name.

Exodus 20:7

When you hear people use God's name as a profanity or in a flippant way, what assumption do you make about their view of God? Do you think they understand what they are doing? If they really knew the one whose name they carelessly toss about, would it change their language?

Abusing God's name is much more than cursing. It involves anything that takes away from the value of God's name. It is mocking God—showing him contempt rather than the fearful reverence that he deserves. There is more than one way to misuse God's name. Whenever we speak of God in any way other than absolute respect, we misrepresent him. Whenever we try to justify our sinful actions with the argument that we were only acting in obedience to God, we slander his character. Whenever we do anything ungodly in the name of Christ, we disgrace the name of God. Using a Bible verse to justify our own sin tarnishes God's name. Claiming to be a Christian yet living as if God has no power to help us, treats God as less than he is.

There is a price to be paid for mocking the Lord's name. He will not stand for such disrespect. There is too much at stake. He will protect his reputation. If you have been careless in the way you represent God, seek his forgiveness immediately and begin to show him the respect he deserves.

September 13

God's Day

Remember the Sabbath day by keeping it holy. Six days you shall labor and do all your work, but the seventh day is a Sabbath to the LORD your God. On it you shall not do any work, neither you, nor your son or daughter, nor your manservant or maidservant, nor your animals, nor the alien within your gates. For in six days the LORD made the heavens and the earth, the sea, and all that is in them, but he rested on the seventh day. Therefore the LORD blessed the Sabbath day and made it holy.

Exodus 20:8-11

In Old Testament days, the Sabbath was Saturday, the last day of the week. God himself set an example for his people to have one day of rest after six days of labor. Was God tired after having created the universe? Of course not, but he insisted that his people stop working long enough to focus on him regularly, so he established the Sabbath. The New Testament church celebrated God's day on Sunday, the first day of the week, in honor of the day Jesus was raised from the dead.

Why do we need a Sabbath? For at least three reasons. First, we need a regular time set aside to focus on worshiping God. We honor God by stepping out of the fast lane and taking time to worship him. Second, we need the break for our bodies, minds, and spirits. We do ourselves no favors by pushing ourselves to the point of breakdown. Third, we need a regular time to check our priorities. In the brisk pace of our daily activities we can neglect the things that are really important. The Lord's day is a good time to stop and evaluate the way we are living, and to make necessary adjustments in our attitudes. "Keeping the Sabbath day holy" means to set it aside and dedicate it to God. Although we look at it as something we do for God, the truth is that observing a day of rest every week has enormous benefits for *us*. How do you observe the Sabbath? Is it just like any other day to you? Ask God to help you to keep the Sabbath holy.

Honor Your Parents

Honor your father and your mother, so that you may live long in the land the LORD your God is giving you.

Exodus 20:12

Depending on what kind of parents you have, you'll find this fifth commandment easy or difficult to follow. Honoring your parents means treating them with respect whether or not they've earned it. That's not exactly the way we do things these days, is it? You've heard the saying, "If you want respect, you have to earn it." Yet God offers no exception clause here; he simply says to honor your parents.

If your parents are loving, kind, and fair, you'll want to return their consideration. If they are cold, critical, even abusive, you are to honor them nonetheless. Does that mean you agree with the way they do things? Of course not. Does it mean you respect the way they live? No. It means you honor them because God loves them. Showing respect to them is an act of obedience to God rather than an act of submission to them. You are treating them as Christ would. If you no longer have contact with your parents, or if they have died, this means treating their reputation or their memory with integrity by speaking about them respectfully.

God understood that this is asking a lot in some cases. Perhaps that's why he attached a promise to this command. It's not always easy, but doing the right thing comes with its own rewards, including a heart free from guilt, anger, and bitterness. Obedience to the fifth commandment brings a double blessing, for both the parents and the children benefit when a son or daughter shows honor no matter what.

September 15

Murder

You shall not murder.

Exodus 20:13

God is clear about the evil of murder. The Bible says that we do not have the right to take revenge (Deuteronomy 32:35; Hebrews 10:30). Before you conclude that surely this is one commandment you'll never break, let's take a closer look at it. In his Sermon on the Mount, Jesus shed light on the Law that the Jews had worked long and hard to keep to the letter. Imagine what went through the minds of the pious Pharisees when Jesus said anyone who harbored anger in his heart toward another was guilty of murder. That meant that they, as well as each one of us, would be guilty. At the root of every murder there is anger, whether it is anger at oneself or at the victim. Few people reach a point so desperate that they actually take a life, but Jesus tells us to deal with anger at the very outset, long before it reaches such a point.

The saddest thing about murder is its finality. No matter how repentant the killer, there's no bringing the victim back. How many suicides happen because the person thought there was no hope? Maybe the next day everything would have changed, but now it's too late.

Rather than skimming over this commandment in the assumption that it doesn't apply, give it some serious thought. Are you holding on to anger against someone? Against yourself? God wants to remove it so your heart is free to enjoy the life he wants you to have.

Sexual Purity

You shall not commit adultery.

Exodus 20:14

Sex is usually associated with pleasure, not pain. God created sex. He designed it to be a good thing. But why are there so many painful side effects to this God-given pleasure? When we abuse our privileges, we are inviting disaster. That is the problem with the popular view of sex. Most people don't see the big picture. In today's culture we are told that sex is for the moment, that there are no aftereffects, and there need be no strings attached. The important thing is that the two people involved are both willing partners.

Adultery (having an intimate relationship with someone other than your marriage partner) is much more than a physical act. It is betraying the trust and commitment that is the foundation of marriage. Entering a sexual relationship with anyone outside of marriage leads only to heartache. There is a huge cost involved, one that is not always clear until it is too late. Adultery hurts everyone involved. The circle of pain extends much larger than the two people involved in the act. Sex was meant to bring union; but adultery destroys trust and leaves division. Sex was designed to bring joy; adultery causes intense sorrow. Proverbs 7:23 warns that adultery can cost you your life. The scars that adultery leaves remain until the grave.

The Ten Commandments are hard, but Jesus was even harder when it comes to adultery. In fact, he declared that desiring in your heart someone who is married, or someone other than your own spouse, is adultery whether or not you actually get physically involved.

We have been warned. God has made it abundantly clear that using sex in ways God did not intend invites disastrous consequences. Now is the time to heed the warning and decide to remain sexually pure. The rewards for keeping sex within marriage are worth the effort.

September 17

God's Word for Thieves

You shall not steal.

Exodus 20:15

Stealing, whether it involves something large or small, reveals a character flaw. It demonstrates a selfish disregard for what belongs to others. It shows a preference for taking shortcuts rather than working for what you want. Stealing reveals self-centeredness—an inclination for satisfying your own desires at the expense of others. Taking what belongs to someone else violates them. It demeans them. It also comes at great risk. If your theft is discovered, you stand to lose your reputation. Others will no longer trust you. It could cost you a relationship.

Theft comes in many forms. Gossip robs other people's privacy; it can even destroy their reputation. Criticism takes away another person's sense of self-worth. Anger directed toward others steals their joy. What makes us want to take away from others in order to benefit ourselves? We may justify our thievery by telling ourselves we deserve what we took from someone else. We may feel that we are needy and that the other person can afford the loss. But is that really true? Don't we simply want what we want? Meanwhile, we grow more and more calloused to the needs of others.

Have you been stealing from others without realizing it? Are there ways you've been seeking to better yourself at the expense of someone else? Ask God to give you a healthy respect for what is yours and for what is not. When you take time to recount the many ways God has blessed you, you'll be less inclined to desire things God has given others.

Lies

You shall not give false testimony against your neighbor.

Exodus 20:16

A person's reputation is a priceless treasure. Take away his money, and he will still have his good name. Remove her possessions, and she will still have her character. But damage someone's reputation, and you have taken away something extremely precious.

How do you steal someone's reputation? By jumping to conclusions about the motives behind his actions. By passing along a rumor about her. By taking a kernel of truth about the person and distorting it to leave the wrong impression. There seems to be a need deep within us to make ourselves look better by bringing down others. We feel threatened when someone else is smarter, wealthier, more talented, or better looking than we are, so we try to find and expose any flaw that we can. This sin is rooted in insecurity. The ironic part is that whenever we lie about another person, we are hurting ourselves. Jesus explained that God will treat us by the same standard that we apply to others (Luke 6:37–38). Therefore, we should treat others in the very same way we want them to treat us.

If you are tempted to leave a false impression about someone, stop to consider why this person threatens you. Think about your motives. Ask God, who loves truth and hates lies, to help you give that person the benefit of the doubt. Assume the best, the way you would want others to do for you. In doing so, you will save two reputations.

the Commandments

September 19

Contentment

You shall not covet your neighbor's house. You shall not covet your neighbor's wife, or his manservant or maidservant, his ox or donkey, or anything that belongs to your neighbor.

Exodus 20:17

Be satisfied! One of the worst things that can happen to you is to become dissatisfied with what God has given you. To *covet* is to long for something that someone else has. Perhaps your friend has something you don't have (it could be anything: a relationship, a material thing, a talent), and you are envious. You want what your friend has. The more you think about it, the more you want it! After a while, jealousy consumes you, and all you can think about is what you don't have. The longer you dwell on this, the more miserable you become. Regardless of how many good things you do have, it doesn't matter because you lack the thing you really want.

Coveting is not only self-centered; it is a sign of ingratitude to God. Envy is a waste of time and effort. It turns our focus to what we don't have and away from the things God wants to give us. We usually fail to consider that the very thing we are yearning for would ruin us. How often do we long for something, only to thank God later that he didn't give it to us! God is blessing us in ways he knows are best for us, but we waste our energy pining for what he is giving someone else.

The real command here is to trust God. Trust that he loves you. Trust that he wants what is best for you. Trust that he knows what you can handle. If you plant this truth firmly in your heart, there will be no need to look jealously over the fence at what your neighbor has.

thoughts Chapter 18 odly living

Chapter 18
Thoughts on Godly Living

What does it mean to live a godly life? What does a godly life look like? Let's say you've made it your goal to live a godly life; how do you go about it? Do you find the nearest monastery, take a vow of silence, and spend the rest of your days in prayer and solitude? You could do that. Or you could find someone you consider to be a godly person and imitate everything that dear saint does. Maybe you could tote a huge Bible around everywhere, smile serenely, and address everyone as "my child." How about getting a conservative haircut and wearing only T-shirts with Christian slogans? We're digressing, aren't we?

Living a godly life is a lofty goal, yet Jesus said he wants us to be perfect. That's right—perfect (Matthew 5:48). He didn't say he wanted us to act perfect; his desire is for us to be perfect. But isn't that impossible? Not according to the Scriptures (Philippians 4:13). As we take a look at what it means to live a godly life, keep in mind that godliness begins in the heart. Godliness is not a set of rules to be followed or a religion to adopt. Godliness grows out of an intimate, life-changing relationship with God. For the next couple of weeks, we'll delve into several passages from both the Old and New Testaments to see what the Bible has to say about living the way Christ would have us live.

thou ... uing

September 20

Help to Pray

In the same way the Spirit also helps our weakness; for we do not know how to pray as we should, but the Spirit Himself intercedes for us with groanings too deep for words.

Romans 8:26 (NASB)

Sometimes life becomes so complicated and problems become so bewildering that we aren't even sure how we ought to pray about them. We want the best for ourselves and our friends, and yet we're not always sure what God's best would be. Would it *really* be best if our friend got that job, or made that team, or took that trip? We're not sure. What if we ask God to give something to our friend that goes against God's will? God has an answer for that.

God has given each Christian his Holy Spirit, and God's Spirit always knows God's will. As we pray, the Spirit will guide us to ask for what God wants to give. At times we'll be at a loss to know what to pray. We won't even be able to put our prayer into words. Yet the Holy Spirit will take our groanings and translate them into an effective prayer.

When you don't know what to pray for someone, pray anyway. You may need to be quiet and allow God to speak to you first. It may be that you need to let God put thoughts and prayers into your mind so that you can pray. Perhaps you can only groan in anguish over a friend's suffering. Whatever it is you feel you need to do, begin praying and ask the Holy Spirit to guide you. Remember that God doesn't need your words to know your heart.

Loyalty to God

Though he slay me, yet will I hope in him.

Job 13:15

How deep does your loyalty to God go? Is it shallow? You trust God, but only if he doesn't ask you to make any sacrifices. Is your loyalty to God mediocre? You'll tolerate a little discomfort for the sake of your faith, but there's a pretty clear line in the sand, and you won't go beyond that. Or is your loyalty deep? No matter what happens or what God asks of you, you'll stay faithful to him.

Of all the heroes in the Bible, Job stands out as a model of faithfulness in the midst of adversity. We all experience tragedy of some kind in our lifetime. But not like Job. Everything happened to Job! He was a loving father; his children were killed. He was a generous man; he lost all of his possessions. He was a loyal friend; his friends turned on him. He was a hard worker; he lost his health. Even his wife lost hope. When he could have used some real encouragement, she told him to curse God and die. But Job didn't curse God; he didn't even get angry or blame God for his predicament. Instead, he uttered the greatest loyalty statement in human history: "Though he slay me, yet will I hope in him." Job is so famous for his perseverance that to this day even non-Christians speak of "the patience of Job."

Job's loyalty to God ran as deep as loyalty can go. In spite of disaster after disaster, Job refused to turn his back on God. On a scale of "one to Job," how deep is your loyalty? If it's on the shallow end, don't be discouraged. Take it as a sign that you don't yet know God as you should. Job could trust God the way he did because he knew him so well. Keep getting to know God better, and ask him to help you trust him more and more, regardless of your circumstances.

thoughts on godly living

A Gentle Whisper

The LORD said, "Go out and stand on the mountain in the presence of the LORD, for the LORD is about to pass by."

Then a great and powerful wind tore the mountains apart and shattered the rocks before the LORD, but the LORD was not in the wind. After the wind there was an earthquake, but the LORD was not in the earthquake. After the earthquake came a fire, but the LORD was not in the fire. And after the fire came a gentle whisper. When Elijah heard it, he pulled his cloak over his face and went out and stood at the mouth of the cave.

Then a voice said to him, "What are you doing here, Elijah?"

1 Kings 19:11-13

Sometimes we look for God in the wrong places. We assume there has to be a hundred-voice choir singing before we can hear from God. We look for God in thunder and lightning, trumpets and billowing smoke. That's not always God's way. God can speak through fire or earthquakes or any way he chooses, but he knows we're really listening when we hear him whisper. The hardest thing to do sometimes is to be quiet and listen. We don't like silence. We'd rather be doing something than sitting still, so we immerse ourselves in noise and activity, then we wonder why we don't hear from God. God should not have to shout in order to be heard. He is God; he shouldn't have to compete with the other noises in our lives.

King David, who's known as a man after God's own heart, knew the secret of silence. As a boy, he spent many hours in solitude, listening to God's voice while the sheep grazed in the meadows. His advice? "Be still before the LORD and wait patiently for him" (Psalm 37:7).

We mistakenly assume God is not pleased with us unless we're active, so we're always looking for things we can do for God. We confuse stillness with idleness. Idleness is doing nothing; spending quiet time with God is doing something. If we want to hear from God, we need to stop making so much noise. We must stop our activity long enough to listen for his whisper. If we're quiet, we'll hear it.

Good News

For, "Everyone who calls on the name of the Lord will be saved."

How, then, can they call on the one they have not believed in? And how can they believe in the one of whom they have not heard? And how can they hear without someone preaching to them? And how can they preach unless they are sent? As it is written, "How beautiful are the feet of those who bring good news!"

Romans 10:13-15

We learn early in our Christian life that salvation is a free gift, available for the asking (Ephesians 2:8). Yet we all know some people whom we consider too far gone even for God. We don't bother telling them about Jesus because we're convinced that they're not interested. Could it be that the only thing standing between our lost friends and salvation is the fact that we've not told them the good news?

God is the only one who really knows a person's heart. We don't know what they are like behind the mask they may be wearing. That's why it's important that we obey when God tells us to share the good news of Christ, no matter what outcome we anticipate. No doubt we'd be surprised at the people who would accept God's salvation if only it were presented to them!

If God is leading you to share your faith with an unlikely candidate, do it now. Don't wait for someone else to go and tell them. You go. Perhaps you, yourself, were once a long shot for God's kingdom. Aren't you glad that God didn't consider *you* a hopeless case?

thou   iving

September 24

What You Set Your Mind On

Those who live according to the sinful nature have their minds set on what that nature desires; but those who live in accordance with the Spirit have their minds set on what the Spirit desires.

Romans 8:5

The poster in the elementary school classroom reads like this: I can do it if I set my mind to it! In other words, if I continue to concentrate on that spelling list, I'll learn to spell the words. If I continue to focus on the math facts, I'll memorize the times table. The poster is right. Setting your mind on something means opening your mind to regular input from that source. That's great if the source is a good one, such as spelling or math, or the things the Bible teaches (love, truth, peace). But what if you're repeatedly subjecting your mind to something evil? You will internalize whatever it is that your mind is taking in. You'll form values and attitudes based on the input you allow into your mind.

The world is obsessed with proving there's no connection between the sinful practices we observe through literature, television, and movies and the resulting escalation in sinful lifestyles and crimes of violence. That's not only nonsense, it's nonbiblical! The apostle Paul understood the connection between what we allow into our minds and the way we live. He realized it is critical for Christians to focus on the right things. Paul divided everything into two categories. He said some things belong to the sinful nature and others belong to the Spirit. The category that dominates your thoughts will dominate your life.

Don't be naïve. Don't be cavalier and assume it's safe to dabble in sin without being affected. Pornography, movies, and songs that elevate sexual deviance, crime, and violence—these do much more than entertain you. They entice you into evil. Be smart and take control of what's going into your brain. Set your mind on those things God's Spirit desires.

God's Purpose for You

For when David had served God's purpose in his own generation, he fell asleep.

Acts 13:36

You have one life to live. It can only be invested once. How you invest your life is up to you. If you spend your time pursuing your own goals and ambitions, your life will bear testimony to how you sought to fulfill your dreams. If you live your life trying to please other people, your life will be a reflection of the plans that others made for you. However, if you seek to fulfill every purpose God has in mind for you, your life will be a tribute to the glory of God.

David became king of Israel in a difficult time. The Philistines had badly defeated Israel and killed the previous king. The nations close to Israel were looking for opportunities to take advantage of them. Even the city of Jerusalem was controlled by David's enemies. David's own people were divided between the north and the south. Some did not want David as their king. David inherited a lot of headaches along with his crown, but he trusted that God had made him king for a reason.

David set about to carry out every purpose God had for him. He defeated his enemies. He united his people. He encouraged his nation to worship the one, true God. By the time David reached old age, Israel had achieved a measure of greatness that it has never reached again. When David died, an old man, he was confident that he had completed everything God desired of him. The result? God received glory in the accomplishments of his nation, Israel. As for David, he is known to this day as a man after God's own heart.

You are at a perfect point to decide where to invest your life. God has plans for you. He wants to use your life in ways that will make a significant difference, not only now, but for eternity. As you make important educational, career, and life choices, let God set your agenda; then follow it carefully.

thoughts on godly living

God's Plans

"For I know the plans I have for you," declares the LORD, *"plans to prosper you and not to harm you, plans to give you hope and a future."*

Jeremiah 29:11

No one knows you like God does. He's known about you since before time began. He was present at your birth, and he's been intimately acquainted with every detail of your life right up until now. He's aware of your weaknesses as well as your strengths. He knows your fears and your joys. He knows how to make your life fulfilling and how to make it really count for something. That's why he has a plan for you. He didn't create you, then abandon you to figure out life as you go along. He loves you far too much for that!

God has a perfect plan for your life. It's tailored just for you. It matches the things he's building into your character right now. The plan he has for you is not the same as his plans for your friends. All of your experiences, both good and bad, fit into his plan. The promises he has made to you and the things he has taught you are part of his design for your life.

How tragic to live your life and accomplish all of your own goals, yet never discover what could have been if you had sought God's direction! Be sure to spend time consulting the Master in your decisions. He will show you options you never considered. You will have no regrets when you allow God to direct your steps, for his path leads to abundant life (John 10:10).

Seek God September 27

"You will seek me and find me when you seek me with all your heart."

Jeremiah 29:13

Have you ever wondered what life was like before everything became instant? Before computers, microwaves, and remote controls? Previous generations were not used to having their needs met immediately. Most things took time and hard work. We, on the other hand, are accustomed to convenience at our fingertips. Unfortunately, we can subconsciously transfer this mind-set to our relationships as well. We want to be respected, or trusted, right away—even before we prove we are respectable or trustworthy. We put pressure on friendships that have not had enough time to develop. Worst of all, we treat God as though he were at our beck and call. We treat him almost like a genie that we summon whenever we're in need.

It's crucial to understand that God comes to us on his terms, not ours. We must learn to spend the time necessary in God's Word and in prayer, or we will never truly know him. When we condition ourselves to stay focused as we seek out God, when we block out the distractions and concentrate solely on our time with him, then we will experience God. God will honor our search with his presence, and we'll know him in ways that we never knew before.

Whenever you feel as though God is far away, consider whether you've been truly seeking him, or just living under the assumption that he's as close as your next distress call. Have you been spending enough time in prayer? Studying the Scriptures? Going to church? God has provided many ways to hear from him. All you need is a willing heart.

No Condemnation!

Therefore, there is now no condemnation for those who are in Christ Jesus.

Romans 8:1

Paul knew something about condemnation. He had been responsible for the torturous deaths of devout Christians, including the martyr Stephen. Others he had condemned to imprisonment. Now, as a Christian, Paul had to live forever with the memories of what he'd done. No matter how many good things he did for the sake of Jesus Christ, Paul could never undo the treacherous acts he'd committed as a zealous, but misguided, Pharisee. How could he live with himself? How could he stand the shame that he'd been such a sinner? There was only one way: Paul understood God's heart. The great news for Christians is that God does not condemn the repentant sinner. Salvation through Jesus Christ wipes away the guilt and shame of even the most hardened rebel. Once we repent of our sin and confess it to God, he throws it away. He doesn't hold it against us; as far as God is concerned, it never happened.

Yet, why does guilt so often haunt us? Why do we do so many things motivated by a guilty conscience? Feelings of guilt for things God has already forgiven do not come from God. They come from Satan. Guilt comes from misunderstanding who God really is. God dealt sin a fatal blow on the cross, so that it has no mastery over us. He is that powerful. Even sin is under his authority. That's why we can live free from guilt—not because we're so good but because God in his mercy chooses to make us spotless and blameless.

If you've been carrying the weight of guilt and shame over something you've done, now is the time to take it to God. Confess your sin to him, leave it with Jesus, and walk away from it. Experience the truth that Paul understood, and take joy in the reality that you are clean, pure, and forgiven in God's sight.

Witnesses

"But you will receive power when the Holy Spirit comes on you; and you will be my witnesses in Jerusalem, and in all Judea and Samaria, and to the ends of the earth."

Acts 1:8

He could have sent a host of angels to proclaim salvation from the highest mountains. He could have written his saving message across the sky with the clouds. He could have sent fire, or shouted out the good news with thunder from heaven. But these are not God's way. His plan is for people like you to be witnesses to his love. Quietly, like a pebble thrown into a pond, his people are to spread the news of his saving grace. As we are obedient to share his message, the circle grows and grows.

We must understand that God doesn't use us because we're his only option. He offers us a tremendous privilege when he invites us to be his witnesses. Nor does God intend for us to share the gospel on our own strength. He enables us, through his Holy Spirit, to have a part in his divine purpose of drawing people to himself. His Spirit prompts us to spread the good news. His Spirit fills us with power, so we see amazing things happen when we obey his prompting.

Do you sense God's Holy Spirit leading you to be an ambassador for Christ? Perhaps he is prompting you to tell your own salvation story to a friend who is searching. It could be he's leading you to pack your bags and go on a mission trip. Maybe God is calling you to prepare for a full-time career in the ministry. Be sensitive to the ways the Spirit of God leads you, and trust that he will empower you to obey his leading.

thoughts on Godly Living

September 30

Separation

Surely the arm of the Lord is not too short to save,
*   nor his ear too dull to hear.*
But your iniquities have separated
*   you from your God;*
your sins have hidden his face from you,
*   so that he will not hear.*

Isaiah 59:1-2

You pray . . . no answer. You pray again . . . silence. You pray harder. You pray longer . . . nothing. Doesn't God love you? Of course he does. When it seems as though God is far away, remember first of all that he loves you. That will never change. Second, understand that he wants what is best for you, so his answer may be "no," or it may be "yes, but not now." The silence may also indicate that you've drifted away from God and that the relationship needs to be restored before you will hear from him again.

Since the time of Adam and Eve, sin has separated us from God. When we cling to sin and refuse to seek God's forgiveness, God will not listen to our prayers. God is pure. He is holy; he will not overlook blatant disobedience and continue as if nothing has happened (Isaiah 1:13–16). God seeks a repentant heart before he will listen to our requests in prayer.

Always be sensitive to the condition of your heart. If your prayers seem to go unheard, that's your cue to examine your life. Is there a sinful attitude or behavior that you've known was wrong, yet you refused to let it go? If there is, repent of it immediately. Confess it to God. Don't expect God to pour out his blessings as long as you cling to your sin. Thank God for his silence because it highlighted your need to seek his forgiveness. Get rid of the sin and enjoy your relationship with God once again.

Not One

He saw that there was no one,
  and he was appalled that there was no one to intercede;
so his own arm worked salvation for him,
  and his own righteousness sustained him.

Isaiah 59:16

It never hurts to run a pronoun check on yourself when you pray. What's a pronoun check? It's when you check to see how often the words *I* and *me* come up in your prayer compared to *you*, *he*, *she*, and *they*. If you find your prayers are heavy on the first person and light on the second and third persons, you'll want to adjust the way you pray.

Prayer is much more than asking for things. It's thanking God for what he's already given you and praising him for who he is. That's where the *you* comes in. Prayer is also your opportunity to intervene on behalf of other people. As you pray, think about your family, friends, classmates, and coworkers. If you're sensitive, the Holy Spirit will prompt you to pray specifically for several individuals. He may bring to your mind a friend who doesn't know Christ or a classmate who's searching for meaning in life.

Isaiah spoke of a nation that was disobeying God. God was preparing to punish them, but mercifully, he looked for one faithful person who would intervene and pray for Israel. If he could find just one believer lifting up the nation in prayer, God would have reason to withhold his judgment. Sadly, there wasn't even one intercessor.

You may assume your prayers for others make no difference to God. Why would God show mercy to someone else because of your prayers? The answer to that is a mystery. Only God knows why, but he has shown mercy to those who deserved judgment, not because of them, but because of the faithful prayers of an intercessor. This truth may not be news to you at all. Perhaps long before you knew Christ, your parents or your grandparents or your friends were praying for you. God answered their prayers, and the rest is history. Be sure your prayer circle includes more people than just you and God. Be sensitive to the needs around you, and be faithful to pray for others as God leads you.

thou... ...iving

October 2

Living and Active

The word of God is living and active. Sharper than any double-edged sword, it penetrates even to dividing soul and spirit, joints and marrow; it judges the thoughts and attitudes of the heart.

Hebrews 4:12

The Bible is unlike any other book ever written or ever to be written. In fact, *book* is an inadequate description of the Bible. The dictionary describes a book as a printed work on sheets of paper, bound together within two covers. The Bible is that, but it's so much more! The Bible consistently tops best-seller lists. For centuries, even unbelievers have studied the Bible as in intriguing piece of literature. They know it contains everything good literature should include: love, romance, mystery, murder, intrigue, and advice on everything from parenting to prosperity. But what is it that sets the Bible apart from other literature? Christians know the answer to that question.

Why can Christians read the same verses on the same pages day after day, year after year, and still get something new out of them? Because we aren't just reading a book. We are interacting with almighty God through his written Word.

Every word in every chapter, from Genesis to Revelation, is there by God's inspiration. When you read your Bible, the Holy Spirit will apply the verses you read to your life. As you read about holiness, the Spirit will make you aware of areas that you've not given over to Christ. As you read about love, the Spirit will assure you of God's love for you. You will find encouragement in God's Word, just when you need it the most. Don't neglect your Bible reading just because you've read it before or because you think you already know what it says. God's Word is alive, and it can change your life today if you let it.

Without Faith

And without faith it is impossible to please God, because anyone who comes to him must believe that he exists and that he rewards those who earnestly seek him.

Hebrews 11:6

One thing that keeps many people from coming to know Christ is—are you ready for this?—they're too nice. They live moral lives. They give to charity. They treat others well. They may even go to church and read the Bible on occasion. This gives them false security. They assume that God must be pleased with them because they are good people. They really only lack one thing, but it's the one thing they need to please God—faith.

The Bible says you can live the cleanest life possible; you can do all sorts of good deeds; you can even memorize the Bible from cover to cover, but without faith you will not please God. The Pharisees did all of these things, yet Jesus was anything but pleased with them! What does it mean to have faith? According to the last part of the verse, faith means you not only believe God exists, but you also earnestly seek after him. It's not enough to be a good person or even to acknowledge that God exists. The Bible indicates that the demons know God exists, but that is not enough (James 2:19). They don't put their trust in him.

The good news is this: God promises to reward those who earnestly seek him. If you trust God, he'll provide for your needs. If you seek his will, he'll guide you into his perfect will. If you seek his love, he'll pour out love unlike anything you've ever experienced. You hold the key that unlocks everything God has for you. It's your faith.

October 4

Discipline

And you have forgotten that word of encouragement that addresses you as sons:

"My son, do not make light of the Lord's discipline,
*   and do not lose heart when he rebukes you,*
because the Lord disciplines those he loves,
*   and he punishes everyone he accepts as a son."*

Hebrews 12:5-6

Living things grow. Plants grow. Animals grow. People grow. Every parent's main job is to help their children reach maturity, so they see that their young ones get enough food, enough rest, and enough exercise to stay healthy and to grow stronger. You have a heavenly Father who wants to help you reach spiritual maturity. Therefore, he will lead you to do all the things that help you grow as a Christian. He'll invite you to spend time with him through prayer and through his Word. He'll strengthen you through healthy relationships and through wholesome activity that brings emotional rest.

An important part of growing up is to learn where danger lies. When a child is young, he can't perceive danger as well as his parents do. That's why his parents set limits and discipline him when he breaks those limits—to protect him from his own inexperience. Likewise, God disciplines his sons and daughters because he loves us and wants to protect us from ourselves!

How can you tell if you're experiencing God's hand of discipline or if you're just going through bad circumstances? Examine your life. Have you been taking part in things that could hurt you? For example, if you were growing increasingly dishonest and now you're ashamed because you've been found out, perhaps God is helping you break this habit before it gets you into really big trouble. It could be that you allowed pride to motivate you, and God has let you experience a taste of failure to help you rearrange your priorities. However God gets your attention, the important thing to remember is that his discipline is a sign of his love for you. No matter how unpleasant discipline is, its goal is not to harm you but to help you grow. Thank your heavenly Father that he loves you enough to be involved in your growth.

Worldly Wisdom
October 5

Do not deceive yourselves. If any one of you thinks he is wise by the standards of this age, he should become a "fool" so that he may become wise. For the wisdom of this world is foolishness in God's sight.

1 Corinthians 3:18

Are you familiar with A *Tale of Two Cities* by Charles Dickens? The opening paragraph in that novel contains Dickens's famous lines: "It was the best of times, it was the worst of times, it was the age of wisdom, it was the age of foolishness . . . it was the season of Light, it was the season of Darkness." Doesn't that sound like our world today? There is so much affluence and prosperity in our world, yet millions still languish in poverty. There is so much knowledge, yet ignorance is still prevalent. We've managed to travel to outer space, yet we don't know how to keep peace with those on our own globe. Dickens was describing society in the year 1775—over two centuries ago. Times haven't changed much! Two hundred years from now, historians will marvel at how little we knew! One thing will remain unchanged, however. True wisdom, then as now, will not depend on technology, or learning, or worldly wisdom. Since the beginning of time, true wisdom has been found only in God. That truth will never change.

After two centuries, shouldn't we be more civilized than we were in Dickens' day? Yet we seem to be more confused and hostile than ever. There is a lot of good in society, but there is also much evil. Why is that? Over two thousand years ago, Paul warned of the danger when the world sets its own standard for morality. No matter how wise we think we are, our best thinking is foolishness to God.

There are a lot of opinions out there on what's right and what's wrong—on what's permissible and what's unacceptable. You're a young person; to whom should you listen? How will you know what to do? Jimmy Carter, former American president and a devout Christian, said, "We must adjust to changing times and still hold to unchanging principles." It makes no difference whether it's the first century, the eighteenth century, or the twenty-first century, God's principles remain the same. If you want wise direction, bypass the world's "wisdom." Open your Bible. Don't get your wisdom from the world. Get it from the Word.

October 6

Far More

Now to him who is able to do immeasurably more than all we ask or imagine, according to his power that is at work within us.

Ephesians 3:20

What dreams do you have for your life? Do you plan to get an education, establish a career, get married, have children, buy a house? Those are great goals. But did you know God has even bigger plans for you? He wants to do great things through your life!

Some people talk about dreaming big dreams for God. They have it backwards. God has big dreams for us—far bigger than we can even imagine! That's why it's crucial to check with God before settling merely for what looks good to us. It's possible to become so focused on our plans that we miss out on what God has for us. For example, we may pursue our career as an end in itself, but God has big plans to use our career for his glory. Perhaps he'll use our skills in construction to help the homeless. Maybe he'll take us to the mission field to share Christ, along with our agricultural expertise. He might use our counseling knowledge to share his message of hope to those in crisis. Whatever his plan is, we can count on one thing—it's *big!* Bigger than anything we could come up with.

As you're dreaming your dreams and making your plans, remember this truth: God has far more in store for your life than you could possibly know. Be open to the many ways he wants to use your life. Your own plans may look good to you, but they might, in fact, be second best. Never settle for what is merely good. God wants you to enjoy what is best. Trust *his* plans. Trust *his* timing. He has plans for you that will amaze you!

Lessons from the Lord's Prayer

Prayer is one of the most important things a Christian will ever do. In prayer, we talk directly with the God of the universe. He speaks to us, and we tell him our concerns. It's not difficult to pray, yet few Christians claim to pray as much as they should.

It is interesting that during all the time the disciples spent with Jesus, they never asked him to teach them how to preach, even though he sent them out to preach throughout the countryside. They never asked him for instructions on how to teach or how to perform miracles or how to cast out demons, even though they would have to do all these things. Their one request for instruction was for Jesus to teach them how to pray (Luke 11:1). Something about the way Jesus prayed compelled the disciples to want to be like him. Some of the most profound times in Jesus' life happened right after he prayed.

When Jesus taught his disciples the Lord's Prayer, he was not giving them a prayer to memorize and recite every time they prayed. He was giving them a model for their own prayers. As you study the model prayer that Jesus gave, compare it with the prayers you offer to God. What can you learn from the way Jesus prayed that can help you to be more effective in your own praying?

October 7

Our Father

This is how you should pray:

"'Our Father in heaven,
hallowed be your name.'"

Matthew 6:9

Everyone wants to be loved. God designed the family to be a source of love and encouragement. If you have a family that loves you and that is in your corner, you can take on life with confidence. But what if that isn't your experience? What if, to you, family means criticism, anger, and even abuse? There is another family that longs to love and to support you. It's your Christian family.

The Lord's Prayer opens with the words "Our Father." Jesus wants us to remember every time we pray that we have a heavenly Father who loves us unconditionally. The word *our* tells us that we are not alone: we are part of a family. We share our heavenly Father with every other believer. We have brothers and sisters in the spiritual family God has given us. Through them, we can find the strength and encouragement we need to face the ups and downs of life. Likewise, God has called us to love and to serve our Christian family members in the same way Jesus did (John 13:34).

If we pray with selfish motives, without concern for our fellow believers, the Bible says our prayers are of the devil (James 3:14–15). If we pray while we are angry and unforgiving toward other Christians, God will frown on our prayers (Matthew 5:22). We ought never to pray with only ourselves in mind. Every time we pray, God wants us to remember that we are a part of a family that is precious to him.

Our Father . . .

"'Our Father in heaven.'"

Matthew 6:9

If you want an enlightening experience, ask five or six people to describe their view of what God is like. You'll probably get five or six very different answers! One person may see God as a kindly old gentleman. Another may picture him as a harsh and demanding taskmaster. The Bible describes God as a loving father. He is not a hardened jail warden or an exacting slave driver. Nor is he a doddering old grandfather.

When you hear the term *father*, what comes to your mind? Without realizing it, you may equate God's character with the way you view your earthly father. Perhaps your father is nurturing, affectionate, and reliable. If so, you will probably see God that way too. Sadly, some fathers are harsh and critical, even cruel. Even fathers with the best of intentions are imperfect. They make mistakes. They have weak moments. If your father neglected you or did not express love toward you, you may tend to think that God is uncaring. When you go through hard times, you may assume it's futile to seek comfort from God. After all, why should he care? When you have a need, you might conclude, *There's no point in asking God. He won't provide for me.*

If your experience with your earthly father has been unpleasant, you may need to reverse your thinking. Rather than trying to fit God into your image of what a father is like, realize that God is the pattern for earthly fathers to follow. God loves his children perfectly. He's never too busy or too preoccupied or too self-centered to care about you. Also, because he loves you, he will discipline you. (It *is* possible to be too lenient as a parent.) God wants only what is best for you. Because he is all-powerful, God can provide everything you need to live a joyful, abundant life. In other words, he can afford it. Since God's love is unconditional, no matter how many times you blow it by sinning, you will always find forgiveness when you seek it. That's what God is like. That's the goal that human fathers strive toward. But even the best earthly father is only a pale reflection of the kind of heavenly Father you have. Spend time getting to know your Father in heaven. Allow him to love you as only he can. He wants so much for you to experience the peace and joy that he can give you.

October 9

In Heaven

" 'Our Father in heaven.' "

Matthew 6:9

Where is God when you pray? In another dimension? Above the clouds? Far away? What did Jesus mean when he said that his Father was "in heaven"? He did not mean God is up there somewhere where you can't reach him. When Jesus told his disciples to pray to their Father "in heaven," he was reminding them that God is not limited like we are. We should approach God much differently than we approach others. Other people, even our friends and family, are restricted by what they can, or will, do for us. When we speak to God, however, we talk with one who is loving, powerful, merciful, wise, holy, and righteous. When we speak to God, it is not like when we speak to our best friend. Our best friend is not eternal, ruling the universe, and preparing to judge humanity!

Think and meditate on God's greatness before you pray. Remember that nothing is impossible for God. Keep in mind that he is holy and righteous, so he will not overlook your sin. Remember that he is merciful and will forgive you when you ask. Remember also that he loves you more deeply than you can even imagine and that he will answer your prayers in his perfect love and wisdom, in the way that is best for you.

Don't be in a hurry to rush in and out of God's presence. When you pray, the knowledge that you are talking to almighty God should dramatically affect the way you conduct yourself.

Hallowed Be Your Name . . .

"'Our Father in heaven,
hallowed be your name.'"

Matthew 6:9

Names aren't what they used to be. In biblical times, parents gave their children names they hoped would reflect the child's character. They believed that knowing a person's name gave some insight into his or her personality. For example, when Jacob was born, he was grasping his twin brother, Esau, by the heel (Genesis 25:26). Because he was tripping up his brother, he was named Jacob, meaning "he grasps the heel," or "deceiver." True to his name, Jacob grew up to take advantage of his brother at every opportunity. In keeping with this practice of giving names describing character, people sometimes had their names changed after they became adults. When God came to Gideon, Gideon was hiding from his enemies. God referred to him as "valiant warrior!" (Judges 6:12 NASB). Was Gideon a valiant warrior at that time? No. But God intended to make him one.

With this cultural background in mind, we can see the importance in Jesus' words regarding God's name. Because God is perfectly holy, whenever we call on his name, we are acknowledging the sacredness of his character. The very name "Lord" was a reminder that the one we address is divine and worthy of our deepest reverence.

Jesus wants us to know that when we pray we are speaking to almighty God. If we realize this at the front end of our prayer, we'll be less inclined to ask him for anything that would dishonor his holy name. Furthermore, we'll understand why he will not help us achieve anything that would disgrace his name. A solid recognition of the perfect, holy character of our God leads naturally into the next phrase that Jesus gave us: "Your will be done."

LESSONS PRAYER

October 11

Your Will Be Done . . .

" 'Your kingdom come,
your will be done
on earth as it is in heaven.' "

Matthew 6:10

There are no arguments in heaven over obeying God's will. The angels don't spend weeks mulling over whether or not they'll do what God is telling them. They obey—immediately, completely, and cheerfully. If only people would do the same! We know God loves us and wants what's best for us: the cross proved that. And our problem is seldom that we don't know what to do; we usually know only too well what God desires. Too often we just don't want to do it! Some people spend a lot of time seeking God's will. The truth is, if they spent as much time doing what they already know God wants them to do, the rest would take care of itself.

Jesus reminds us to turn our gaze away from ourselves and outwards to the work God is doing around us. "Your kingdom come" is really a request that God would bring about his rule over every person on earth. Presently, not every person calls Jesus Lord, but one day everyone will (Philippians 2:10–11). Of course, we cannot pray earnestly for God to have his way over every other person's life if God is not the Lord of our own life. This prayer must begin with me. I have to ask, "Does God rule over *my* life?" If he does, then I should pray that he would have complete rule over my family, my neighbors, my classmates, and my friends, until everyone on the face of the earth obeys Jesus as Lord.

When we pray this prayer, we must be prepared to be part of God's answer. If God is to rule in our friend's life, God may want to use us to make her aware of his love. We will be Christ's ambassadors, working to expand God's kingdom wherever we go (2 Corinthians 5:20). Praying for God's kingdom to come is not enough: we must be prepared to get up on our feet and go out as Christ's messenger to those who have not yet claimed him as their Lord.

Daily Bread · · ·   October 12

" 'Give us today our daily bread.' "

Matthew 6:11

We know God can do big things when we ask, but we assume some requests are beneath him—too small to bother the Lord of the universe. Not so. Jesus used the example of bread to teach us this truth.

Bread was the most common element of a Jewish meal. Ordinary. They didn't always eat rich, elaborate feasts, but they had bread every day. To the disciples, daily bread represented the unspectacular. They'd seen Jesus heal disease, calm storms, and walk on water; they knew God could deliver the big-ticket items. But Jesus was telling them not to leave God out of the seemingly ordinary parts of life.

Praying every day for God to meet our needs does not annoy him—it pleases him. Asking for our daily bread also reminds us regularly that we rely on God for everything—not just the big things, but the everyday needs in life.

Don't ever worry that God will consider your needs too small for him. He loves you. He wants to take care of you whether you need a miracle or a piece of bread. Remember that everything in life comes from God. Don't forget to thank him today for meeting your needs.

LESSONS ... PRAYER

October 13

Forgive Us Our Sins . . .

" 'Forgive us our debts,
as we also have forgiven our debtors.' "

Matthew 6:12

What's your reaction when someone hurts you or mistreats you? Do you immediately start planning your revenge? The world has lots of phrases to describe this response: "I'll get you for that!" "One day you'll get yours!" "Don't get mad, get even!" That's the world's way of dealing with conflict. Jesus shows us a better way. It's called forgiveness. He calls on us to forgive those who offend us, just as God has forgiven us and continues to forgive our sins against him.

God promises us that we will be treated the same way we treat others (Matthew 7:2; Luke 6:37–38). That can be a welcome promise or a worrisome thought! If we're generous toward others, we'll experience God's generosity. If we refuse to forgive those who wrong us, God will not forgive our sins. Why would God do this? Because he loves us, and he refuses to let us live with sinful attitudes that will eventually destroy us. He wants to develop our character to match his own. God is also perfectly just. He won't treat us one way and yet allow us to treat others in a different way. The Lord's Prayer holds the reminder that if we hope to receive forgiveness and grace we must be willing to extend mercy to those who offend us.

If you are holding on to bitterness, refusing to forgive someone, review in your heart how God overlooked your sin when he made you his child. Now he asks you to do likewise and excuse the sin of your debtor. When you let go of a grudge, you will experience the joy and freedom that comes with forgiveness.

Lead Us Not into Temptation . . .

"'And lead us not into temptation,
but deliver us from the evil one.'"

Matthew 6:13

A time will come, or may have come already, when you find yourself facing intense temptation. You may be asked to compromise in the area of sex, lying, stealing, or gossiping. Others may pressure you to get into alcohol, drugs, or gambling. You may not have been looking for it, but suddenly the powerful voice of temptation is calling out to you, and you are on the edge of giving in.

God knows about the temptations we will face. He sees all that we, and others, are doing (Psalm 53:2). Knowing the dangers we will encounter, he can direct us around them, or away from them, and keep us safe. However, we must want to avoid temptation and evil. Sin is a serious thing; its goal is our destruction. Too often we like to get as close to temptation as we can without actually giving in. We think we'll be strong enough to pull back at the last minute. Then, to our dismay, we discover that temptation is not as easily resisted as we thought. Sin is a much more powerful foe than we realize.

When you pray, ask God to protect you from evil. Don't walk blindly through life, spiritually weak and unprepared for the temptations you will meet. Daily, ask God to keep you from situations that can overpower you. Ask him to guide you into his will and away from anything that could sidetrack you or destroy you. David prayed this with great sincerity (Psalms 23:4; 25:4–5; 27:1). Don't wait until you are hopelessly entangled in sin to ask God to help you. Ask him to deliver you from evil now, while there is still time to avoid disaster.

Lessons from the Psalms

Chapter 20

Lessons from the Psalms

The Psalms hold the mirror up to life itself. Life is not a flat line: it has its ups and downs. Everyone's life has times of victory and times of failure. There are times of celebration and times of mourning.

As you study the Psalms, you'll be able to relate to the words you're reading, because the Psalms come straight from the heart and soul of those who wrote them. David wrote many of the psalms; some were written in caves as he hid from a demented and dangerous enemy. Others were praise songs, composed during times of great joy and triumph.

Regardless of whether you're presently experiencing good times or bad, the Psalms have a message for you. They'll give you an example of what it means to love God in all situations and to trust him in spite of your circumstances. As you walk through the Psalms, you'll learn more about your own relationship with God.

Get ready for a time of personal growth as you spend some time in the Psalms.

Blessed Is the Man   October 15

Blessed is the man
  who does not walk in the counsel of the wicked
or stand in the way of sinners
  or sit in the seat of mockers.
But his delight is in the law of the LORD,
  and on his law he meditates day and night.
He is like a tree planted by streams of water,
  which yields its fruit in season
and whose leaf does not wither.
  Whatever he does prospers.

Psalm 1:1-3

It is no accident that some people consistently experience God's blessing on their lives and others do not. Is it because God loves some people more than others? You already know the answer to that one. What is the difference then? It all depends on people's choices.

The Bible says there are things we can do and things we can avoid doing that will determine God's blessings in our lives. One extremely important factor is the friends we choose. If we allow sinful people to influence us, we shouldn't be surprised when God doesn't bless our lives. It's impossible to spend prolonged time in the company of ungodly people without being affected by their sinful attitudes. Even if our motivation is to provide a positive influence on them, we need to have our eyes wide open and be extremely cautious of the dangers, or the influence will end up going the wrong way. When we sit down with mockers, it takes great effort to avoid being dragged into a cynical, sinful spirit ourselves.

On the other hand, if we choose the friends we know God wants us to have, we'll find our lives overflowing with blessings. As we spend time with those whose lives please God, we'll find strength and encouragement to live pure, meaningful lives ourselves. When we make the effort to seek direction from his Word, we'll not wander down dangerous roads that lead only to despair. We'll know where we're headed, and we won't be lured off the right path by others. God does not arbitrarily choose to bless one person and not another. We determine, by our own choices, whether we'll open our lives up to the good things God has in store for us.

Lesso Lessons from the Psalms salms

October 16

Big Prayers

Ask of me,
> *and I will make the nations your inheritance,*
> *the ends of the earth your possession.*

Psalm 2:8

Do you pray big or do you pray small? If you pray big, you understand what God is like. Powerful. Almighty. All-knowing. Eternal. If you pray small, could it be you're afraid God can't deliver? Think about the way you pray. If you never ask God for anything more than a good day, or for your friend's cold to get better, you're missing out on much of what God wants to do in your life! He wants to give you more than a good day. He wants to give you the ends of the earth! Don't doubt that God wants to do big things in your life. Pray with confidence. Pray with anticipation. If you pray little prayers, you'll get little answers.

As Paul reminded his friends in Ephesus, God is able to do "immeasurably more than all we ask or imagine" (Ephesians 3:20). That's a lot more than curing the sniffles. Jesus encourages his followers to step out in faith and ask. The more you understand who God is, the bigger your prayer life will grow. God is not a distant, untouchable being; he's more willing to be involved in your life than you might think. Jesus said, "For everyone who asks receives; . . . Which of you, if his son asks for bread, will give him a stone? Or if he asks for a fish, will give him a snake? If you, then, though you are evil, know how to give good gifts to your children, how much more will your Father in heaven give good gifts to those who ask him!" (Matthew 7:8–11).

If God hasn't been doing anything big in your life, it's not because he's not able. It may be that you simply haven't asked him. When you pray, go beyond vague, safe prayers, such as "Lord, be with me today." That one's a given. Think about the one to whom you're addressing your prayer. God is big! Don't be afraid to pray big!

All Day Long

Morning by morning, O LORD, you hear my voice;
  morning by morning I lay my requests before you
  and wait in expectation.

Psalm 5:3

After you've prayed, what you do next reveals what you really believe about God. When David prayed to God every morning, he didn't get up off of his knees and go about his day as if he'd never prayed. He waited to see how God answered his prayers. He watched in anticipation for the answer he knew would come. He prepared himself to obey whatever God asked him to do next. That's the difference between just saying prayers and truly praying. David began each day by talking with his Lord. For the rest of the day, he was aware of God's presence as he experienced God at work in his life.

If you pray in the morning for your unbelieving friend to become a Christian, but then don't share your faith with him when God gives you the opportunity, you've merely recited a prayer. You haven't really prayed. If you ask God in the morning to increase your faith, then don't look for the opportunities he'll give you to trust him, you don't understand what prayer really is. Prayer is not an isolated event. It's an ongoing activity that flows out of your relationship with God. If you don't understand this, you'll fail to make the connection between the events of your day and the things you prayed that morning. In other words, you'll be oblivious to God's activity in your life.

If you've been in the habit of reciting prayers instead of truly praying, you've been practicing a ritual, not enjoying a relationship. When God speaks to you in the morning, or when the Holy Spirit prompts you to pray for something, watch expectantly throughout the day for God's answer. Walking with God is not something you do for fifteen minutes each morning before getting on with your life. Walking with God is your life! It's an exciting adventure to be lived all day long!

Lessons from the Psalms

October 18

A Good Night's Sleep

I lie down and sleep;
I wake again, because the LORD sustains me.
I will not fear the tens of thousands
drawn up against me on every side.

Psalm 3:5-6

We're never more vulnerable than when we sleep. When we sleep, we let our guard down, and we're oblivious to what's happening around us. David uses the image of peacefully sleeping in the midst of a legion of enemies to show how trustworthy God is. David had so many people after him day and night, trying to take his life, he should have turned into an insomniac. On the contrary, he slept like a baby because his life was in God's hands. He was able to let his guard down because he was confident that God was watching over him. That's what trusting God means. Real trust doesn't say, "I trust you, Lord, as long as I'm aware of any danger around me, so I can fight against it." Real trust says, "I trust you, Lord, to take care of me, even when I don't know what's happening all around me."

It's our nature to think we're solely responsible for our own well-being, but trying to stand guard over our own lives is futile for two reasons. One: we're not always aware of the dangers around us. Two: even if we know what we're up against, we don't always have the power to do anything about it. That's where anxiety comes in. We fear what we don't know and what we can't control. We find it hard to sleep at night because we're preoccupied with our present situation or we're afraid of what tomorrow might bring. It's impossible for us to relax because we feel we're the only ones watching out for our own safety. We are spending needless hours tossing and turning. God wants to take over as night watchman and let us rest. When we learn to hand over our anxieties to God, as David did, and let him stand guard over our lives, we'll find the peace and security that lets us rest.

If you find yourself fretting about what's happening around you or worrying about tomorrow, take the night off. Get some sleep, and let God relieve you of your post. He's far more qualified for the job than you are.

David's Priority List   October 19

But I, by your great mercy,
*   will come into your house;*
in reverence will I bow down
*   toward your holy temple.*
Lead me, O LORD, in your righteousness
*   because of my enemies—*
*   make straight your way before me.*

Psalm 5:7-8

What does it take to have a close walk with God? The right priorities. David knew God better than most people. Let's take a look at his priority list:

To worship. David was a king, but he considered it his highest calling to honor God. David didn't merely go to the temple as a matter of ritual. He considered it a great privilege to be invited into the presence of holy God to worship him. David's psalms of praise bear testimony to the high priority he placed on praising God.

To confess his sins. David wasn't perfect; in fact, he committed some pretty major sins, including adultery and murder. However, he acknowledged his sins and humbly confessed them to God. He couldn't bear to be separated from God by his own sinfulness, so David made confession a priority as well.

To follow God's guidance. David was a bright man, a gifted leader, and an accomplished warrior, yet he consistently turned to God for guidance. He understood that life is too complicated for even the smartest person to figure out on his own, so he gave God's plans precedence over his own.

To seek God's protection. David had plenty of enemies and plenty to fear. He prayed daily for God's protection, and he relied on God for peace in spite of his tumultuous life. In answer to David's prayers, God guided him through many intensely dangerous situations.

To thank God. David's life was characterized by thankfulness. He recognized God as the source of every blessing in his life, and he developed a habit of thanking God regularly. The Book of Psalms is a record of David's grateful heart.

When you lay it out, it's not hard to see why David grew so close to God. Look at the things he valued the most: worship, forgiveness, wisdom, guidance, and gratitude. Do you want to know God better? Take David's priority list and make it yours as well.

Lessons from the Psalms

October 20

Better than Lions

The LORD is my shepherd, I shall lack nothing.

Psalm 23:1

According to the Scriptures, it's better to be a sheep than a lion. Lions are fierce and strong; sheep are weak and defenseless, but they don't have to fear for their safety. Lions are mighty hunters, yet it is the sheep that doesn't go hungry. That's because the sheep has something the lion doesn't have—a shepherd. The lion must depend upon its own strength and cunning; the sheep belongs to one who will lay down his very life for its safety. Psalm 34:10 observes: "The lions may grow weak and hungry, / but those who seek the LORD lack no good thing." In other words, even the strongest, most ambitious people may not always have all they need, but those who trust God to provide for them will have all their needs met and more.

God himself is the greatest security you have. No enemy can succeed against you when you are under God's care. You will never lose your way in life when God is the one guiding you. No crisis you face will be too difficult for God to overcome. It's all a matter of where you put your trust. Have you put your trust in prayer instead of putting it in God? Is your faith based on your religion? Do you put your faith in other Christians? Your church? These things are all part of your Christian life, but your ultimate trust should be in your Shepherd. God is the only one you can always depend on to meet your needs.

If you wander away from your Shepherd, you will miss out on what the Shepherd wants to give you. Even then, however, he will not abandon you (see Psalm 139:7–12). He is your Shepherd by choice—his choice (John 15:16) as well as yours (John 14:15). If you have drifted away from the Shepherd, he urges you to return to him today (Matthew 11:28–30). Under his care, you will find strength, purpose, and security.

Green Pastures

He makes me lie down in green pastures,
he leads me beside quiet waters.

Psalm 23:2

Some people will gladly run your life for you if you let them! Some people have a way of always bringing you down rather than building you up. They encourage you to get involved in destructive things. They take advantage of you. Their concern is what you can give them, not what they can give you.

There is another kind of friend. This friend actually cares about what's best for you. It may be a teacher, classmate, coach, teammate, pastor—anyone God brings alongside you to help you make smart choices. These friends are your "green pastures," your "quiet waters." They are God's provision for you. They will encourage you to slow down when you take on too much. They will challenge you to get busy when you're too idle! They care about you enough that they'll warn you when you're heading into danger.

The Christian life is not meant to be difficult. If you find that your Christian life is wearing you out and leaving you distressed, you have wandered away from the "green pastures" and "quiet waters" your Shepherd has prepared for you. God will see that you have all the spiritual help that you need. He knows exactly what you need and when you need it. He knows where he's leading you. He has placed people around you who will guide you along the best path. If you've been wandering in the wrong direction, return to the Shepherd. He wants to give you peace and rest.

Restoring Your Soul

He restores my soul.
He guides me in paths of righteousness
for his name's sake.

Psalm 23:3

Do you sometimes feel spiritually worn out? It can happen to anyone. Maybe you're carrying an unusually heavy load of problems. Perhaps you've been battling a nagging temptation, or you've been on the receiving end of unfair criticism. Whatever it is, it has beaten you down. Way down, deep within your soul, there's a weariness that you think you can't overcome.

Spiritual exhaustion can catch you by surprise. It seems invisible; you can't see it coming. It can happen so gradually that before you know it; you've become disoriented to God. Perhaps you've gotten so far from God that you're not sure you even care about spiritual things anymore. Your problems have distracted you from spending time with God as you used to, and now he seems like a stranger.

God can help you. God has a way of strengthening you at the deepest levels of your life. His Spirit searches out the most private corners of your mind to renew your thinking. Your Good Shepherd can lead you to people and to places where you'll be refreshed and energized. God may teach you something about himself that will give you a fresh excitement about being a Christian. He'll guide you back into a life that reflects his own righteousness. He'll give you a fresh start. The way he chooses to restore you is as unique as you are, but your Shepherd will revitalize your soul if you ask him. Don't be afraid to ask.

Shadows

Even though I walk
through the valley of the shadow of death,
I will fear no evil,
for you are with me;
your rod and your staff,
they comfort me.

Psalm 23:4

According to Webster, a shadow is the darkness cast by something cutting off light. It's an illusion. There's no substance to a shadow, but shadows can be terrifying because they play tricks on you. When you were a child, did you ever hide under your bedcovers to get away from the frightening shadows in your bedroom? When you turned on the light and the shadows disappeared, you saw that you had nothing to fear.

David's beautiful psalm about the Good Shepherd is one of the Bible's most well-known passages. The Twenty-third Psalm is probably read or recited as much out of church as in it. Why? Because it gives an inspiring message of hope in a way that all of us can understand. David did what every good writer does; he wrote about what he knew. He knew lots about life's shadows, and he was intimately acquainted with shepherding; he masterfully joined the two together to pen some of the most comforting words of hope ever written. David faced many dangers in his life—times when he didn't know if he'd live out the day; times when he was misunderstood, threatened, and attacked; times when the shame of his own sin sent him into the depths of despair. Through it all, he experienced the unwavering presence of God. Just as he used to lead his sheep through the valleys, David's Shepherd guided him through the dark times in his life. Just as David's sheep used to recognize his voice through the darkness and follow the sound, God's voice brought comfort and direction to David when he didn't know where to go.

Life is full of shadows. There is evil out there. There are dangers. There are frightening valleys where the mountains block out the light. Death casts a shadow of fear across life. But Jesus, your Good Shepherd, will walk with you through the valleys. He'll dispel the shadows of fear because he is the Light (John 1:4).

Lesso Lessons from the Psalms salns

October 24

Don't Miss the Banquet

You prepare a table before me
  in the presence of my enemies.
You anoint my head with oil;
  my cup overflows.

Psalm 23:5

Soldiers don't usually sit down for a picnic in the middle of a raging battlefield. They either fight to the death, or they turn and run! The scene David paints is one of total security. In the midst of the worst his enemies could dish out, David found peace and joy in God. He found reason to celebrate. He enjoyed more blessings than he could even take in. His enemies were trying to keep the crown from him, but they couldn't stop God from making him a king.

Sometimes going through life's hardest times teaches us the most about God. When our enemies are after us and we want to panic, God gives us peace. He lays out a banquet to celebrate the victory that's already ours. He reminds us who we are—royalty—because the King has claimed us as his own. He pours out his goodness, so our lives overflow with his blessings. When everything is going well, we might take God's presence for granted; but when life is hard, we can see his presence more clearly. That's because he gives us peace and cause for celebration when we'd expect only despair.

If you're experiencing some of the difficulties that life throws at you, look to see what God is doing. He hasn't gone anywhere. He's preparing a table for your victory party. He's getting ready to honor you in front of your enemies. He's pouring out his blessings on you. You don't have to leave the battlefield to have your picnic, for God is with you and your enemies don't intimidate him.

The Right Perspective

Surely goodness and love will follow me
all the days of my life,
and I will dwell in the house of the LORD
forever.

Psalm 23:6

People say we can only count on two things in life: death and taxes. Maybe so, but Christians can add two more absolutes to our lives: God's love and his goodness. It's important for us to establish these truths firmly in our lives once and for all: God loves us, and God is good to us.

We run into trouble when we try to look through our circumstances to understand what God is like. We have a bad day, so we conclude God doesn't love us. If it's a really bad day, we may even decide God is picking on us. When things are going well, we assume God has decided to be good to us that day. It's crucial to our spiritual growth that we always look to God first and let him show us our circumstances from his perspective. When we do this, life will take on a whole new dimension. For example, that bad day that proved God doesn't love us becomes something totally different when we see it through God's eyes. It becomes an opportunity to trust God. It provides an occasion for God to reveal his power, to encourage us with his presence, and even to do a miracle. Mature Christians often find the worst situations to be times they experience God the most!

If circumstances determined God's character, David would have wanted to run as far away from the house of the Lord as he could, not dwell in it! He lived through some terrible hardships! Instead, he discovered that the right perspective gave him a completely different view of his life. He was free to experience God deeply in both good times and in bad.

Don't focus on your problems and miss God's goodness. Focus on God's goodness instead. Take note of the many ways he's expressing his love to you in spite of your problems, or even through them. When you look at life from the right perspective, you'll see God as he really is. Thank him that on good days or bad, you can always count on his love and goodness.

Chapter 21
Lessons from Peter

Peter lived on a steady diet of his own words. He was an impulsive, outspoken extrovert, eager to speak his mind and quick to take action. He always meant well; it's just that his demonstrative personality often got him into trouble! Peter must have been an exasperating character at times. He certainly knew what it felt like to fail. Yet Jesus never gave up on him. The longer Peter knew Jesus, the more these changes became obvious in Peter's life. Peter developed from a brash, opinionated man into an articulate, confident leader (see Acts 2:14–40). He never lost his boldness; Jesus just redirected it. If Christ could work this miracle in Peter's life, there's hope for the rest of us!

As you read Peter's words, take note of the wisdom and maturity that is evident in his writing. Peter is an inspiring example of what Christ can do with a person whose heart is devoted to him.

Use Your Head!

Therefore, prepare your minds for action; be self-controlled; set your hope fully on the grace to be given you when Jesus Christ is revealed.

1 Peter 1:13

One difference between Christianity and cults is that Christianity encourages you to think for yourself while cults often depend on brainwashing you into following without thinking. Christianity does not ask you to stop thinking in order to believe. On the contrary, the greater the thinker you are, the better you will be able to grasp the enormous truths God wants you to understand. God wants you to love him with all your heart, soul, strength, and mind (Mark 12:30). That means he wants you to use your head!

Satan thrives on deception; God has nothing to hide. Every Christian ought to be a thinking person. We need to do as Peter says and "prepare our minds for action." We don't know what the day will bring. God does, and he can prepare us. We must fill our minds with truth so we're not deceived by falsehood. If we allow others to do our thinking for us, we're at the mercy of their opinions and their values. If we waste our days in front of a television set, we'll soak up the world's thinking like a sponge.

If your mind is lazy, you'll miss out on so much that God wants to teach you! Exercise your brain: read a good book, rent a thought-provoking movie, spend time with people who know how to think, attend conferences, ask lots of questions. Look for opportunities to stretch your mind. It takes an active mind to appreciate fully God's greatness!

October 27

Holy Like God

But just as he who called you is holy, so be holy in all you do; for it is written: "Be holy, because I am holy."

1 Peter 1:15-16

Being like God could come in handy! If you were all-knowing, you'd never have to study. If you were omnipresent you could go to school and to work without leaving your cozy bed. If you were all-powerful, no one could bully you or take advantage of you. God calls you to be like him, but (alas!) not in these ways. He wants you to be holy as he is holy.

Only Christians can be holy. Non-Christians can be good, and nice, and decent, and thoughtful, but they can't be holy. When you accepted Christ as your Savior, God cleansed your soul and made you a saint. You may not think of yourself as a saint, but the Bible says that's what you are (1 Peter 2:9). When you became a Christian, Christ entered your life and began living out his life in you. God is holy by nature. He is pure; there is no evil in him. He is good; he operates by truth and love. Now that holy Christ lives in you, you have access to his holiness. You now have the capability of holiness in your own life.

The way you treat others should be an extension of the way God treats you—with love, patience, and forgiveness. The way you conduct yourself should be worthy of the Spirit of God who lives within you. This means you'll respect God's presence in your life by the choices you make, by the movies you see, by the books you read, and by the company you keep. Being holy is not striving to follow a list of moral rules. Being holy is living in a way that honors your holy God.

Royal Priests

But you are a chosen people, a royal priesthood, a holy nation, a people belonging to God, that you may declare the praises of him who called you out of darkness into his wonderful light.

1 Peter 2:9

In Old Testament times, priests did two things: First, they brought God to the people: that is, they brought God's Word to the people and helped the people to know what God was like. Second, the priests brought the people to God; that is, they helped people who were searching for God know how to find him and experience God's forgiveness.

God has chosen you to be part of his royal priesthood. God wants everyone to know him as you do, so he's called you to act as intermediary to help others find him. Many people don't know Jesus personally. They've never spent time with him. They've never read their Bible. They don't know what God is like. You have a relationship with him, so you can help them by showing them who God is. You can help them learn that God loves them, that he offers forgiveness for their sins and new life through Christ. If you live a holy life, others will catch a glimpse of the Christ you represent. They'll connect the name of Jesus with love, kindness, and forgiveness because of your example. They will be drawn to Christ because they will learn what he is really like. This is bringing God to the people.

When others are seeking to know God, your job as a priest is to show them the way. Even if you don't know your Bible thoroughly, you know enough to help them get started reading theirs. You can tell them what Christ has done for you. You can lead those who are hurting to the One who can heal their pain. You don't need a seminary degree to help others find God. Simply introduce them to your Savior. That is bringing people to God. Take God to the people; take the people to God. That is what priests did. That is what God asks you to do.

LESS LESS ETER

Cast Your Anxiety on Him

Cast all your anxiety on him because he cares for you.

1 Peter 5:7

Anxiety develops when you worry about things beyond your control. Sometimes other people make decisions that affect your life. Awaiting the results of a job interview, for example, can be agonizing because your future is in someone else's hands. Fear of the unknown can cause you anxiety; days can seem like weeks when you're anticipating a doctor's diagnosis.

Anxiety is unhealthy. It takes a toll on you mentally, emotionally, and physically. Depression, ulcers, and high blood pressure are just a few of anxiety's side effects. Anxiety is a spiritual problem as well. As long as you're clinging to your worries, you're not trusting God to take care of you. God wants you to give your anxiety to him. Things may be out of *your* control, but nothing is beyond God's control. The imagery Peter presents is that of *throwing*, or *hurling*, your cares on God. It's not a halfhearted undertaking; it's deliberate, and it's dramatic.

Picture yourself beside a lake. You have a fishing rod in your hand, and whatever it is that's been eating away at you is attached to the hook. Now imagine yourself drawing your arm back, then casting forward as far as you can. The fishing line flies across the water and your problem lands way out in the lake. Now, drop the rod on the beach and walk away. That's the way God wants you to treat your anxiety. Don't pray to God about your problems and then take them with you at the end of your prayer time. Leave them with God; he can handle them.

A Thief in the Night

But do not forget this one thing, dear friends: With the Lord a day is like a thousand years, and a thousand years are like a day. The Lord is not slow in keeping his promise, as some understand slowness. He is patient with you, not wanting anyone to perish, but everyone to come to repentance.

But the day of the Lord will come like a thief. The heavens will disappear with a roar; the elements will be destroyed by fire, and the earth and everything in it will be laid bare.

2 Peter 3:8-10

There's been endless speculation about Jesus' Second Coming. Hundreds of books predict when it will be and what it will be like. Speakers travel across the globe sharing their insight into this intriguing event. Some have immersed themselves in the topic, trying to unlock the mystery of Christ's return. Many calculated an exact date when the trumpet would sound and Jesus would come in glory. The given date came and went, and it was back to the drawing board! Members of some religions have been so sure the Second Coming would happen immediately that they quit their jobs and waited for him on their rooftops or on hillsides. Later, they were lining up at employment agencies. It's a fascinating subject. In fact, Christ's return has mesmerized people since his resurrection. Even in Peter's day, people were spending a great deal of time speculating on the subject.

Peter had three things to say about the matter. First, he pointed out that God's timing is not like ours. A thousand years is like a day to God. That means Jesus walked the earth only two days ago! Second, Peter noted that Christ's return will be as sudden and unexpected as a prowler sneaking into a house under cover of darkness (Luke 12:40). Thieves don't tell you what time to expect them! Therefore, there's no point in trying to determine exactly when Christ will come. In fact, the Bible says even Jesus himself did not know when the Second Coming would be (Matthew 24:36). Third, Peter said Christ will come in dramatic judgment, with fire, and the world will be no more. Every secret and every sin will be laid bare. On that day, according to the apostle Paul, believers and unbelievers alike will all bow in humble worship to the King of kings (Romans 14:11).

How does all this relate to us? Rather than wasting our time on endless speculations about Judgment Day, we need to understand one thing: it *is* coming, and it will be like nothing we could even imagine! Let's live each day in such a way that no matter when Christ returns we'll be ready.

Living with God's People

T o walk in love with saints above, O! That will be glory!
To walk below with saints we know, now that's another story!

The person who wrote this poem was an astute observer of God's children. The Christian life is always easier to study than it is to practice. If all we ever had to do was to affirm that it's good to love our enemies, we would all be spiritual giants. But when God asks us to love one of our real enemies, that's when our theories fly out the window!

Learning to live in harmony with other believers is an essential part of being a Christian. God does not call us to be Lone Ranger Christians. He wants us to work together. He commands us to love one another and to forgive our fellow believers when they sin against us. He instructs us to love even those who seem unlovable. That's God's intention for the church. The church is a place where Christians work together. We meet each other's needs. We carry each other's burdens. We pray together and study the Bible together. We learn together in the church how to be Christian. The church isn't perfect because its members aren't perfect. But it is God's way.

As you read the following devotions, ask yourself if you are serving God in your church the way the Bible says you should.

Blame

The man said, "The woman you put here with me—she gave me some fruit from the tree, and I ate it."

Genesis 3:12

"The devil made me do it!" That line was popularized in a comedy routine by the comedian Flip Wilson. He grew famous for taking on the outlandish persona of "Geraldine." Time after time, Geraldine would absolve herself of any blame for her latest shenanigans with this classic line. Like most comedy, it was funny because it struck so close to home. This habit of looking for a scapegoat is nothing new. After Adam and Eve ate from the forbidden tree, the first thing they did was look around for someone to blame. It was slim pickings since they were the garden of Eden's entire population, but each managed to find someone:

Adam: "This woman you put with me, she. . . ."

Eve: "The serpent deceived me, and I ate."

It didn't work, but that hasn't stopped generations of sinners from trying the same trick: "I didn't know it was a sin." "My friends tricked me." "My parents never taught me right from wrong." "I don't have a strong support network in my church." "I got caught in my one area of weakness." "Everyone makes mistakes." And of course, that old classic, "Satan was oppressing me!" Making excuses for our sin may be amusing in a comedy act, but it's a very real obstacle that separates us from genuine repentance. God didn't fall for Adam's excuse, nor was he fooled by Eve's. Why do we waste our breath?

When God confronts you with your sin, you'll never find forgiveness as long as you're blaming someone else. You can offer God a thousand reasons for why you did it, but only one will hold up: "Forgive me, Lord. I was wrong." It's incredibly freeing when you go ahead and admit your fault and seek forgiveness. Think of how different this world would be if every one of us accepted responsibility for our own behavior!

November 1

The Spirit

All of them were filled with the Holy Spirit and began to speak in other tongues as the Spirit enabled them. . . .

"Then how is it that each of us hears them in his own native language?"

Acts 2:4, 8

Have you ever been in a foreign place where you didn't understand the language? Did you feel frustrated? How did you communicate? Were you relieved when you found someone else who spoke English?

Not long after Jesus' resurrection, God sent his Holy Spirit to the believers in Jerusalem. When they received the Spirit, they began to speak in languages they had never spoken before. At the time, there were many foreigners in Jerusalem whose native language was not Hebrew. When these visitors heard a commotion, they gathered around the early church believers to see what was going on. To their astonishment, each of them heard the gospel presented in his or her native tongue. They were flabbergasted! There were over a dozen countries represented in the crowd, and every person heard the good news that day, even though those who spoke did not know their languages.

When God wants you to share his message, don't be intimidated by the circumstances. You may feel inadequate to share Christ's love because you don't know what to say. If you're a new Christian, you may feel you don't know your Bible well enough. Don't let that stop you. God gave you his Holy Spirit to help you spread his good news effectively (Acts 1:8). Don't assume God will only use you to reach out to people who are just like you. He may ask you to tell people from another culture how they can know him. He may even lead you to be his witness in a foreign country. His Spirit will guide you so you know how to share his love, even with those who are very different from you. The important thing is that you're open to talk about your faith as the Holy Spirit prompts you.

We're usually far more likely to underestimate what God wants to do through us than overestimate it. The disciples probably had no idea on Pentecost morning that by sundown there would be three thousand new Christians in their midst! When God wants to move in power, no barrier can prevent him—not even a language barrier.

The Model Church

They devoted themselves to the apostles' teaching and to the fellowship, to the breaking of bread and to prayer.

Acts 2:42

There are all sorts of churches. Some meet in ornate buildings with stained glass windows; others gather in more modest buildings, school gymnasiums, huts, or even outdoors. Some congregations sing hymns to organ music; others sing choruses to guitars and drums. Still others have immense choirs and full orchestras. Some Christians meet together in secret, after dark, because Christianity is against the law in their country. Other churches assemble in the most public of places—downtown, in civic centers, even in public swimming pools.

Churches can have very different personalities, and therefore express worship in a variety of ways. But it makes no difference what the building looks like or whether the pastor wears robes or blue jeans. The important thing is that the church is biblical. Churches based on the Bible have at least four things in common.

Learning. A biblical church is a learning church. God has so much to tell his people! The apostles were set aside as teachers in the early church because they had walked with Jesus and because Jesus had commanded them to make disciples (Matthew 28:19–20). God still calls out and equips people to teach others about Christ.

Fellowship. Fellowship was vital to the early church's survival, just as it is today. God didn't design the Christian life to be a solitary venture. He wants us to encourage one another. God wants his people to enjoy one another and to build wholesome relationships with other Christians. Some of that happens at church, but it can also happen over a soft drink at a local fast-food restaurant.

Worship. The breaking of bread probably referred to the Lord's Supper. The early church met regularly to worship together and to remember Christ's death and resurrection. In other words, they gathered to remind themselves why they existed.

Prayer was the lifeline of the first church, as it is for us today. If our church is not a praying church, we will not know what Christ wants us to do. There is too much at stake for us to think we can survive without prayer.

How would you describe a model church? There are all sorts of opinions about that. Don't get distracted by the differences between your church and someone else's. The Bible tells us what things are really important.

Living with God's People

November 3

The Way Church Was Meant to Be

All the believers were together and had everything in common. Selling their possessions and goods, they gave to anyone as he had need. Every day they continued to meet together in the temple courts. They broke bread in their homes and ate together with glad and sincere hearts.

Acts 2:44-46

Early Christians loved to be together. Christianity was so new and exciting to them that they wanted to celebrate their faith with other believers (Acts 2:43). They wanted to be together as much as possible. To first-century Christians, church was not a once-a-week thing; it was an everyday occurrence.

The first church was characterized by a *we* mentality. Those who had something to give shared it willingly. They wouldn't think of enjoying a full pantry while their fellow believers went hungry. If someone needed shelter, others opened their homes. If someone needed money, others sold what they had to get it for them. Persecution was a reality in their lives, not a concept. Some would lose their lives for their faith. They needed each other for strength and moral support. The early church demonstrates church as Jesus meant it to be: Vibrant. Alive. Supportive. Loving. Giving. Sharing. Fun.

Did you know you're a part of your church because God put you there? Do you realize how important you are to your fellow church members? Do you understand how important they are to you? If you've been holding back, preferring to remain on the fringe, it's time to get involved! Here are a few suggestions to get you started: invite people from church into your home; find a way to share something you have with someone who needs it; make it a habit to linger after each service and meet someone you don't know; go to a church function in addition to the Sunday morning service; offer to serve in a church ministry. As you open yourself up to your church, an amazing thing will happen. You'll see your church more and more as a family and less and less as an institution. You'll discover the joy that God meant churches to bring.

It's Great to Be a Christian!

November 4

They broke bread in their homes and ate together with glad and sincere hearts, praising God and enjoying the favor of all people. And the Lord added to their number daily those who were being saved.

Acts 2:46-47

Some Christians feel embarrassed about their faith. They live the Christian life as if it were a burden to carry. They don't want to stand out in any way, so they try to hide their faith in order to fit in with the crowd. They think they have to coerce others to accept Christ, but they're such unenthusiastic Christians themselves it's a tough sell. What a tragic misconception! That's not at all what Christianity is all about.

Loving God is not a burden; it's a joy! Following Christ is not something to be hidden; it's an incredible adventure to be shared! Christ brings believers joy that the world can't come close to matching. The first Christians stood out because they were different—but in a positive way. The world was desperate for what the early church had. It was a time of war and unrest, yet the Christians had peace. Poverty was widespread, yet the early church shared generously. First-century believers were noted for the way they loved one another. They were conspicuous because of their joy. They loved to be together. Their relationships went past the superficial; they were more like family than just friends. In other words, they were genuinely happy people! And, guess what? The Bible says they found favor with all the people. That's right, people *liked* them. How could they not? God added new people to the church daily. They didn't have to coax others to accept Christ. Their faith was irresistible!

As a Christian, you never have to be embarrassed about what you believe. People all around you are searching for something to fill the emptiness within them. They're looking for exactly what you have! Don't think it's your burden to cajole others into accepting Christ. God will draw people to himself. Concentrate instead on living the Christian life with enthusiasm, and be ready to tell others how they can find the same joy they see in you. If you're enjoying Christ as he wants you to, others won't be able to resist seeking him too.

Living with God's People

November 5

Divine Appointments

*Now an angel of the Lord said to Philip, "Go south to the road—
the desert road—that goes down from Jerusalem to Gaza."*

Acts 8:26

Divine appointments can occur at the most unexpected
times and places! You never know when God has scheduled
an appointment for you. Philip was enjoying tremendous
success preaching in Samaria. Many people were turning
their lives over to Christ. Philip could reasonably conclude
God wanted him to continue preaching there until as many
people as possible had become Christians. Instead, God
sent word to Philip to leave what he was doing and to go
out into the desert. Philip could have assumed the angel got
his wires crossed: *The desert? When I'm doing so much for the
kingdom of God right here? I'm a pretty good preacher! Who's
there to preach to in the desert?* Yet as strange as God's instructions may have seemed, Philip trusted him and did as he
was told.

While Philip was traveling down a desert road, he met an
influential Ethiopian in a caravan. The Ethiopian was reading the Old Testament, but he couldn't understand it.
Immediately Philip realized what God wanted him to do.
People don't search for answers in the Bible unless God is
working in their lives, so Philip helped the man become a
Christian. In doing so, Philip had no idea how many others
this one man would also lead to Christ. Philip simply recognized God's activity and joined in on it.

You never know when God has plans for you to share
Christ with someone. You may happen to sit next to him
on the bus or stand next to her in line. The person you
introduce to Jesus may be influential in leading many others to know him as well. If you're sensitive to God's leading,
even when it doesn't seem reasonable, you'll discover the
joy of getting involved in God's activity. By keeping one
divine appointment, you can have a part in spreading the
gospel far beyond yourself!

Paul's Word to the Galatians and Ephesians

The newspapers periodically report about people who suffer from amnesia. A man went hunting and disappeared for two years. When he returned, he had no memory of what took place while he was gone. A woman suffered a traumatic shock, and her memory was erased. She no longer remembered her family or her friends. She had to relearn everything, from brushing her teeth to driving a car. Some people experience times of identity crisis, when things they assumed about themselves are proven false, and they grow confused as to who they really are.

As you read through the Books of Galatians and Ephesians, you get the distinct impression Paul didn't want his fellow Christians to be confused about who they were! In case the believers in Galatia or Ephesus were unclear about their identity, Paul made it crystal clear for them. They were transformed people, saved by God's grace, not by their own efforts. They were filled with the Holy Spirit, as should be evident by the fruit in their lives. Paul reminded them of their special identity as Christians.

Unfortunately, we Christians sometimes suffer from spiritual amnesia. We forget all that God has done for us. We begin to believe the world's propaganda that we are no different than non-Christians. We begin to question whether anything really changed in us when we became Christians. Paul's words can put such doubts and fears to rest. He wants us to understand our identity as God's children, and to experience the abundant life available to us through Christ.

With Paul's help, get ready to take a good look at who you are, who you are not, and who God wants you to become!

New Life

"I have been crucified with Christ and I no longer live, but Christ lives in me. The life I live in the body, I live by faith in the Son of God, who loved me and gave himself for me."

Galatians 2:20

When you became a Christian, you didn't adopt a new lifestyle or join a new religion. You didn't take on a new set of morals or commit yourself to be a better person. The Bible says you died. The person you were no longer exists. Even if you were very young, even if you weren't living a blatantly sinful life, you were a stranger to God then, and you are now his child. When you turned your life over to Christ, he began to live through you, and things will never be the same again.

Calling ourselves "reformed sinners" is inaccurate. We're not reformed; we're *reborn!* We're not just improved versions of who we used to be; we're completely new creations. We're not the same persons anymore. Then, we lived by our own strength; now, almighty God is living through us. Then, our goals were short-term; now, they are eternal. Then, sin's power held us captive; now, we are free to overcome temptation. Then, we were strangers to Christ; now he lives within us. Then, we were enemies of God; now, we are his beloved children. Then, we had no hope for the future; now, our future is filled with incredible joy! Then, we were condemned to eternity separated from God; now, we look forward to eternal life, face-to-face with God. We are not better people than we were before; we are *different* people than we were before!

Your Sins Are Showing

The acts of the sinful nature are obvious: sexual immorality, impurity and debauchery; idolatry and witchcraft; hatred, discord, jealousy, fits of rage, selfish ambition, dissensions, factions and envy; drunkenness, orgies, and the like. I warn you, as I did before, that those who live like this will not inherit the kingdom of God.

Galatians 5:19-21

Occasionally it's a good idea to take inventory of your lifestyle. Do you live as someone who belongs to God, or does your life show no evidence that you are a Christian? According to Paul, a sinful lifestyle reflects a heart that's not right with God. Paul didn't say Christians never sin, nor did he say that Christians lose their salvation by sinning. He did say that those who persist in sinful activity are proving by their behavior that they don't belong to God's kingdom, regardless of what they claim.

Some people think they are Christians because they prayed a sinner's prayer once, maybe at camp or in a church service. Yet their lives bear no evidence that they know Christ. Perhaps they heard what awaits nonbelievers in the afterlife, so they wanted to take out a little insurance. In actuality, nothing really happened in their hearts. It may have seemed like a good idea to have Jesus as Savior, but they had no plans to make him their Lord. Praying the sinner's prayer without genuine repentance is just words. Paul said the proof of salvation is a changed life. If the only proof you have that you are a Christian is what you did a long time ago, the evidence is pretty weak. The proof of your Christianity ought to be seen continually as you reflect Christ through your lifestyle each day.

If you examine your life and you see consistent disobedience to God, something is wrong. The worst thing that could happen to anyone would be to depend on false assurance of salvation. Make sure you are under no delusions. Settle things with God today.

November 8

The Fruit of
the Spirit

But the fruit of the Spirit is love, joy, peace, patience, kindness, goodness, faithfulness, gentleness and self-control. Against such things there is no law. Those who belong to Christ Jesus have crucified the sinful nature with its passions and desires.

Galatians 5:22-24

Yesterday, we saw that a sinful lifestyle is evidence of a heart that's not right with God. Today, we'll take a look at the flip side. Paul lists some character traits that should be obvious in a Christian's life. There is a way to tell if people are Christians: look for certain qualities in their lives.

The moment you accepted Christ, your sinful nature died. You became a new creation, free to live the lifestyle God desires. The Holy Spirit will work in you to produce a Christlike character that reflects the new person you are. With Jesus as the blueprint, the Spirit wants to build characteristics into you that have not previously been part of your personality so that you can become like Christ. For example, you may have a reputation as a hot-tempered fireball. The Spirit can give you self-control. You may be prone to bursts of anger; the Spirit can give you patience. If you were self-centered, the Spirit can sensitize your heart to the needs of others. The Spirit can bring peace where there was anxiety, joy where there was discouragement, and gentleness where there was hatred.

Review the fruits of the Spirit listed above. Are they all a part of your life right now? If you allow the Holy Spirit to do his job, every characteristic listed in these verses will describe you, and you will be well on your way to becoming like Christ.

Carrying Burdens

November 9

Carry each other's burdens, and in this way you will fulfill the law of Christ.

Galatians 6:2

When someone we know is struggling under a heavy weight, we can do one of three things. We can pretend not to notice, we can criticize the person for being weak, or we can offer to help carry the load.

People carry all kinds of burdens; some are piled on them by life's circumstances. Maybe they're dealing with grief, or an abusive parent, or a broken home. Others have made foolish choices, and now they struggle with the consequences: pregnancy, addiction, public embarrassment. You may think their burdens are none of your business: they have their problems, you have yours. Are you tempted to look down your nose at them for getting themselves into such a mess? Paul says helping them is not only your business; it's your obligation. You can ease their load by showing love, acceptance, and encouragement rather than indifference or criticism. When you are a friend to those in need, you help ease the load they are carrying.

There should be no room in the Christian's heart for selfishness when so many people need help with their burdens. If we are surrounded by hurting people and we are not moved by compassion, the love of Christ is not in us. It's a great joy and an unparalleled privilege to get alongside someone who is heavyhearted and help lift the burden. Ask God to lead you to a hurting person today, and then watch to see how God wants you to help.

November 10

Something or Nothing

If anyone thinks he is something when he is nothing, he deceives himself. Each one should test his own actions. Then he can take pride in himself, without comparing himself to somebody else.

Galatians 6:3-4

Why is it so easy to see faults in others and so hard to see our own shortcomings? We can easily spot imperfections in other people: they talk too much, they eat too much, they're lazy, they're mean, they're rude, they're thoughtless, they're selfish, and so on. It's not that we claim to be perfect ourselves, but when we compare our tiny flaws to the blatant faults in other people, we look pretty good! We can explain away our own weaknesses and rationalize our own failures, but we're reluctant to give anyone else the benefit of the doubt. We tend to assume the worst of others and assume the best of ourselves.

Why do we do this? As long as we can find people who are worse than we are, we feel good about ourselves. When we measure ourselves against the worst sinners out there, we come out looking pretty good. Paul says we're using the wrong standard.

There is one standard for determining whether your life is pleasing to God. It's found in the Bible, not in comparisons with other people. You must place your life next to the life of Jesus. Only when you are like him will you no longer have to be concerned with your own shortcomings. Don't waste your time finding fault with others. Instead, take an honest look at your own behavior. Are you pleased with what you see? Do you think Jesus is pleased with what he sees?

Reaping What We Sow

Do not be deceived: God cannot be mocked. A man reaps what he sows. The one who sows to please his sinful nature, from that nature will reap destruction; the one who sows to please the Spirit, from the Spirit will reap eternal life.

Galatians 6:7-8

Have you ever wondered why some people seem to get away with their sin without ever having to pay the price? The truth is, they don't. God has built certain principles into this life; one of them is: you reap what you sow. It may not be immediately obvious, but it's a fundamental rule of life; you can count on it.

To put it in more familiar terms: what goes around comes around. If you continually mistreat your friends, you'll end up alone. If you're in the habit of telling secrets, people will stop confiding in you. If you're a liar, people will learn to mistrust you. The principle applies in your spiritual life as well. If you live in continual disobedience to God's ways, you'll destroy your life. On the other hand, if you show kindness to others, you'll never lack for friends. If you're reliable, people will learn to trust you. If you're honest, they'll respect you. If you live in a way that honors God, he will honor you in return.

Some people never connect what is happening to them with how they are living. They complain that they have no friends, but they never realize this is because they have not been a friend to others. No one trusts them because they have been untrustworthy. No matter how things appear in this life, there will come a day when every one of us will have to answer for the way we lived. The sooner we understand that today's choices determine tomorrow's rewards, the better off we'll be. Are you happy with your life right now? Could it be that you are reaping what you have sown?

November 12

Don't Give Up!

Let us not become weary in doing good, for at the proper time we will reap a harvest if we do not give up. Therefore, as we have opportunity, let us do good to all people, especially to those who belong to the family of believers.

Galatians 6:9-10

Farmers are patient people! They prepare the soil and plant their crops in the spring. Day after day they labor, from sunrise to sundown, getting the seeds in the ground. Then, when everyone else goes on vacation, they work through the summer tending their crops. Finally, the fall comes, and it's harvesttime! Not everyone has the patience to be a farmer. Many of us want to see our efforts rewarded much more quickly. We can learn an important life lesson from the farmer: good things take time.

Doing what God asks can be hard work. Sometimes we don't see the results we want soon enough to suit us, so we're tempted to give up. We share our faith with a friend and pray for his salvation. When he doesn't accept Christ right away, we get discouraged and quit praying. We try to help a friend overcome a problem, but we don't see any change, so we get frustrated and move on to another project. Our problem is we give up too soon. Can you imagine a farmer preparing the soil for his crop, then never planting the seeds because he felt he had already worked hard enough? Or planting the crop but growing impatient when it wasn't ready to harvest after just one month?

We need to be patient, like the farmer. As long as we keep praying for people, encouraging them, and helping them grow, God promises we will see a harvest. If we faithfully study God's Word and obey what it says, we will grow more and more like Christ. It won't necessarily happen overnight, but it will happen. Don't grow tired of doing the right things. God's Word promises that if we persist in doing what is right, we *will* be rewarded.

Your Calling

As a prisoner for the Lord, then, I urge you to live a life worthy of the calling you have received.

Ephesians 4:1

Some people seem to sense early on in life what they are called to do. Have you heard people say, "Since I was in elementary school, I always knew I'd be a _____" (fill in the blank: pastor, youth leader, missionary)? Others go through their entire lives searching for their calling. Some people assume they haven't been called to anything in particular. Paul explains that each and every Christian has received a calling.

As a Christian, your calling is to glorify God with your life. Regardless of what vocation you take, your calling remains the same. Pastors, missionaries, youth leaders, and student ministers are not the only ones God has called into the ministry. They may have been called to a more visible ministry than others, but they are not the only ones with a calling. There are Christian schoolteachers who have realized that their calling was to honor God, and over the years, they have encouraged many students who passed through their classroom. Christian police officers and lawyers have realized that they were called to represent Christ in the world of criminal justice. Parents have understood that they were called to model a Christian lifestyle for their children.

Whatever vocation God leads you into (dentist, doctor, plumber, trapeze artist), keep your eyes fixed on your calling to honor God with your life. Whether you're repairing teeth, bodies, or sinks, you'll have endless possibilities to show others what Christ is like by your example. Always keep Paul's advice in mind, and live a life worthy of your calling.

November 14

Watch What You Say!

Do not let any unwholesome talk come out of your mouths, but only what is helpful for building others up according to their needs, that it may benefit those who listen.

Ephesians 4:29

Unwholesome talk is like vomit; it spews out of the depths of your being and makes a nasty mess wherever it lands. Sometimes it makes you feel better, but it's an unpleasant experience for whoever happens to be in the way! Unwholesome talk is impure, ugly, and evil. It includes gossip, criticism, sarcasm, lies, bragging, and crude humor. The result of unwholesome talk is never good; someone always gets hurt.

The words that come out of your mouth have the power to do more damage than you might realize. They also have potential for immeasurable good. Your words of encouragement can lift a heavy heart. Your words of kindness can boost someone's damaged sense of self-worth. Your words of truth can bring others closer to God. Your words of wisdom can help others make smart choices.

Don't underestimate the power your words hold just because you're young. God can use you to build up those around you if you will guard your mouth and pay careful attention to what comes out of it. Over the next few days, listen closely to the kind of talk that comes from your mouth. If you don't like what you hear, ask God's forgiveness, and look for ways to build others up instead of tearing them down. If your friends are in the habit of causing damage with their words, set an example for them by the way *you* talk. You'll feel better about yourself, as will those who listen to you.

Be Kind

Be kind and compassionate to one another, forgiving each other, just as in Christ God forgave you.

Ephesians 4:32

The world suffers from a severe shortage of kindness. We learn cruelty when we're very young. Remember some of the cutting words you heard on the playground? It's really no wonder; adults aren't always great role models. We say vindictive things; we accuse each other of all sorts of sins. We spread rumors and hold grudges. Over the centuries, the world has experienced incomprehensible violence because of people's refusal to treat one another the way God intended.

Jesus knew firsthand how cruel people can be. He was abused, rejected, tortured, and killed—all in the name of God! If there were a limit to how much cruelty one had to take before striking back, Jesus would certainly have passed it. If anyone had cause to be bitter and unforgiving, Jesus did. But he set the standard for us when he hung on the cross. Every breath was bringing indescribable pain, but he cried out, "Father, forgive them" (Luke 23:34).

Christians ought to be conspicuous by our kindness. We should stand out as people known for our forgiveness. We should be characterized by gentleness. We should have a reputation for our compassion. If we are known, instead, for our bickering and our cruelty, we are unworthy to call ourselves by the name of Christ.

Forgiveness is the ultimate act of kindness. It's one thing to show kindness toward someone who has treated you kindly, but it's quite another to show kindness to someone who has hurt you. That's forgiveness; when you can do that, you are loving the way Christ loved.

What Pleases God?

And find out what pleases the Lord.

Ephesians 5:10

Do you know what pleases God? Are you sure? Some Christians spend their lives assuming God is pleased with them simply because they are Christians. They never stop to consider that they might actually be disappointing God with their attitudes and their behavior.

Before his conversion, Paul thought he was the model of righteousness. He assumed God wanted him to rid the world of heretics, so he poured his life into persecuting Christians. Paul was mortified when Jesus opened his eyes and he saw how displeasing his life had been. He was determined never to misunderstand God's will again. He was adamant that his friends not make his mistake, so he warned them about living under false assumptions. He advised them to find out what pleases God and then do it!

We can be like Paul and mistakenly set our own standards for what we think pleases God; that way we know we can live up to them! We might assume God will overlook our small indulgences as long as we avoid the big sins. So we don't kill anybody, but we do gossip just a little. We don't actually hate anyone, but we occasionally criticize others. We don't pretend to be perfect, but by our own standards, we're not as bad as we could be. The problem is, God is not impressed when we live up to our standards; he expects us to live up to his.

If you've never investigated what is pleasing to God, now is the time to do so. As you read your Bible and pray, God will make clear how he wants you to live. Let that—and nothing less—be the standard for the way you live.

Be Careful

Be very careful, then, how you live—not as unwise but as wise, making the most of every opportunity, because the days are evil. Therefore do not be foolish, but understand what the Lord's will is.

Ephesians 5:15-17

Since we are limited creatures, we mortals sometimes miss the big picture of what God is doing. Rather than looking around us to see how God is at work, we focus inward, as though the rest of the world revolves around us. We ask, "What is God's will for my life?" when we should be asking, "What is God's will, and how can I adjust my life to it?" The difference is subtle, but it's very important. God's will is always bigger than we are. God has the entire world on his heart, not just our part of the world. The Creator of the universe does not spend all of his time trying to figure out ways to make us happy. He is concerned with making people from every nation on earth his children. The key is not what we are going to do but what God is going to do and how we can be involved in it.

God has a plan for this world, and you're a part of that plan. You're surrounded by opportunities to get involved with God's activity, but if you're too busy focusing on your own concerns, you'll miss them. How tragic it would be if you invested your life trying to build a career when God wanted to use you to build his eternal kingdom! God knows the past, the present, and the future. His plans are vastly superior to your best thinking. Trust that he knows what he's doing, and join him. When you invest your energy into his activity, you're investing in eternal things that are far bigger than you are.

Be Strong

Finally, be strong in the Lord and in his mighty power. Put on the full armor of God so that you can take your stand against the devil's schemes. For our struggle is not against flesh and blood, but against the rulers, against the authorities, against the powers of this dark world and against the spiritual forces of evil in the heavenly realms.

Ephesians 6:10-12

If you are a Christian, it's crucial that you understand something: Christianity is spiritual warfare. Satan and his hosts are alive and active, and they're seeking to cancel out your witness for Christ. Be very careful, or you'll become a prisoner of war. Satan's powers are limited and certainly no match for God, but he can still harm you if you are not careful.

It's vitally important that you remain spiritually strong. Satan is no match for God; therefore, if your strength is from God, you can withstand the devil's schemes. But if you try to resist him on your own, you'll end up as a casualty. That is why God gives you spiritual armor. With the spiritual weapons found in prayer and God's Word, you can face any spiritual battle with confidence. It's also crucial that you recognize who your enemy is and who it isn't. At times it may seem as though people are your enemies. They will attack you for your faith and try to weaken your resolve to follow Christ. You'll be tempted to get angry with them and fight back. Don't do it. Pray for them instead, and love them. They are not the enemy; Satan is. It may be that they are in bondage to him, and they need you to help set them free.

Don't take spiritual warfare lightly. When you become careless in your faith, you are vulnerable to the attack of spiritual forces. But as long as you remain close to Jesus, you are safe. Understand that you are in the middle of a war, and remain strong in the Lord.

Chapter 24

Thoughts from John's Gospel

If anyone really knew Jesus, it was John. He was one of the first people Jesus called to be his disciple (Mark 1:16–20). John belonged to Jesus' inner circle of friends. John, Peter, and James had special times with Jesus that even the other disciples did not experience (Matthew 17:1; 26:37). When the other disciples fled from the authorities on the night Jesus was crucified, John stood at the foot of the cross caring for Jesus' mother (John 19:25–27). It's no wonder that, in his Gospel, John never refers to himself as John, but as "the disciple whom Jesus loved" (John 13:23). What an incredible honor!

As John listened to Jesus teach, John heard things he would never forget. He saw Jesus do things that would remain vividly etched in his memory for the rest of his life. As you read some of what impressed John most about the life of Jesus, remember that he wrote as an eyewitness. He's telling you what he heard, what he saw, and what he experienced. As you consider John's observations, try to see the picture of Jesus that John is painting for you. As you look at Jesus through John's eyes, you, too, will be captivated by the love and majesty of your Lord and Savior.

It's Up to You

November 19

When Jesus saw him lying there and learned that he had been in this condition for a long time, he asked him, "Do you want to get well?"

John 5:6

It seems like a strange question to ask a lame man: "Do you want to get well?" Of course he wanted to get well! He'd been crippled for thirty-eight years, unable to work, and forced to beg for his food. He was dirty and weak. Who wouldn't want to be well again? All the same, it's curious that he didn't reply with an emphatic, *Yes!* Instead, he gave a reason for why he'd not been healed yet. He'd spent years lying within a stone's throw of healing waters, yet he'd not managed to work his way into the pool when it supposedly brought healing. We're not privy to the lame man's true feelings. Perhaps he did want to be healed. Perhaps he didn't. It's possible he was afraid of being well. He had no trade; if he couldn't beg, how would he live? He belonged to a community of disabled people; would he lose his friends? Jesus knew without asking how the man really felt, yet he asked this seemingly rhetorical question. Maybe he asked because the man needed to settle the answer in his heart.

At times, we ask for God's help, but deep down we don't really want it. We may beg to be delivered from our sin, but deliverance is the last thing on our agenda. The truth is, we're comfortable in our sin. We have no desire to stop, but we ask because we want to shift the focus away from our guilt. Now it's God's fault for not delivering us as we asked. We may even enlist others to pray for us so we appear remorseful, but we choose to persist in our sinful behavior. Sometimes, even in bad situations, we grow so used to our misery that we're afraid to let it go. We don't ask for help because we fear the changes that might come along with it. Familiar misery is better than unknown freedom.

Once he was healed, the lame man had a new lease on life. But along with wellness came big changes, different expectations, and new responsibilities. First of all, he was unemployed. In those days there were no talk-show circuits or lucrative book contracts to sell his story. He no longer had the sympathy of others; in fact, many were probably jealous of him now. He didn't fit in with his old crowd anymore. And, though he had a new body, he still had the same old sin problems (John 5:14).

When you pray for something, be sure you really mean it. Jesus can help you, but his help will bring changes in your life. Be ready to let go of your old way of life and make the adjustments that go along with healing.

Giving All You Have

Philip answered him, "Eight months' wages would not buy enough bread for each one to have a bite!"

Another of his disciples, Andrew, Simon Peter's brother, spoke up, "Here is a boy with five small barley loaves and two small fish, but how far will they go among so many?"

John 6:7-9

The world does a good job of making us feel inadequate, doesn't it? Movies are built around glamorous characters, with beautiful faces and perfect bodies. The sports world has its own standard of perfection: whoever is the fastest or the strongest is most admired. The global media keeps us up-to-date on who are the richest, smartest, and most talented people in the entire world. Then we look in the mirror, and we see ordinary written all over us. We know there are needs all around us; in fact, there are needs all around the world, but we feel hopelessly insignificant to make any worthwhile contribution. As today's passage shows, the important thing is not what we have or what we can do, it's who we know.

Try to imagine the scene from Philip's perspective: Jesus had been teaching the crowds for hour after hour. Jesus' teaching was so spellbinding that no one thought to stop and make lunch. Now it was late. The teaching was finished, and the multitude was famished. Jesus turned to Philip and asked if he had any ideas on how to feed them. Poor Philip! Picture his face—his eyes like saucers, his jaw somewhere around his knees. "You've got to be kidding! Let them get their own dinner! We don't even have anything to feed ourselves!" We're told that Jesus already knew what he was going to do; he only asked Philip to test him. Apparently, Philip didn't pass the test.

How would you have responded? The Bible says the crowds were following Jesus because of the miracles he'd performed on the sick. But this was different. These people were hungry, that's all. Would you have drawn the same conclusion as Philip: "That's impossible!"? Perhaps you would have responded like Andrew, with tentative faith, but at least not flat doubt: "Here's a bit of food, but it's not much." Both Philip and Andrew learned an important lesson that day. So did a little boy who shared his lunch. It's not how much or how little you've got; it's who's in charge of it. Jesus not only fed the multitudes; he had leftovers! Don't focus on how much or how little you have to offer. Just give it to Jesus and watch to see what he does with it.

November 21

Drawn by the Father

No one can come to me unless the Father who sent me draws him, and I will raise him up at the last day.

John 6:44

If people you know are searching for God, that's a sign that God is already at work in their lives. People's natural tendency is to move away from God, not toward him (Romans 3:11). Whenever Jesus met someone who was seeking to know God, he immediately recognized his Father at work in the person's life. When Jesus spotted Zacchaeus in the tree, he understood who had motivated him to make the effort to know him, so he promptly left the crowd of people in the streets and invited himself to Zacchaeus's house for dinner (Luke 19:1–10).

We Christians often share our faith using the shotgun approach to witnessing. Whoever crosses our path when we're on a hunt for converts gets blasted with the Good News! We hope we'll hit a target somewhere if we shoot enough gospel bullets. The truth is, we don't snare Christians; God draws them to himself. Witnessing is not something we do for God. It's something we do in response to what God is doing. When we begin to recognize God's activity in the lives of people around us, we will become much more intentional about how we share our faith with others. It's not wrong to share Christ with a complete stranger. Nor is it wrong to share a Christian witness with each person we meet. Our problem, at times, is that we are surrounded with people and we aren't sure who is ready to respond to the gospel.

If you pay attention, you'll see God at work in lives all around you. Perhaps a friend will begin asking you questions about the Christian life, or a coworker will observe you during a crisis and want to know where to find such peace. Maybe you'll notice a family member reading books about spiritual matters. Real witnessing doesn't involve selling Christ as though he were a product; it involves learning to recognize the Spirit of God working in someone's life and joining him in his activity.

Free Indeed!

So if the Son sets you free, you will be free indeed.

John 8:36

From the outside looking in, living for Christ might seem restricting. Unbelievers often think of the Christian life as a set of rules—all the things we can't do. This distorted perspective is nothing new. The rich young ruler concluded that following Jesus was not for him because it meant he couldn't hold on to his wealth (Luke 18:22–23). He missed what Jesus had to offer him because he focused on what Jesus asked him to give up. The world still sees Christianity as a set of strict rules that keep people from having fun.

Christians know nothing could be further from the truth! We know that Jesus came to set us free from bondage, not to trap us into it. We know from experience that sin is the real slavemaster, and we know that Christ paid the penalty to set us free from sin's entrapment. We see all that Christ has given us. The only things he's taken from us are things we're glad to be rid of: despair, guilt, shame, and death. We've tasted the abundant life that Jesus offers, and we wouldn't trade this joy for anything. Some of us were at the brink of suicide, with death looking better than life, but Jesus gave us hope. Some of us were fighting losing battles with addictions, but Christ gave us victory. Some of us were estranged from our own families. Jesus brought us together again. All of us were headed for eternity without God. Jesus turned us around, and now we look forward to joining him in heaven.

Christianity is all about freedom, not bondage. If you're still living in bondage, then there is a truth about Jesus you have not yet experienced. Remember, Christ came to set you free. No matter what it is that's got a hold on you (drugs, anger, fear, guilt), Jesus has the power to release you so you'll be free to enjoy life as God intends. Will you let him?

November 23

The Father of Lies

"You belong to your father, the devil, and you want to carry out your father's desire. He was a murderer from the beginning, not holding to the truth, for there is no truth in him. When he lies, he speaks his native language, for he is a liar and the father of lies."

John 8:44

Satan is an intriguing character. Movies, songs, and books portray him in a wide variety of personas, from a harmless cartoon character to a powerful, grotesque monster. The world, for the most part, dismisses his existence, except as a character in horror movies. Christians fear him. Some cults worship him. Across the board, there seems to be great confusion about who Satan really is and how much power he has. That shouldn't surprise us because he's the master of confusion.

Jesus revealed exactly who Satan is and what he's about. He's a liar. His primary weapon is deception. Christians often credit Satan with powers he doesn't have. We talk as though he can be everywhere, like God, or as though he can read our minds. We refer to him as God's evil counterpart, with God using his power for good, and Satan using his for evil. We've watched too much science fiction! Satan is not, and has never been, God's equal. Satan is a heavenly, created being. He sends out his demons because he can only be in one place at a time. Satan is an expert in understanding how we think, but nowhere does the Bible say he can read our thoughts. Christians cannot be demon possessed, as some say, because Jesus dwells within us. Satan has no power over Jesus (Matthew 12:29). We can be tempted to use Satan as a scapegoat, blaming him for our sin. We act as though we're the powerless victims of Satan's manipulation. That's an excuse. Christ's death on the cross freed us from sin's bondage; when we sin, we deliberately choose to disobey God. The devil can't make us do it!

Where did you pick up your ideas about Satan? Only the Bible presents Satan as he really is—the father of lies. Don't become preoccupied with Satan, giving him credit where it's not warranted. Stay close to Jesus, the Truth, and you'll not be deceived by Satan's trickery.

Thieves

"The thief comes only to steal and kill and destroy; I have come that they may have life, and have it to the full."

John 10:10

Listen to the way people around you talk about God. Often, people talk as though God were a thief, obsessed with taking things away from them. When someone dies, they say, "The Lord took him." When someone suffers a financial setback, they say, "The Lord giveth; the Lord taketh away." People are reluctant to accept Christ because of all the things they'll have to give up. Church members see the offering as the time when God takes their hard-earned money. It's as though God's goal is to make sure we never have too much.

Nothing could be further from the truth! There are thieves out there, to be sure—con artists who'll take your time, poach your possessions, and snatch your self-worth. You need to watch out for those who are out to hurt you or steal from you. But God is not one of them! God's purpose in creating you was to give you abundant life, overflowing with joy, filled with good things. If God were interested in taking from you, he would never have sent his Son to the cross.

If you've pictured God in your mind as a taker, you don't know him very well. People may have hurt you and robbed your joy, but God is completely different. The more you get to know him, the more you will experience the extraordinary, abundant life he wants to give you. Talk to God, and see if he wants to give you something new today.

thoughts from John's Gospel

November 25

Life

Jesus said to her, "I am the resurrection and the life. He who believes in me will live, even though he dies."

John 11:25

If you've ever had someone you love die, you know how real death is. It's one thing to read about traffic fatalities, war casualties, or murder victims in the newspaper. It's another to attend the funeral of someone who died—someone you knew personally and loved dearly. Death can seem unreal unless it strikes close to home. However, one thing is sure. Death is real, and it will come.

In Jesus' day, funerals were heart-wrenching events. As a show of respect for the deceased, people would weep and wail as loudly as they could so they could be heard a great distance away. Some families would even hire mourners to come to the funeral just to make sure there was a respectably loud level of mourning. Funerals were deeply somber because death was a symbol of hopelessness. Death is the one human struggle that no one escapes. Significantly, it was at a funeral that Jesus made this profound statement: "I am the resurrection and the life." He didn't say he knew how to be resurrected. He said he *is* the resurrection!

This is incredibly good news! Jesus takes the power away from death. Christians will still experience physical death, but we have nothing to fear in death because Jesus promises us life everlasting. Have you been worrying about death? Do you realize the enormity of today's verse? Read it again. Think about it. Thank God for defeating death and for giving you life everlasting!

When It's OK to Cry

Jesus wept.

John 11:35

How often do heroes show their emotions? Do you recall many movies where the hero, especially if it was a man, cried? In the old westerns, a cowboy could lose his friends, his ranch, and his family, but as long as nothing happened to his horse, he wouldn't shed a tear. He'd simply wince, scowl, and reach for his gun. Times have changed, somewhat. Now it's okay for real men to show emotion, but we're still a little embarrassed when they do, aren't we?

Jesus showed tremendous self-control when he was baited by the Pharisees and taunted by the crowds. The Bible doesn't record that he cried when soldiers pounded spikes into his hands and feet. The Bible never tells of Jesus' weeping for his own suffering, but it tells us he wept for other people's pain. Lazarus and his sisters were three of Jesus' closest friends. After Lazarus died, Jesus saw the sorrow of Mary and Martha, and it moved him deeply. Jesus could, and would, bring Lazarus back to life. Nonetheless, John records that Jesus *was* "deeply moved in spirit and troubled" when he saw Lazarus's family and friends overcome by grief and despair (John 11:33). Lazarus had been Jesus' friend too; Jesus wept with them. Jesus didn't weep because Lazarus had died, for Jesus was about to raise him back to life. Jesus wept because he saw the anguish and hopelessness of his friends.

Your family and your friends will go through times of pain and loss. Because you care deeply, you'll want to do something to help. You may grow frustrated when you can't think of the right words to say. Perhaps your compassion will move you to seek answers to their suffering or to find ways to alleviate their pain. But there may be times when there is little you can do to change their circumstances. Sometimes the best thing you can say is nothing; the best thing you can do is simply to listen and share their sorrow (1 Corinthians 12:26). Tears aren't always a sign that you've lost your self-control. Sometimes they show that you, like Jesus, have the capacity for true compassion.

November 27

Unbelief

Even after Jesus had done all these miraculous signs in their presence, they still would not believe in him.

John 12:37

Do you ever think, *If I could just see Jesus in the flesh, hear his voice, and watch him perform miracles, it would be much easier to have faith in him?* In Jesus' day, people were able to walk with him and observe him firsthand. They were eyewitnesses when he touched a blind man and gave him sight, or healed the rotting flesh of a person with leprosy. They saw him take a young boy's lunch and feed five thousand men with it. Most astonishing, they were there when Lazarus walked out from the tomb, very much alive, four days after his death! These were astounding signs of miraculous power! But the most incredible thing of all was this: even after what they saw and what they heard, some people still refused to believe in Jesus.

Others trusted Jesus so readily it compelled him to remark on the depth of their faith (Matthew 15:28). What was the difference? The difference was the condition of their hearts. People see what they want to see. Those whose hearts are closed to Christ will not trust him even if people come back from the grave in order to convince them (Luke 16:27–31). But those whose hearts are sensitive to God will not need to see miracles in order to believe in Christ and follow him.

Look around you. There are signs of God's power everywhere if you have the eyes to see them. If you are waiting for God to perform miracles so that your faith is increased, you may wait a long time. If, however, you are putting your faith in God, regardless of what happens, you may be surprised at how many miracles occur around you.

Peace

"Peace I leave with you; my peace I give you. I do not give to you as the world gives. Do not let your hearts be troubled and do not be afraid."

John 14:27

Most of us aren't looking for fame, fortune, or power. We just want to be happy. But somehow, circumstances keep getting in the way! Just when we think we've got it together, another problem hits us.

Lots of things can send your life into turmoil. You're caught in the middle of your parents' divorce. Someone you love dies. You're overloaded: too much to do in too little time. A friend rejects you. You're the victim of a crime. Your health fails. How can you have peace when people and situations keep conspiring against you? The world offers lots of ways to cope. Bookstores overflow with advice on how to find happiness. Drugs and liquor promise to numb the pain. Money promises to buy your way out of troubles. Movies tell you what you need is a good romance. Some religions direct you to seek tranquillity within yourself.

You can try every solution the world offers, and you still won't have peace. Peace doesn't come from the world, nor does it come from within yourself. Peace comes from God. God wants to give you the same peace he gave Jesus—a peace that carried him through the worst torment the world could dish out. Even while Jesus was being tortured and ridiculed on an excruciating cross, he had peace. God's peace goes deep down into your soul where nothing and no one can touch it. If you're looking for real peace, go to Jesus. He wants to give you peace that can never be taken away.

November 29

Abide in the Vine

"I am the vine; you are the branches. If a man remains in me and I in him, he will bear much fruit; apart from me you can do nothing."

John 15:5

If Jesus were making this point today, he might talk in terms of electricity. Even the most powerful electrical tool is useless unless it is plugged into an electrical outlet. Without power, the tool is of no use to anyone. Jesus' point that we can do nothing without being "plugged in" to him seems so obvious we might wonder why he even mentions it.

God wants Christians to do two things: grow in our personal relationship with him and spread his good news to others. As ridiculous as it seems, we often try to do both of these things in our own strength. We get too busy to spend time with God, and prayer seems to slow us down, so we try to have a relationship with him through other ways. We go to church, spend time with Christians, and talk about Jesus as if we know him. We assume that since we are Christians, we must know Christ. We might even try to convince a friend to become a Christian. But we never seem to experience victory in our lives, and we don't understand why God does so little through us. Our lives lack power. We are so busy trying to do things for God that we have no time to spend with God.

Jesus' message is straightforward. Just as an electric tool is useless without electricity, so the Christian life is impossible without the presence and guidance of Christ. Jesus says, "Abide in me." Don't try to live the Christian life without Christ; it can't be done.

The Vine

"I am the vine; you are the branches. If a man remains in me and I in him, he will bear much fruit; apart from me you can do nothing."

John 15:5

Are you seeking to do great things for God? Or would you rather God did great things through you? There's a world of difference in the two. The first is dependent upon your strength and your ability, which are both limited. The second is based on the inexhaustible strength and ability of God.

Jesus says we need to take a lesson from a branch. A branch doesn't worry about producing fruit. It simply stays attached to the vine. It is through the vine that all the nutrients flow from the roots to the branches. When a branch is receiving everything the vine has to give, the fruit comes naturally and effortlessly. The key to the Christian life is not how hard we try to be spiritual but how closely we stay connected to Christ. We don't need to worry so much about what we are doing. Our focus should be on staying close to Christ.

If you find that living the Christian life is wearing you out, you could be trying to live it in your own strength—doing things *for* Christ rather than enjoying a relationship *with* him. When you enjoy a close relationship with Christ, he is able to produce all kinds of good things in your life. Focus on strengthening your relationship with the vine and the fruit will follow naturally. Remember, apart from the vine, the branch is only a decoration.

December 1

A Life That Glorifies God

"This is to my Father's glory, that you bear much fruit, showing yourselves to be my disciples."

John 15:8

You may be a brand-new Christian, or perhaps you've known Jesus for years. Regardless, it should be obvious to others that you belong to Jesus. Jesus said that when people look at you, they should see evidence of God at work. What kind of evidence? Jesus called it fruit. When you put others first instead of yourself, that's fruit. When you get rid of an ungodly habit and seek to live a pure life, that's fruit. When you refuse to gossip but choose instead to build up others, that's fruit. When you control your temper, even when others are losing theirs, that's fruit. When you forgive someone who hurt you, that's fruit. The types of fruit are endless.

God doesn't expect you to produce all this fruit on your own. In fact, Jesus said you're not capable, apart from him, of living a life that glorifies God. He wants to live through you, as a way to show others that he is alive and powerful. In fact, the only way Christ will not produce fruit in your life is if you resist what he is trying to do. If, on the other hand, you cooperate with all Christ is doing in your life, you will see amazing things taking place in your life.

Think back to when you first became a Christian. Are you the same person you were then, or have you allowed God to produce fruit in your life as a testimony to his greatness?

Joy

"I have told you this so that my joy may be in you and that your joy may be complete."

John 15:11

Whoever thinks Christians don't enjoy life doesn't know what the Christian life is really about! Jesus didn't come to earth to take away your happiness but to fill your life with a joy that overflows! Jesus was not interested in the kind of joy that the world gives. In the world, joy depends on how things are going. If life is going well, then you can be happy. If life is difficult, joy evaporates. Jesus wants you to be filled with his kind of joy. His joy doesn't depend on what is happening around you; it depends on what is going on inside you.

No one could rob Jesus of his joy. They could reject him, beat him, even crucify him, but the certainty that he still belonged to God and would be rejoining his Father in heaven filled him with joy. Christians ought to have more joy than anyone else in the world. We know the living God! We are assured of an eternity with him in heaven!

Jesus isn't satisfied with your living only a mediocre life. He said he came so you could enjoy life to the fullest (John 10:10). So rejoice! Celebrate! Don't let anyone convince you that the Christian life should be dull and somber. You are vitally connected to the Creator of life itself. Focus on him—not on what people around you are doing—and you will have the same joy Jesus had.

December 3

Laying Down Your Life

"Greater love has no one than this, that one lay down his life for his friends."

John 15:13

Many people are confused about what true friendship means. These people don't want to spend much time or effort on someone else's behalf, so they stay away from friends who appear needy. Instead, they look for those who'll give lots but won't ask for much in return. They evaluate their friendships according to how much they can get out of them, not how much they can give. Their friends are objects, designed to provide fun and pleasure, but not worth any sacrifices in return. Relationships based on this assumption are not friendships; they are self-serving entanglements where one person uses another or where both parties use each other. The problem comes when one of them has a need or faces a crisis. A genuine friendship will weather the storms that are part of life, but a false friendship will collapse at the first sign of pressure.

Jesus modeled true friendship. True friendship comes at a cost. It costs time, and it costs energy. According to Jesus' standard, a true friend looks for ways to give in a friendship, not ways to get. A true friend doesn't resent it when his friend is in need. A real friend doesn't use her friends to serve her own purposes. Jesus knew what it meant to be a true friend. He left the glory of heaven to take on the weaknesses of a human body—that's what he was willing to do for his friends. He subjected himself to betrayal, torture, and murder. That's how far he was willing to go for his friends. When Jesus said there is no greater way to love your friends than to lay down your life for them, he spoke from experience.

Examine your friendships in light of Jesus' example. Have you been treating your friends as possessions—using them for your benefit? Or do you look for ways to give up your life for them? The way you view your friends will be evident in the way you treat them.

Friends of God

"You are my friends if you do what I command."

John 15:14

Have you heard people say, "Jesus is my best friend"? Perhaps you've said it yourself. If, by that, you mean Jesus loves you more than anyone else does, that is true. But have you ever asked yourself, "Does God consider me *his* friend?" Like any relationship, friendship is a two-way street. It's easy for us to count God as one of our friends, but it is quite another thing for God to look upon us as his friend.

You could simply accept all the gifts Christ has for you without ever considering what you could do for him. You could pray to him and regularly ask him for things that would meet your needs. But if you want to express your friendship to him, Jesus tells you how to know if you are a friend to him. If you do what he says, you are holding up your end of the relationship. Those who follow his commands are more than just his disciples; they are his friends. To be a friend to God, you must have a heart like his. You must be like him in spirit. God takes great delight in those who love what he loves. You may protest, "I am Jesus' friend, but I just don't always do what he says!" Jesus said this isn't what his friends do.

Jesus demonstrated his friendship for you on the cross, and he continues to confirm it daily. Ask him today what he wants you to do to show your friendship to him.

December 5

Chosen

"You did not choose me, but I chose you to go and bear fruit—fruit that will last. Then the Father will give you whatever you ask in my name."

John 15:16

Have you ever been specifically chosen for a special honor or award? Do you remember the thrill of knowing that out of all who could have been selected, you were the one preferred to receive the honor? Often, we hear adopted children tell of the joy they find in knowing they were specially sought out by their adoptive parents.

You may feel that you've not been chosen for anything significant in your life. Well, if you are a Christian, you've been selected to receive the highest honor and blessing possible, you're a child of the King. You are God's child for one reason alone; God chose you. Of all the millions of people who populated the earth—past, present, and future—God noticed you and determined that you should be his. The time came when you realized that God was reaching out to you and you reached back. Now you are his, bought with a price and profoundly valuable to him. As God's chosen child, you have a new purpose—to make a difference in God's kingdom. Jesus referred to this as "bearing fruit that will last." God did not choose you to grant you eternal life and then forget about you. He wants your life to become like Christ's life. He wants you to live forever in an intimate relationship with him, bringing him glory in all that you say and do.

Take time to reflect on the incredible honor that is yours as an adopted child of God. Reflect on whether your life is producing lasting fruit for the glory of the one who has chosen you.

The Spirit of Truth

"But when he, the Spirit of truth, comes, he will guide you into all truth. He will not speak on his own; he will speak only what he hears, and he will tell you what is yet to come."

John 16:13

One thing about being young is that there are so many decisions to be made: decisions about school, decisions about relationships, decisions about career, decisions about marriage, decisions about where to spend your money, decisions about where to spend your time, and the list goes on. Of all the options available, how do you know what is right for you?

God loves you far too much to have you waste your life on foolish choices. When you became a Christian, God gave you his Holy Spirit to guide you in his truth. The Holy Spirit, who is your perfect counselor, knows the mind of God. Life can be confusing sometimes. When you find yourself in a dilemma and you don't know where to turn, turn to God. When others are putting pressure on you to do something, the Holy Spirit will help you discern whether it's right or wrong to do as they say. Counselors, pastors, parents, and friends can all be helpful as you make decisions, but ultimately, the decisions are yours, as are the consequences of those decisions. Don't make your choice until you've heard from the Spirit of Truth.

It's human nature to seek advice when you're not sure what to do. It can be very helpful to get advice from those you respect, but don't ignore the counselor who lives within you. People make mistakes; God does not. Whenever you're overwhelmed, it means you don't know the truth of your situation, and you need to hear from the Spirit of Truth.

thoug

December 7

Ambition

"I have brought you glory on earth by completing the work you gave me to do."

John 17:4

Ambition is the strong desire for something. It can be any-thing—power, fame, wealth. But whatever it is, ambition is the drive that compels people to go after what they want. Depending on what the goal is, ambition can be a good thing or a bad thing. You probably know people who seem to devote all their time and energy to the pursuit of one thing. Such people are single-minded in their zeal to accomplish their goal. Did you know Jesus was one of those people? He had one ambition in life: to glorify his Father. Everything he did, he did with this goal in mind. Every word he spoke, every relationship he formed, every miracle he did was for a single purpose: to show the world what his Father was like.

Yes, he wanted blind people to see and lame people to walk, but that wasn't the primary reason he healed them. It was so they'd see how powerful his Father is and put their trust in him. Yes, he needed friends, but that wasn't what moti-vated him to spend time with his disciples. He wanted to show them how much his Father loved them and to help them to bring glory to God. Fortunately for us, Jesus accom-plished his goal. History was changed forever when he cried out triumphantly from the cross, "It is finished!" (John 19:30).

The apostle Paul had the same goal Jesus did, and he, too, could say with satisfaction, "I have fought the good fight, I have finished the race" (2 Timothy 4:7). Now it's our turn. We should have one ambition in life: to bring honor to our Father. Everything else should be secondary to this one goal.

One

"I have given them the glory that you gave me, that they may be one as we are one."

John 17:22

Shortly before his arrest and crucifixion, Jesus spent several hours praying in the Garden of Gethsemane on behalf of his disciples. He knew they'd soon be scattered because of his death. He knew persecution would separate them. His prayer was that they'd remain unified, just as he and the Father were unified, in spite of all that was in store for them.

Jesus has the same prayer for all Christians: that we act as one body. There's a difference between unity and uniformity. Uniformity means everyone acts and thinks exactly alike. Jesus didn't ask for this; God designed us to be different and to think for ourselves. Rather, Jesus prayed that Christians would be united in one Spirit. We ought to agree that Christ is Lord. We ought to understand that as children of God we are spiritual brothers and sisters. God expects us to treat one another with Christian love, even though we may disagree on some things. Since all Christians have experienced Christ's love and forgiveness, we ought to share the desire that others will come to know him as well. With these common bonds in place, we are free to disagree on things of lesser importance. Whether to give the announcements at the beginning or at the close of the service is hardly reason for division in the church!

One of the greatest scandals of modern Christianity is that some Christians refuse to love one another. When we bicker and fight, we break Jesus' command (John 15:17), and we mock his prayer in Gethsemane. There is no excuse for two Christians having animosity toward one another. We have the same Lord and the same Spirit living within us. There are so many significant ways to channel our combined energy; it's crucial we don't allow petty squabbling to distract us from reaching the world for Christ.

If you are at odds with a fellow believer, get your heart right with God, and do what God tells you to do to restore unity. Jesus prayed that you would.

December 9

Why Cry?

They asked her, "Woman, why are you crying?"

"They have taken my Lord away," she said, "and I don't know where they have put him."

John 20:13

Mary Magdalene was distraught. Jesus had meant everything to her. He was her teacher and her Lord. Now he was dead, and life seemed hopeless once again. This was a familiar feeling for Mary; she'd known despair before. Her life had been miserable and hopeless until Jesus freed her from Satan's power and taught her about God's love. He'd given her hope where she'd known only despair. How it had pierced her heart to see him beaten—to watch his agonizing death when she knew he was no criminal. At least she could see that he was buried with dignity as he deserved. But now the empty tomb denied her even this small comfort. What was Mary supposed to do?

As Mary wept, she had no idea that the very One she mourned was not dead at all! Jesus was alive, and he was standing right behind her! If Jesus were dead, there would, indeed, be reason for tears. But as Mary was about to discover, it was a day of rejoicing! A day of celebration! A day of victory! There was no reason to weep beside an empty tomb. Jesus told her instead to go tell the others the good news!

Things aren't always what they seem. You may be going through a hard time right now, and life may look hopeless. Perhaps recent events have shaken you and left you bewildered. All you know to do is weep. Jesus may ask you the same question he asked Mary: "Why are you crying?" Dry your tears. Don't give up. Jesus, the Lord, is alive. He's powerful; nothing is too difficult for him. Best of all, he loves you. He doesn't want you to weep beside an empty tomb. He wants you to celebrate his resurrection! If you're discouraged, look and discover that Jesus is standing right next to you. *He* is your hope!

Sent

Again Jesus said, "Peace be with you! As the Father has sent me, I am sending you."

John 20:21

Obeying God requires changes in every person's life. Jesus himself made some radical adjustments to go where his Father sent him. He left the glory of heaven to be born in a cattle stall and raised in poverty. He stepped down from his heavenly throne to take on human frailties. He was a king, yet he willingly suffered indescribable degradation at the hands of those who should have been worshiping him. What motivated him to make such major adjustments? Obedience. His father had an assignment for him, and Jesus set out to do it, no matter what it cost him.

You, too, have to choose what adjustments you're willing to make in order to go where God is sending you; you cannot stay where you are and follow Christ at the same time. Ultimately, Jesus' assignment took him right back to his throne in heaven. For all eternity Jesus will rule the heavens and the earth from his seat at the right hand of his Father. Even while you are following God's will, Jesus promises that he's preparing a place in heaven for you too.

In the meantime, Jesus promises something else—peace. No matter where your obedience leads you, God's peace will be there. In the good times and in the hard times as you obey your Lord, you'll know a peace that defies description (Philippians 4:7). Jesus went to the cross because that's where his Father sent him. Where is the Father sending you? Are you willing to make the necessary adjustments so you can go?

thoug̲ Thoughts from John's Gospel ospel

December 11

But What about John?

Jesus answered, "If I want him to remain alive until I return, what is that to you? You must follow me."

John 21:22

It starts as soon as we're old enough to tell the difference between what belongs to us and what belongs to someone else. We begin comparing. We go on the alert to make sure our siblings never get more than we do. We keep track of who gets away with what. We check to see how our life matches up with the lives of our friends or classmates. Unfortunately, we often carry this habit into adulthood. We're not happy with our career, our home, or our car because we see what the neighbors have.

When Peter denied Jesus, he experienced the humiliation of disobedience. He was grateful for a second chance. He desperately wanted to get it right this time, but when he heard what was in store for him, he wasn't so sure. When Jesus told Peter he was to glorify God by dying a martyr's death, Peter's first reaction was to ask what Jesus had planned for John! Jesus' response might seem harsh, but Peter had to focus on his own walk with God and leave others to do the same.

Whatever God has given you, whatever he has called you to do, and wherever he is leading you, let that satisfy you. Don't look around to see if others have a better life. Only God knows what is best for you, so don't waste your time comparing your life with others'. Understand that it's an incredible privilege to serve God, no matter how he asks you to do it.

Chapter 25
Paul's Advice to the Philippians

When Paul wrote to the Philippians, he was writing to friends. The first person in Europe that Paul helped to know Christ was Lydia, a woman from the city of Philippi. Lydia and her family became the nucleus of the first church in Greece. The local jailer, the one who almost committed suicide after a miraculous earthquake freed Paul from his jail cell, was also a part of the church. Paul had introduced him and his family to the joys of knowing Christ; now they were serving Christ in the Philippian church. A young woman in the church had been demon possessed, but she had met Christ when Paul cast out the demon and set her free from her bondage. Needless to say, the people in the Philippian church dearly loved Paul!

When Paul wrote to his friends in Philippi, he wasn't trying to make their lives miserable. He wasn't being legalistic or unrealistic. He was giving loving counsel to his friends so that they could experience all the wonders of God's love and presence. Over the next several days, you'll see the loving guidance Paul gave to his friends in this brand-new church. Paul's advice to them still holds true. If you want to experience the love and joy that Christ has for you, pay close attention to Paul's words in the following devotions.

Paul's   Philippians

December 12

Humility

Do nothing out of selfish ambition or vain conceit, but in humility consider others better than yourselves.

Philippians 2:3

What's the difference between having a healthy self-esteem and being conceited? If you have a healthy self-esteem, you will be humble. You'll know that you are who you are because God loves you. You'll understand that God has blessed you because of his goodness, not yours. Because you aren't preoccupied with your own importance, you won't mind when others get the attention. You'll ask others about themselves instead of monopolizing conversations with information about yourself. You'll be comfortable serving others rather than always insisting on what you have coming to you. You'll have a quiet confidence that allows you to build others up instead of tearing them down to make yourself look better.

Conceit, on the other hand, is thinking more of yourself than you should. Another word for it is *pride*. Whereas humility puts others first, pride stems from self-centeredness. It's the tendency to put yourself before others and to focus on your own importance. Pride can actually grow out of a low self-esteem; if you don't like yourself, you might feel the constant need to brag about your accomplishments just to prove to others and yourself that you're worth something. Or, you might feign humility in an attempt to get others to build you up:

You: "I'm just a good-for-nothing schmuck!"

Your audience: "Oh, no you're not. You're a wonderful person."

You (blushing): "Gee! I guess you're right!"

Make sure you understand that humility is not a sign of weakness or insecurity. It's the sign of a healthy self-esteem. Ask God to remove your pride and give you true humility. You'll save yourself from embarrassment, for God promised that he will humble those who are incapable of humbling themselves (Matthew 23:12).

What Does It Matter?

But what does it matter? The important thing is that in every way, whether from false motives or true, Christ is preached. And because of this I rejoice.

Yes, and I will continue to rejoice.

Philippians 1:18

Paul had a gift for keeping things in perspective. He was chained up in prison for preaching the gospel: you'd think he'd have been discouraged. You'd think he'd have questioned God's wisdom for sidelining one of his best players. After all, who worked harder to spread the gospel than Paul? Why not send one of the weaker players to the bench and leave Paul on the field? But Paul didn't question God's game plan. He concentrated on staying faithful, wherever he was, and trusted that God knew what he was doing.

Christ's enemies chained Paul to the wall of a prison cell in order to stop him from sharing the gospel, but to Paul's delight, his detainment actually helped spread the gospel. Palace guards heard about Christ's love for the first time. Paul's friends were inspired by his example to proclaim the gospel. Even Paul's enemies preached about Christ in an attempt to stir up anger against him. Paul's conclusion? "If Christ is being lifted up because of my suffering, then it's worth it." Paul was thrilled that the gospel was still being presented, even by his enemies, while he was imprisoned.

When you experience loneliness, criticism, or rejection because you've spoken up for Jesus, don't conclude that God has abandoned you. Trust him to use you in the midst of your situation. Perhaps your critics will be moved by your forgiving attitude, and they'll seek Christ themselves. Your experience might help you learn to be more compassionate toward others who are suffering. Maybe your courage will inspire your friends to take a stand for their faith as well. The important thing is to keep your perspective. God is in control, so you have every reason to rejoice!

Paul's Philippians

December 14

Work Out Your Salvation

Therefore, my dear friends, as you have always obeyed—not only in my presence, but now much more in my absence—continue to work out your salvation with fear and trembling, for it is God who works in you to will and to act according to his good purpose.

Philippians 2:12-13

This verse is often misunderstood. Some will tell you that you must work hard to attain salvation. In other words, salvation will come as a result of your good behavior. That's not what working out your salvation means. In fact, it means the opposite: good behavior will come as a result of your salvation.

Everyone comes to the point of salvation from a different experience. Some who accept Christ have been abused, and they've carried bitterness in their hearts for years. Through Christ's example, they learn how to forgive and are no longer slaves of their past. Others have lived a life of deception; gossiping and lying are second nature to them. When they meet Christ, the Truth (John 14:6), they learn to be honest with themselves and with others. The changes are as unique as the person who accepts Jesus as Savior, for the Holy Spirit works in each heart to bring wholeness where there used to be emptiness.

What areas in your life need to be transformed? Perhaps you've never known a father's love: your heavenly Father longs for you to experience his indescribable, unconditional love. You might be filled with anger: Christ can take it away and give you peace in your heart. Are you ashamed of the way you lived before you knew Christ? He invites you to enjoy the new life that his forgiveness has made possible. You are a new creation. When you accepted Christ, your new life was just beginning. For the rest of your life, God wants to help you experience this new life to the fullest. Whatever it is that prevents you from living the way God desires, turn it over to him. Let him work in you until your life is completely transformed!

Garbage

What is more, I consider everything a loss compared to the surpassing greatness of knowing Christ Jesus my Lord, for whose sake I have lost all things. I consider them rubbish, that I may gain Christ.

Philippians 3:8

What matters to you more than anything else? Your family? Your friends? Your reputation? Your health? These are all good things; they should matter to you. But there's one thing that should come before any of these: knowing Christ.

Before Paul was a Christian, he placed high importance on who he was and where he came from. He took great pride in his pure Jewish heritage, in his excellent education, and in his flawless behavior (Philippians 3:4–6). His reputation in the community was everything to him. Then he met Christ, and everything that used to be on the top of his priority list fell to the bottom. Once he experienced Christ, nothing else could come close to that experience. From the moment of his conversion, Paul put everything else below his goal of knowing God more intimately. As far as Paul was concerned, everything else in his life was as valuable as garbage compared to the value of knowing Christ. That's why he could willingly endure ridicule, physical abuse, and loneliness, as long as he still had Christ.

Is knowing Christ important to you? No one is asking you to stop loving your family, or to hate your friends, or to harm your body. But knowing Christ should be the first item on your priority list. When you choose to place Christ first in your life, you will see everything else in your life in its proper perspective. How important is knowing Christ to you?

December 16

Count Your Blessings

Rejoice in the Lord always. I will say it again: Rejoice!

Philippians 4:4

Have you heard the words to the old hymn?

> When you are discouraged, thinking all is lost,
> Count your many blessings, name them one by one,
> And it will surprise you what the Lord hath done.

The phrase "count your blessings" is familiar, even outside of church circles. There's wisdom for all of us in that old hymn. Sometimes when we focus on our problems, we lose sight of the good things in our lives. It's as though we are under a gigantic cloud that blocks out the sun. We get irritable and depressed and, worst of all, lose perspective. That's when it's time to review all the reasons we have for rejoicing, and get our perspective back.

If you're under the cloud, don't grumble and complain. Count your blessings instead. Here's a list to get you started:

God loves you.

Jesus died for your sins.

You're a new creation.

You'll spend eternity in heaven with Christ.

You're part of God's family; you have brothers and sisters who love you.

God has promised never to abandon you.

Now, list some unique ways God has blessed your life.

Is the cloud gone yet?

Don't Worry!

Do not be anxious about anything, but in everything, by prayer and petition, with thanksgiving, present your requests to God. And the peace of God, which transcends all understanding, will guard your hearts and your minds in Christ Jesus.

Philippians 4:6-7

Anxiety is a thief: it robs our joy, our peace of mind, and even our health. So why do we worry? Because there are so many things to worry about! We all have our pet worries: we worry about getting sick; we worry about getting caught; we worry about dying; and we worry about living. We worry about what has happened, what will happen, what might happen, what isn't happening, or that nothing will happen.

We might as well face it: there'll always be stuff to worry about. So rather than wishing for a problem-free life, we should take Paul's advice: instead of worrying and fretting about everything, we should take our concerns to God.

Paul made a promise: if you pray about your problems instead of worrying about them, God will give you peace. Paul couldn't even describe the peace God gives because it's beyond human description. He did say that God's peace will set up guard duty around your heart and your mind so that no troublesome worry can disturb them. When God's peace guards your mind, you do not have to brood about things that worry you. When God's peace guards your heart, you will be free to experience joy because you are free from the burden of worry you've been carrying. God's peace frees you to live life as God wants you to. You'll experience supernatural calmness, no matter what your circumstances. Why not pull out your favorite worry today, and turn it over to God?

Paul's Advice to the Philippians

December 18

What's On Your Mind?

Finally, brothers, whatever is true, whatever is noble, whatever is right, whatever is pure, whatever is lovely, whatever is admirable— if anything is excellent or praiseworthy—think about such things.

Philippians 4:8

Paul seems a little bold here. It's one thing to tell us how to act, but now he's telling us how to think! He's right though. The things we put into our minds will come out in our character. If we deny it, we're not facing reality. We're also contradicting what the Bible teaches. Paul is doing us a huge favor by cautioning us about the way we fill our minds.

If you feed your mind with things that are pure and good, you'll have a healthy mind and good character. The most important way to do this is to read your Bible each morning so you'll have God's Word in your mind all day. You may want to read a chapter from the Gospels each day so that you are always learning from the life of Jesus. You might also want to read a chapter from Proverbs each day (since there are thirty-one, you can read one each day of the month). You will eventually want to read every part of the Bible so you will benefit from everything God has said. Another way to fill your mind with good things is to spend time talking with other Christians who are also striving to live a pure life.

Have you put some standards in place to make sure you don't let sin creep into your life through your mind? If you decide now what sort of movies you'll watch, what kind of books you'll read, what forms of music you'll listen to, and what type of humor you'll tolerate, it'll save you from getting caught off guard by temptation in the future. Set your sights high for yourself: don't let anyone else talk you into allowing garbage to enter your mind. Instead, decide today that you'll only allow into your mind things that please Jesus.

Enough Is Enough

I am not saying this because I am in need, for I have learned to be content whatever the circumstances.

Philippians 4:11

There was a phrase floating around Christian circles a few years back. You'd see it here and there, on posters and bumper stickers: "A Christian is just one beggar telling another beggar where to find bread." Although it presented Christians as humble people, as indeed we should be, this saying wasn't totally accurate. Christians are not beggars! Christians are wealthy beyond description—wealthy in a way the world doesn't understand.

Paul had been the epitome of success. He had climbed the ladder pretty well to the top. He was making a name for himself as a mover and shaker in the Jewish world. He had power, influence, and an impressive reputation. Then he met Jesus and his ambition did an about-face. Worldly success no longer meant anything to him. He was content whether he had money or no money, shelter or no shelter, food or no food, because his contentment came from within.

Our society works hard to keep us discontent. Advertisers have one goal: to convince us that we need something. And we fall for it. We work harder and harder to get more and more—then we spot something else we don't have. More might be better, but it's still not enough. It's said that when Alexander the Great conquered the entire known world, he wept because there were no more worlds to conquer! We need to learn that outward things will never satisfy our inner longing for contentment. Only God can do that.

If you've been dissatisfied with your circumstances, don't ask God to change your circumstances. Ask him to change your heart.

Paul's Paul's Advice to the Philippians ppians

December 20

Everything

I can do everything through him who gives me strength.

Philippians 4:13

A preschooler asked to do something that was beyond his capabilities. Fearing he would get hurt, his mother refused to let him do as he asked. With a scowl, her little son crossed his arms, stomped his foot, and retorted, "I can do *all* things through Christ, who strengthens me!"

Just like the little boy, we sometimes get confused about God's promises. Paul didn't say we can decide to do anything we want to do and God will put his power behind our wishes. God does promise to carry out his desires through us. This means whatever he asks us to do, we can do it—not because we're extraordinarily gifted, but because he will give us the strength.

Bottom line? If you decide you want to be a millionaire, don't count on God to fulfill your desire. But if God has called you to do something, only one thing will prevent it from happening: your disobedience. If God wants to use your life to bring joy to a lonely person, or to teach a Bible study, or to be a missionary, the only thing standing in your way is your own unwillingness. When God asks you to do something, don't waste your time deciding if it can be done. Just do it! Paul didn't say, "I can do some things through him who gives me strength." He said, "I can do everything through him who gives me strength."

All Your Needs

And my God will meet all your needs according to his glorious riches in Christ Jesus.

Philippians 4:19

Christians ought to be the most generous people in the world. We can afford to be generous because of the way God does math. God's math is different from ours. We think the more we give away, the less we have. God says, "Go ahead and be generous because the more you give away, the more I will give you."

Paul was writing a thank-you note to his good friends in Philippi. They'd taken up a collection to help him continue serving as a missionary in another city. As he commended them for their generosity, he also assured them that God would, in turn, be generous with them.

You can never outgive God. If you struggle to show generosity to others, keep in mind who it is that asks you to share your resources. When God asks you to give away something or to share what you have, don't worry that you'll come up short. He promises to take care of you, and his storehouse never gets empty. If you're not already tithing, giving at least 10 percent of your income to your church, make that a personal goal. Tithing is more about faith than it is about money. When you give the first portion of what you earn, you are showing God you trust him to take care of you. God may not need your money, but you need to give it.

Christians talk a lot about God meeting our needs. We need to be sure we put our money where our mouth is.

Lessons from the Life of Mary

Twenty centuries ago, when the Jewish people were expecting the Messiah, the highest honor a family could hope for was that he be born into their family line. Young women from wealthy families undoubtedly harbored the hope that they might be the one chosen to give birth to the Savior. It made sense that such a hero be raised in a noble family and have all the advantages that money and position could offer.

Mary was a young teenager when her parents arranged her marriage to a man much older than she was. No doubt she expected to have children and live quietly as a carpenter's wife in the backwater town of Nazareth. Mary may have seemed like an ordinary young woman, but God saw her in a totally different light. He saw a heart that was devoted to him. He saw a gentle girl who trusted him. He saw the perfect woman to nurture the Son of God.

This average teenager could have had no idea what God would do through her life. For centuries afterward, her name would be symbolic with godly love and devotion. We can learn much from examining her life to see how God can work through ordinary people to do extraordinary things.

Surprised by God

In the sixth month, God sent the angel Gabriel to Nazareth, a town in Galilee.

Luke 1:26

Mary was just a small-town girl planning her wedding. In her culture, girls typically married in their teens to a man chosen for them by their parents. It was not unusual for the groom to be several years older than his bride. Nazareth was an insignificant little village in the world scheme of things. Joseph and Mary probably planned to live out their days quietly in their little corner of the world. Then one day their lives were radically and irrevocably changed!

God dispatched an angel with an incredible message for Mary. Of all the women of her day or of any age before or after, God had chosen *her* to bear the Savior! She wondered, *Why me?* Mary was under no delusions. She was not the prettiest or the wealthiest woman in the world. She was smart but uneducated. And she was so young! She still had much to learn about life. Predictably, she was completely taken by surprise when the angel Gabriel relayed this awesome assignment.

Why *did* God choose Mary? He saw her humility and her quiet faithfulness to do what he asked her. This was exactly the kind of person he could trust to raise his Son. Outward things—looks, money, power—none of those mattered. What mattered was a heart yielded to do the will of God.

You may see some similarities between your life and Mary's. Yes, times have changed. But, like Mary, you may be going about your business expecting to do all the ordinary things: finish your education, find a job, get married, have children. But, in the midst of your ordinary life, God may surprise you with something extraordinary. You may not consider yourself to be anyone special, but God does. He sees your heart. He knows how faithful you've been to him. He may decide he can trust you with something unusual. Seek to be faithful, and watch expectantly to see what he does in your life!

Scared to Death!

But the angel said to her, "Do not be afraid, Mary, you have found favor with God."

Luke 1:30

When God shows you what he wants to do with your life, it may scare you to death! The angel God sent to tell Mary of his plans for her had to calm her down first. The sight of Gabriel terrified her! His message overwhelmed her! It was too hard to take in!

If God were to reveal to you everything he has in store for your future, you, too, might be overwhelmed. That's why he tells you only what he wants you to do now. Don't be limited by looking at your situation in human terms. When God does things, they are God-sized. They are impossible for you to do apart from his help. If there is nothing unusual about your life right now, consider whether you have been inadvertently leaving God out of it.

Whatever it is that God has asked you to do next, don't be afraid. Nothing else is as exciting as walking closely with God. Those who think the Christian life is boring are not living it the way God intended! Walking with God will stretch you in ways that nothing else will. Trust him and don't fear. As you obey him step by step, day by day, week by week, year by year, you will look back on your life and be amazed at where he has taken you and what he has done.

Nothing Is Impossible

"For nothing is impossible with God."

Luke 1:37

Has God ever spoken to you about something he wanted you to do and you thought, *But that's impossible!?* The angel Gabriel was telling Mary about a plan that not only sounded impossible; it was impossible! Surely she could not be expecting a baby; she was a virgin! Surely God would not choose a mere human to give birth to his holy Son! Surely God would not have peasants raise the Son of God! Yet that's exactly what God was planning, for though these things were indeed humanly impossible, they were entirely possible for the Lord. He created life itself; why should this be impossible for him?

Gabriel did not tell Mary, "Nothing is impossible for you if you try hard enough!" Nor did he say, "You can do anything if you just believe hard enough." He said, "When God wants to do something, nothing is too difficult, and nothing can stop him."

God can do anything he wants in your life. He can get you a job. He can help you overcome an addiction. He can protect you from harm. He can even change your heart! Has he told you something he wants to do in your life? Do you believe him? The moment you say, "But that's impossible!" when you know what God is saying to you, you have just revealed what you really believe about God. Remember, with God all things are possible! Is your life living proof that God can do the impossible?

December 25

Not Like You Expected

And she gave birth to her firstborn, a son. She wrapped him in strips of cloth and placed him in a manger, because there was no room for them in the inn.

Luke 2:7

Things don't always work out the way you thought they would, do they? You've probably experienced occasions when you were expecting something good to occur, but when the time came, it didn't happen the way you expected. You may have been disappointed or embarrassed. It may have been needless embarrassment. Perhaps things happened exactly as God wanted.

If you had been Mary or Joseph—expecting the Messiah, the Savior of mankind—what kind of expectations would you have had? Not a cattle shed with a feeding trough for a cradle! Even a modest hotel room would be better than a cold barn! Instead of nurses by her side, Mary ended up with some rough and dirty shepherds, who probably smelled as bad as the barn did.

No, things didn't pan out exactly as Mary and Joseph would have wished. They may have even felt like failures; maybe it was their fault for not providing a better birthplace for a king. But the birth happened precisely according to God's plan. He wanted his Son to be born in a lowly and humble setting, completely the opposite of what generations of hopeful Jews had expected. For his Son did not come to the world to be served, but to serve (Matthew 20:28).

When circumstances happen in your life that are not what you would have chosen and you wonder why God allowed this to happen, trust him anyway. Don't be disappointed. Don't be embarrassed. God never does things the way we would have done them. His way is always better!

Thoughts for Year's End

When we are young, we often wish time would go by faster. As we get older, we'd love to slow down the clock. The end of a year can be a bitter-sweet time. As we survey the past twelve months, we may draw immense satisfaction from all we have achieved, or we may look back with regret at missed opportunities and failures. Some years bring incredible joy that is exciting to recall and relive. Other years are marked by tragedy; these years are black spots that we'd just as soon forget.

God is a God of grace. He is a God of new beginnings. If you have regrets about this past year, give them to God. Ask his forgiveness for the ways you have failed him. Be encouraged, for a new year is beginning—a year filled with new opportunities to love God, to honor him, and to serve him faithfully. Be encouraged because you serve a powerful Savior. He can bring about changes in your life that you never dreamed were possible. Be encouraged because God loves you, and you are not going into the new year alone. Look forward to the exciting adventures God has in store for you as you experience him day by day.

Long-Term Faithfulness

There was also a prophetess, Anna, the daughter of Phanuel, of the tribe of Asher. She was very old; she had lived with her husband seven years after her marriage, and then was a widow until she was eighty-four. She never left the temple but worshiped night and day, fasting and praying.

Luke 2:36-37

You've probably heard about Anna; she's the elderly woman we read about at Christmastime, the one who prayed her entire life for the Messiah to come. Day after day, year after year, decade after decade she prayed, without giving up. Finally, when she was very old, she saw the Christ child—the answer to her prayers. Anna serves as an example of faithfulness in the long haul!

We're often quick to assume God has decided not to answer our prayers. We might pray for an unbelieving friend for a few months or maybe even for a year. But time passes, and our friend doesn't become a Christian, so we lose interest and abandon our prayer. We assume our friend will never come to know Christ or it would have happened by now. How easily discouraged we get when we don't see results soon enough to suit us! Our problem is that we pray according to our own agenda, not God's. It's vital to remember that God works by his timetable, not ours.

Have you been praying for someone who doesn't know Christ? Have you been praying for one of God's promises to come about in your life? Don't set a time limit on how soon God should answer. Keep praying. Don't get discouraged. In the long run, when God answers your prayer, you'll enjoy a double blessing because you'll have learned faithfulness in the long term as well.

Nothing Is Too Hard

Ah, Sovereign LORD, you have made the heavens and the earth by your great power and outstretched arm. Nothing is too hard for you.

"I am the LORD, the God of all mankind. Is anything too hard for me?"

Jeremiah 32:17, 27

Exactly how powerful is the God we serve, anyway? We talk about his power. We hear about his power. We even sing about his power. Jeremiah 32:17 has been made into a chorus and sung in churches all over North America. But do we really *experience* his power?

Jeremiah needed a miracle. He was in prison for confronting the king of Judah with a word from God, just as God had told him to do. Everyone was angry with Jeremiah. From the heads of state down to the peasants, everyone in Judah hated him and mocked him for saying unpopular things. But that's exactly what God had told him to do! As Jeremiah was praying, he looked at the sky and contemplated how powerful God must be to have created the heavens and the earth. Then he reviewed in his mind all the miracles God had done through the ages. Jeremiah had heard about the mighty miracles in the history of God's people, but now he needed to see one for himself. He needed to experience God's power. God was faithful to Jeremiah. Not only was Jeremiah freed from captivity, but everything God had predicted occurred exactly as he said they would.

Don't settle for mere talk about God's power—or books and songs about his power. Ask him to show you for yourself. If God has given you a task that looks impossible, do it anyway; then you can experience his power accomplishing his will through your life. Don't consider your own inadequacy. That's irrelevant. Remember, nothing is impossible for God!

December 28

Our Best Thinking

When the disciples James and John saw this, they asked, "Lord, do you want us to call fire down from heaven to destroy them?"

Luke 9:54

If there's ever a time not to trust your own judgment, it's when you've been hurt. When you think you've been treated unfairly, your first reaction is exactly that—a reaction. It's a defense mechanism: I've been hurt; I need to strike back. In your rush to retaliate, you're likely to blow the situation out of proportion. That's what happened to James and John.

Jesus and his disciples were traveling to Jerusalem when they came upon a Samaritan village. For years there had been bitter animosity between the Jewish people and the Samaritans, so it probably didn't surprise the disciples that they weren't well received in Samaria. However, they weren't about to stand by and have Jesus treated so poorly! James and John quickly came up with a plan to repay these rude Samaritans for their lack of hospitality: "Let's teach them a lesson! Let's pull off a huge miracle and destroy the village in the process. Then they'll be sorry!" Talk about overreacting! Jesus, of course, had other plans. He rebuked his zealous friends, and they carried on with their journey.

Acts 8:14 tells us that the Samaritans later accepted the gospel. Guess who was sent to pray with the Samaritans? Peter and John! As they prayed with the new believers, John, the recovering pyromaniac, must have felt more than a little twinge of guilt. If he'd had his way, his current prayer partners would have been roasted alive!

You may think you know the whole story. You may think you understand people's motives, but you probably don't. Only God knows what's in a person's heart. Only God understands why people say what they say and do what they do. If you take your hurts to God and give others the benefit of the doubt, you'll save yourself from doing something you regret. In addition, you may see God do a miracle after all, but it won't involve burning down a village. Do you tend to jump to conclusions and react angrily when you feel you've been mistreated? Learn from James's and John's mistake. Don't rush to retaliate. Show compassion instead of anger, and watch to see what God does next.

Wait!

Wait for the LORD;
be strong and take heart
and wait for the LORD.

Psalm 27:14

Waiting is one of the hardest things to do in all the world! If you have to wait for someone who is late, or if you're expecting something important in the mail, or if you've applied for a job and you're waiting for the phone to ring, waiting can almost drive you crazy! Why is it so difficult to wait? Waiting means you're not in control. Someone else will determine what happens next. Whether you're waiting on an inconsiderate friend, a slow postal system, or an indifferent employer, sitting helplessly can be excruciating.

Waiting on the Lord is a different matter. God loves you more than you can even imagine. Everything he does in your life shows his perfect love for you. When God delays giving you something, he has a good reason. It's not that he doesn't love you or that he wants to make you squirm. It's a matter of timing. Waiting on God reminds us of just how much our lives depend on him. Every day we wait is another day to realize how helpless we are apart from his strength. Waiting on God can be one of the most spiritually rewarding things we ever do. Waiting on God is not sitting around doing nothing. Waiting on God involves action on our part. We should pray. We should continue doing what God told us last. We should watch for what he does next. We should examine our hearts to see if any sin is hindering God's answer.

If you are waiting on God for something right now, don't consider the time an idle, frustrating experience. Trust that he loves you and that his answer will come. In the meantime, get busy!

Carried to Completion

Being confident of this, that he who began a good work in you will carry it on to completion until the day of Christ Jesus.

Philippians 1:6

In the Book of Revelation, John describes Christ as the Alpha and the Omega, meaning "the beginning" and "the end" (Revelation 22:13). In other words, God is eternal; he is not bound by time. God doesn't just see the future; he's in the future, just as he is in the past and the present. When God begins something in your life, he already knows how it will end because he is there.

When you became a Christian, God's Holy Spirit began the work of making you like Christ. He continues to work in your life to bring about holiness, and he will continue to do so until you arrive in heaven to spend eternity face-to-face with him. You can be absolutely confident that whatever Christ begins in you, he will finish.

If you've received a word from God about something he wants to do in your life, trust that he will make it happen. Don't let circumstances discourage you; God isn't intimidated by your circumstances. Obey him with confidence because God always completes what he starts. If you sensed God telling you he would make you into a missionary one day, believe that he will. He has seen the future. He knows what will happen. If you sensed God saying that he would use your life to encourage others in some way, know that God is perfectly capable of doing what he says. When God says something to you, immediately adjust your life to what he has told you and then watch to see how God makes everything he said become a reality.

What More Could Be Done?

What more could have been done for my vineyard
*   than I have done for it?*
When I looked for good grapes,
*   why did it yield only bad?*

Isaiah 5:4

How would you like to fly a kite without a string? Cut down a tree with a butter knife? Without the right tools or equipment, some things can't be done. Sometimes we feel completely inadequate to do what God expects us to do. We know he wants us to grow as Christians and to show signs of Christian maturity, such as love, peace, patience, self-control, and so on (Galatians 5:22), yet we feel helpless to change the way we think or the way we behave. The truth is that God does not ask us to do anything on our own. He always provides the right tools. There is a story in the Book of Isaiah about this very thing.

Isaiah used a setting that would be very familiar to his audience. He told of a vine grower and his quest for a lush harvest of grapes. This man spared no effort or expense in planting his vineyard. He found the most fertile land, cleared it of all stones and obstructions, then planted only the choicest vines in it. He built a watchtower so he could see intruders coming and thus protect his crop. In eager anticipation of luscious grapes, the vine grower built a wine vat and waited in readiness for the bumper crop that would come. When harvest time came, however, he discovered only worthless grapes. Despite his best efforts, these grapes had no value. Not surprisingly, the vine grower asked, "What more could I have done?"

In case you missed it, God is the vine grower, and we are the vines. God has given us so much in the way of Christian education: books, magazines, seminars, conferences, retreats, etc. He has given us the church for support, encouragement, and fellowship. We have free access to his written Word, so there is no doubt what the harvest is that he expects. Above all, he has given us himself. As a Christian, we have the Holy Spirit living within us, guiding us and giving us strength. In return, God wants us to produce good fruit. He wants us to be holy. He wants us to trust him. God has done his part. Now, he waits in anticipation to see what fruit we will produce.

Index of Readings

Index of Readings

October 3	Hebrews 11:6	Without Faith
October 4	Hebrews 12:5–6	Discipline
October 5	1 Corinthians 3:18	Worldly Wisdom
October 6	Ephesians 3:20	Far More
October 7	Matthew 6:9	Our Father
October 8	Matthew 6:9	Our Father . . .
October 9	Matthew 6:9	In Heaven
October 10	Matthew 6:9	Hallowed be Your Name . . .
October 11	Matthew 6:10	Your Will Be Done . . .
October 12	Matthew 6:11	Daily Bread . . .
October 13	Matthew 6:12	Forgive Us Our Sins . . .
October 14	Matthew 6:13	Lead Us Not into Temptation . . .
October 15	Psalm 1:1–3	Blessed Is the Man
October 16	Psalm 2:8	Big Prayers
October 17	Psalm 5:3	All Day Long
October 18	Psalm 3:5–6	A Good Night's Sleep
October 19	Psalm 5:7–8	David's Priority List
October 20	Psalm 23:1	Better than Lions
October 21	Psalm 23:2	Green Pastures
October 22	Psalm 23:3	Restoring Your Soul
October 23	Psalm 23:4	Shadows
October 24	Psalm 23:5	Don't Miss the Banquet
October 25	Psalm 23:6	The Right Perspective
October 26	1 Peter 1:13	Use Your Head!
October 27	1 Peter 1:15–16	Holy Like God
October 28	1 Peter 2:9	Royal Priests
October 29	1 Peter 5:7	Cast Your Anxiety on Him
October 30	2 Peter 3:8–10	A Thief in the Night
October 31	Genesis 3:12	Blame
November 1	Acts 2:4, 8	The Spirit
November 2	Acts 2:42	The Model Church
November 3	Acts 2:44–46	The Way Church Was Meant to Be
November 4	Acts 2:46–47	It's Great to Be a Christian!
November 5	Acts 8:26	Divine Appointments
November 6	Galatians 2:20	New Life
November 7	Galatians 5:19–21	Your Sins Are Showing
November 8	Galatians 5:22–24	The Fruit of the Spirit
November 9	Galatians 6:2	Carrying Burdens
November 10	Galatians 6:3–4	Something or Nothing
November 11	Galatians 6:7–8	Reaping What We Sow
November 12	Galatians 6:9–10	Don't Give Up!
November 13	Ephesians 4:1	Your Calling
November 14	Ephesians 4:29	Watch What You Say!
November 15	Ephesians 4:32	Be Kind
November 16	Ephesians 5:10	What Pleases God?
November 17	Ephesians 5:15–17	Be Careful
November 18	Ephesians 6:10–12	Be Strong

Index of Subjects

Index of Scriptures